T0330020

Uneven Paths of Development

Dedication

Nadu, Fola, Banke and Koye
and
Krishna, Dayita and Dharmin.
They made it all worthwhile.

Uneven Paths of Development

Innovation and Learning in Asia and Africa

Banji Oyelaran-Oyeyinka

Director, Monitoring and Research Division (MRD), UN-HABITAT, Kenya, and Professorial Fellow at UNU-MERIT, Netherlands

Rajah Rasiah

Professor of Technology and Innovation Policy, Faculty of Economics and Administration, University of Malaya, Malaysia and Professorial Fellow at UNU-MERIT, Netherlands

Edward Elgar

Cheltenham, UK • Northampton, MA, USA

Published by
Edward Elgar Publishing Limited
The Lypiatts
15 Lansdown Road
Cheltenham
Glos GL50 2JA
UK

Edward Elgar Publishing, Inc.
William Pratt House
9 Dewey Court
Northampton
Massachusetts 01060
USA

A catalogue record for this book
is available from the British Library

Library of Congress Control Number: 2008023886

Mixed Sources
Product group from well-managed
forests and other controlled sources
www.fsc.org Cert no. SA-COC-1565
FSC © 1996 Forest Stewardship Council

ISBN 978 1 84720 906 1

Printed and bound in Great Britain by MPG Books Ltd, Bodmin, Cornwall

Contents

Figures

Tables

Boxes

Preface

It is often assumed that East Asia has enjoyed superior institutions to drive rapid growth and structural change while the dismal growth rates recorded by sub-Saharan African (SSA) economies have been caused by inferior institutions. This image falls apart when a careful sectoral assessment is made of the critical institutions and organizations driving learning and innovation in the two geographical regions. Among the countries examined in this book only Taiwan and to some extent China enjoy superior institutions to drive industrial upgrading. While Malaysia has succeeded in stimulating a significant rise in per capita income and enjoys strong basic infrastructure and promotional institutions, the country lags behind Taiwan and China when it comes to high-tech institutions. Indonesia and SSA face a wider set of institutional support problems – though the basic infrastructure in many parts of South Africa is superior to that of a number of East Asian economies. Malaysia, Indonesia and SSA also lag behind in terms of knowledge accumulated due to a lack of commitment to invest in the right kinds of knowledge-stimulating and knowledge-appropriating institutions.

More importantly there is a huge gap in the speed and adjustment capabilities to adopt the right kinds of policies to promote and audit institutions between Malaysia, Indonesia and SSA. Among other things, this book shows that underlying the deep divide between the selected East Asian and SSA economies has been the consequences of the wide lag in policy competences of governments. Also, these divergent outcomes did not result from a lack of planning but from the quality of planning and the depth of commitment to identify which sectors best promote overall economic growth and development. Lastly, there was early recognition in Taiwan and China that change to existing structures of production and distribution was an imperative, and that this would require a Schumpeterian–Nelsonian type of institutional change to transform society. Richard Nelson and Sydney Winter's learning and innovation emphasis through institutional change is the central instrument of analysis in this book to examine the different paths taken by the economies selected. The commitment to experiment and put resources behind technological and institutional innovation in specific sectors in particularly Taiwan and China was markedly different to what we observed in Malaysia, Indonesia and SSA. Information hardware (IH) has been identified among strategic industries for promotion, but the lack of institutional support to drive learning and innovation has stalled upgrading in the industry in Malaysia. In Indonesia and SSA economies the IH sector has been treated as homogenous and technological change has been taken as parametric. The twin evils of progress – namely ignorance and poor commitment to action – have been complicated by the lack of confidence to take autonomous decisions on the part of the Indonesian and African governments. Whereas ambitious governments lacking in a clear institutional focus tended to be responsible for failed industrial projects, the IH industry only received tax incentives to relocate operations in Indonesia, and in addition tax incentives for relocating and stimulating R&D operations in Malaysia.

The focus of this book is therefore on what can be learned in the complex processes of industrial, technological and organizational change in a sectoral system of IH across countries in East Asia and SSA. The IH innovation system is deliberately chosen to illustrate how sectors act as seeds of economic progress.

We carried out detailed firm-level studies in seven countries, three in Africa (Nigeria, Mauritius and South Africa) and four in Asia (China, Taiwan, Malaysia and Indonesia). Rajah Rasiah coordinated the studies in Malaysia, Taiwan and Indonesia, Xinxin Kong in China, Erika Mbula-Kraemer in South Africa, Sawkut Rojid in Mauritius and Banji Oyelaran-Oyeyinka in Nigeria in addition to overall project coordination. The data coordinated by Rajah Rasiah for Taiwan and Indonesia was collected by W.W. Chu, Yeo Lin and himself, and Ari Kuncoro respectively and funded by the Asian Development Bank. We would like to thank Brahm Prakash and Rajiv Kumar for allowing us to use the data on Taiwan and Indonesia. The project was conceived and conceptualized while we were both still with the United Nations University – UNU-MERIT, Maastricht, the Netherlands, which provided intellectual as well as financial support. The success of the project was due in large part to a network of colleagues as well as the different actors in firms, government offices and private organizations who spared time to be interviewed and to fill in questionnaires in the different countries. We are deeply grateful to them all. Erika Moran did a superb job in collecting background data on IH for different countries and worked hard to put the different chapters into a useable form. Finally, we want to acknowledge the invaluable role of our families, their patience and support, in the course of writing this book. Without their tolerance the job would have been much harder.

If there are any shortcomings, of course the usual caveat applies; we take full responsibility for any inadequacies of this book.

Banji Oyelaran-Oyeyinka and Rajah Rasiah

1. Learning to innovate: information hardware sector in Asia and Africa

1.1 INTRODUCTION

This book explores two broad themes and advances one proposition. At a general level, we seek to understand the factors that explain the wide differences in economic growth through divergent paths of development between East Asia and sub-Saharan Africa. The aim is to contribute to the debate on the underlying factors of historical catch-up, an idea that has a long tradition of scholarship (Hamilton, 1791; List, 1885; Gerschenkron, 1962; Amsden, 1989; Amsden and Chu, 2003; Schumpeter, 1934, 1942; Reinert, 2007).

The second theme in this book looks at the process of technological capability accumulation through learning that is now widely accepted as underpinning historical economic catch-up (Nelson and Winter, 1982; Rosenberg, 1976, 1982; Freeman, 1987, 1989; Amsden, 1989; Lundvall, 1988). In taking a comparative historical economic perspective, we are not unmindful of the deep-rooted differences in the history and cultures of the regions and countries as well as the political constituencies and policies that shape the paths of development (see Nelson and Winter, 1982; North, 1990). We feel that these differences may in fact help to shed light on our analyses. We therefore assume that the 'development trajectory of countries is not only non-unique but also malleable'.[1] This informs the title of this book: the paths of development of nations are uneven in the sense that countries chart unequal trajectories depending on where they come from, the processes they adopt (path-dependence), the natural endowment they possess and its consequences for sectoral specialization patterns.

Our broad proposition is that explicit investment in technological capability acquisition, an activity that is central to modern economic development, is underpinned by unique and nationally distinct sets of institutions and organizations. In other words, industrialization is not simply about the purchase of machinery or simply increasing investment in research and development (R&D). If this was the case, the rich mineral and oil-producing countries of the world would not need to exert much effort in achieving modernization. It is also not just about adopting manufacturing as a policy over, say, agriculture or mineral processing.[2] The factors that shape the paths of development are rather complex but there are a few areas of agreement, namely: that knowledge, not just technology alone in its narrow sense, is critical; that certain leading sectors are able to propel economies in the direction of high-growth dynamics; that learning through diversity generation (this is triggered in economic systems through innovation) fosters economic development; and that diversities of institutions and systems of production (and innovation) explain the persistent differences in the paths of development and ultimately the economic outcomes of national endeavours (Schumpeter, 1942; Gerschenkron, 1962; Lundvall, 1988; Dosi, 1982). In other words, sectoral specificities are an outcome of policy decisions arising from political constituencies shaped by the mediation of initial conditions in the manner of integration of host sites in the world economy, institutional development and therefore of the learning and the direction for knowledge accumulation.

One important contribution of the book is the methodological approach we employ. While sub-Saharan African (SSA) and East Asian countries have been compared in the past, the studies have focused largely on examining and comparing Africa at broad macroeconomic levels with the evidently economically successful Asian countries in general, including Taiwan, South Korea and Japan. Past studies include *Asia and Africa: Legacies and Opportunities in Development* (Lindauer and Roemer, 1994), *Asian Industrialization and Africa* (Stein, 1995) and *Africa and Asia in Comparative Economic Perspective* (Lawrence and Thirtle, 2001). However, no study that we know of has approached this subject from the angle of learning and technological capability building. Again, while East Asia has been studied in respect of its 'miracle', studies on SSA have invariably been coded in terms of the 'tragedy' of economic failures and regress.[3] While there are empirical facts to justify both approaches, our focus is different and we look neither to tragedies nor miracles, but to learning. The various country studies leading to this book rely on evolutionary economic theorizing applied to specific sectors that have been influential in stimulating economic growth. In the early 1980s, no one could have predicted that electronics hardware would be one of the drivers of rapid growth of China. Neither could anyone have foreseen that India would become a major exporter of software.

This new dynamic in Asia has implications for both trade and development in Africa. Much of East Asia has become fully engaged in global trade in manufacturing and value-adding services while Africa remains connected largely through the supply of raw materials. Significantly, the terms of trade and volume as well as the destination of raw materials exports are experiencing geographical shifts, by which Africa is progressively exporting more to Asia and, in the process, fueling growth in the continent. But this might happen at the expense of nascent local manufacturing capacity where all efforts are directed at feeding the new factories and workshops of the world based in East Asia. For instance, China and much of East Asia have tremendous strength in low-tech production such as in consumer electronics and computer peripherals, footwear and apparel and clothing. Africa has a fairly long history in textile and garment manufacturing, and the promise of electronics manufacturing in South Africa, Nigeria and Mauritius. The African Growth Opportunities Agreement (AGOA) with the United States in 1999 and the 'everything but arms' agreement between least-developed economies (LDEs) and the European Union in 2001 have given some room for the emergence of foreign-driven garment manufacturing in a number of sub-Saharan economies, but only at the expense of displacement of the older garment manufacturers in these economies. In the background of these agreements is the removal of the Multi-Fibre Agreement (MFA) in 2004. Available evidence shows that much of the AGOA- and EU-related garment manufacturing has remained uncertain and the firms involved pay low wages without social safety instruments.

There is therefore much that connects Africa and Asia and there are lessons of contemporary and historical relevance to be learnt. However, what are of utmost interest for this book are the lessons that our comparative institutional study holds for a better understanding of the theory and policy that promote industrialization in latecomers. Due in part to the complexity of treating national systems together in a multi-country study, we have selected for study a sector characterized initially by low value-added and employment-intensive operations where East Asia has made significant progress, that is, the manufacturing and export of computer hardware. With the exception of a dynamic economy in Japan that had already reached the technology frontier in industries such as shipbuilding, steel, textile and garments before the mid-nineteenth century to act as a driver of the East Asian economies, in some ways like Africa the labour force and institutions in the remaining East Asian economies were also weakly developed initially.

But what justify the selection of the computer hardware sector for study within such contrasting regional settings with such vastly different institutional capacities (and growing wider) are five main reasons:

1. Global growth is currently driven by knowledge-intensive industries (Lall, 2001). At the heart of this 'new economy' are information and communication technologies (ICTs) which are in turn driven by rapid advances in information and computer systems. Africa and other developing countries would have to take stock of this new global dynamic, and understanding how it works is an essential start.

2. Our approach is to examine the industry in a systemic framework within which the complex interactions of actors are involved not just in design and manufacturing but also in assembly and testing, packaging, distribution, marketing and services of computers and components. In a global division of labour, all countries have an entry point in this complex products system as increasingly 'knowledge creation' is separated from manufacturing systems.
3. Beyond design and assembly of computers, the role of the Internet as a general purpose technology (GPT) has spawned a variety of new IH appliances including web phones, game consoles, and so on, through which countries that are far from the global locus of manufacturing (the USA, Taiwan, China) could benefit from value-adding services, which offers African countries considerable opportunities to generate wealth through fruitful networking with Asia.
4. African countries currently have to compete intensely in their home countries with scale-driven products exported from Asia. It is important in an unpredictable world to understand the policy and institutional context of how this competition will be shaped.
5. The processes of learning are expected to drive firms in African countries to move beyond assembly and processing or simply selling computer hardware.

The aim of this book is not to demonstrate how African countries could or should acquire capability development in information hardware (IH) manufacturing and design. The overarching objective is to understand the underlying dynamics of the convergence of institutional, technological and policy factors that shape a latecomer country's attempt to learn from the forerunners to generate economic wealth in a globally competitive sector.

The evolution of the IH sub-sector in East Asia has its roots in production relocation (largely Singapore, Malaysia, the Philippines, Indonesia, Thailand, China and Vietnam) as well as market and technological linkages (Korea and Taiwan) with multinational firms in the United States. Essentially a new global locus of production is emerging which is driven in large part by state actions and strong intermediary links between firms and institutions (Amsden and Chu, 2003; Ernst, 2006; Rasiah, 2000) and sustained by a host of market and non-market phenomena (regional systems, global networks) (Gereffi et al., 2005; Rasiah and Lin, 2005).

This new global division of labour has created a new IH divide:

●   The diffusion of IH into technology-using industries such as textile and garments, and wood and furniture in East Asia has transformed the dichotomy between old and new economies. The diffusion of enabler technologies such as IH, materials and mechatronics by technology creating modern (high-tech) industries into traditional (previously considered low-tech) industries is increasingly removing such dichotomies.

- East Asia continues to attract investment in IH production while Africa and the rest of developing Asia remain as importers. Expansion in the production of export-oriented IH in the transitional economies of Eastern Europe and the continued production operations in Latin America has not slowed down the rapid expansion of production in East Asia (see Rasiah, 2004).

Studies have shown that IH has impacted with varying levels of intensity on traditional sectors such as textiles and garments although the impact seems to be more profound in the computer sector itself which is also the biggest employer of IH skills. In particular, computer use has been more concentrated in services (aviation, banking and financial services) as well as manufacturing. For instance, computer-aided design and computer-aided manufacturing (CAD and CAM) systems are widely used for pattern designing, fabric cutting and stitching, and colour identification. Also, layout and organizational innovations have resulted in considerable IH applications in supply chain management for more efficient warehousing and inventory control, reduction in defects and logistics costs, and more effective qualitative and quantitative demand–supply coordination (between producers and users). For example, integrated materials resource planning (MRP2) has successfully transformed just-in-time production to lower defects and delivery times while absorbing customer taste effectively in both producer-driven value chains (for example automotives) and buyer-driven value chains (for example garments and computers). In some cases it has driven modularization to smoothe production coordination in supply chain management (Gereffi et al., 2005; Rasiah, 2007). In some cases it has quickened the introduction of design changes and strengthened the capacity of shrinking production space to deliver a wider range of product models (Rasiah, 1994). Coordination between small and medium-sized enterprises (SMEs) and large retailers in the US and Europe (Nordstroms, Wal-Mart, Nike) has been facilitated by information technology (IT) through continuous flows of information on design, orders and stock levels, no matter where the geographic locations. These developments have transformed garment value chains so much that in some cases producers coordinate manufacturing, packaging and logistics without affecting the buyers' (brand-holders') position as drivers of the chains (see Rasiah, 2007). In some cases, logistics operators act as the interface between producers and buyers to reduce lead times in the garment industry. African countries have in the main been spectators in this new global order.

A number of Asian countries have progressively become key players in the manufacturing of IH products, although the depth of capabilities, market orientation and the nature of actors vary across countries. For instance, China and Malaysia have a mixed structure where firms produce for both domestic and global markets and are engaged in low value-added production of components, modules and computers. Singapore specializes in foreign-driven high value-added operations in wafer fabrication, designing and logistics (Mathews and Cho, 2000; Wong, 1999). Taiwan specializes in original equipment manufacturing (OEM), R&D and in the supply of global services (see Rasiah and Lin, 2005; Ernst, 2006). Understanding how this new production and innovation dynamics has evolved is the subject of the next section.

1.2   INFORMATION HARDWARE SECTOR: NATIONAL STATUS AND GLOBAL TRENDS

This section sets out the main elements of the computer hardware innovation system. Our conception of 'sector' is different from the notion of an industrial sector where firms are homogeneous, and products are undifferentiated and only distinguishable by the price. According to the perfect competition assumption, individual actors have no role to play and it is infinitesimal in the limiting case (Chang, 2003). In other words the actions of individual agents or states have no effect on the economic outcome, which also means that interactive learning, so central to the systems concept, is irrelevant. Unlike an industrial sector which only consists of firms engaged in the production of sector-specific goods, we define a sectoral system of innovation to include firms and economic agents (including institutions) that connect through market and non-market (that is, social and technical relationships that are not price determined) links. It is underpinned by the following: (1) firms; (2) organizations that support and regulate; (3) networks of actors; (4) institutions; and (5) the knowledge base (Malerba et al., 2001). Using patent data on European economies, Malerba and Orsenigo (1997) and Malerba (1992) expanded the sectoral dynamics to explain the persistence of innovations and how they relate to market structure variables. Sectoral systems also allow the understanding of how a particular knowledge base drives new innovations (see Malerba et al., 2001).

The development of industry-specific knowledge bases often involves considerable knowledge sharing with other industry knowledge bases so that the components of these industries overlap to contain products that can figure in any of these industries. For example, the diffusion of software systems (command navigation systems and smart lights), and electronics components (read-only memory chips and other transistors in car stereo sets), as well as precision tooling (for example moulds) in motorcar assembly has brought together the machinery, electronics and aerospace industries (see Best, 2001; Rasiah, 2002).

A focus on a specific sector such as IH brings out idiosyncratic issues because the nature of markets, the paths of innovation and the challenges faced by states differ considerably depending on the composition of the industry, and the embedding institutions. IH has been a leading sector and, as will be shown in this chapter, a source of considerable wealth creation for the advanced industrial countries and much of East Asia. Whilst key industries have engineered upswings to initiate economic long waves (Schumpeter, 1934; Perez, 1983), successful developers starting from low income levels and from the bottom of the technology ladder often targeted selected lead sectors on the basis of investment generation and linkage potential (see Hirschman, 1958, 1970). The history of successful latecomer industrialization has also been identified with leading sectors (Gerschenkron, 1962) and the computer hardware sector is part of the electronics complex that has driven the economies of East Asia. The East Asian countries, starting with Japan and followed later by South Korea and Taiwan, have all accumulated capabilities at different levels to become major exporters. Whereas local firms using creative duplication and licensing channels have driven production of computer hardware in Japan, Korea and Taiwan, foreign direct investment has been the prime channel of growth in Singapore, Malaysia, Thailand, China, the Philippines, Indonesia and Vietnam.

African countries on the other hand have become major consumers of electronic goods through mastery and adoption of key components of IH (Oyelaran-Oyeyinka, 2006; Oyelaran-Oyeyinka and McCormick, 2007). Table 1.1 shows the indicators of IH knowledge infrastructure and the normalized values of these indicators' basic Internet infrastructure (BII) calculated over the 1999–2004 period.[4] BII CAGR (cumulative over several years) for China, India and Korea top the Asian countries while Ghana, Nigeria, Tanzania and Rwanda have also been growing very rapidly in Africa. The growth rate in Africa reflects the significant investments being made in telecommunications, particularly in GSM (global system of mobile phones).

The IH industry is a complex network of firms that can only be fully understood when considered in a global and regional systemic framework. Components of the industry range from microprocessors, peripherals and

Table 1.1   Average annual growth rate, Africa and Asia

Country	Int. user 2004	PC density 2004	Tel. density 2004	GDP growth (1999– 2004)	BII growth (1999– 2004)
China	72.52	40.88	241.05	7.82	53.09
Hong Kong	505.57	608.34	549.16	2.04	28.32
India	32.41	12.06	40.71	3.98	45.05
Indonesia	7.68	13.88	45.91	0.38	22.37
Korea	2.03	544.92	541.94	3.76	42.63
Malaysia	3.04	196.83	178.60	1.63	18.68
Philippines	3.90	45.13	42.11	1.59	31.29
Singapore	4.89	921.21	439.59	2.18	20.65
Botswana	33.91	45.22	77.13	4.89	31.70
Ghana	16.98	5.16	14.46	2.16	43.45
Kenya	44.81	13.17	8.94	−0.003	17.51
Nigeria	13.74	6.73	7.98	1.08	37.44
Senegal	42.33	21.25	23.13	1.40	33.43
South Africa	78.35	82.18	105.17	1.40	18.31
Tanzania	8.85	7.38	4.27	2.95	53.28
Rwanda	4.27	*	2.58	1.40	32.44

Notes:
*Information not available.
Basic Internet infrastructure (BII) refers to a composite index of Internet users per capita, personal computer users per capita (PC density), and telephone density (Tel). BII = Internet User Index = $\{Xj, i - \text{Min} (Xj, i)\}/\{\text{Max} (Xj, i) - \text{Min} (Xj, i)\}$, Xi refers to the Internet users per capita, and i and j refer to the number of countries reporting data.

Source: Authors' calculations from World Development Indicators, The World Bank 2005.

components to complete systems, operating systems and applications. There are also a plethora of actors: original equipment manufacturing (OEM), original design manufacturer (ODM) and own brand manufacturer (OBM), depending on the level of technology and markets. The activities in which actors are involved are complex and diverse, such as development of new products, design, production, R&D, manufacturing, assembly, logistics, distribution, sales, marketing, service and support. They therefore include the largest multinational corporations (MNCs) as well as small local enterprises.

While the personal computer (PC) has been the flagship of the industry for a long time, the notebook (NB) segment has emerged as a significant component that signals a continuous advance in the evolution of digital technology, which is a shift in form factor. Presently, it is the fastest-growing segment of the industry, located largely in the United States, Japan, Taiwan and China.

The gradual shift of centres of manufacturing production and increasingly design is one of the hallmarks of development in this sector. The move to the Asia-Pacific region and particularly China has been due to a host of factors. Both push and pull factors working simultaneously have been instrumental in the global spread of manufacturing and design, as well as R&D activities. Foreign direct investment (FDI)-driven IH manufacturing began relocating in economies such as Singapore, Malaysia, Thailand, the Philippines, China, Indonesia and Vietnam, with literate low-cost labour in sites endowed with good basic infrastructure, political stability, security and fairly efficient bureaucratic coordination (especially approvals and customs). Singapore managed to stimulate considerable upgrading in the industry through its leveraging strategy. Malaysia, Thailand, the Philippines and Indonesia have remained entrenched in low value-added operations. Vietnam's experience with IH manufacturing is still recent while China has managed to attract both types of operations: low-cost operations in unskilled labour-abundant sites and fairly high-tech operations in science parks.

Taiwan and Korea have relied on preferential policies to stimulate upgrading in local IH firms, accessing MNC know-how through licensing and appropriating learning and innovation synergies through creative duplication (see Amsden, 1989; Amsden and Chu, 2003; Kim, 1997; Rasiah and Lin, 2005). Taiwan, Korea and China have developed the capabilities to sustain export success. These include the availability of a knowledge and skills base, the creation of unique organizational and institutional structures, as well as policy and state coordination that fostered the growth of the sector. From the early 1980s, IH industry space in the world which had been dominated by US companies is now shared by Japanese, Korean, Taiwanese and Chinese companies.

The dynamics of foreign operations in developing economies have also changed over the years. American, European and Japanese firms relocated only assembly and test operations to East Asia in the late 1960s and 1970s. The decomposition of manufacturing operations that started in the 1980s led to the contracting out of components and completely knocked down (CKD) parts operations to other American firms. American and European firms subsequently began contracting out wafer fabrication (for example Taiwan Semiconductor Manufacturing Corporation and United Microelectronics Corporation), computer manufacturing (for example Tatung) and related components to Taiwanese firms from the mid-1980s. OEM operations had become important players in the IH value chain

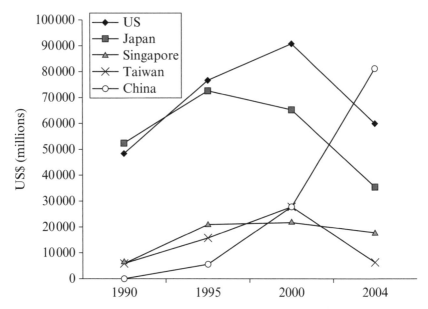

Source: Reed Electronics Research, Yearbook of World Electronics Data.

Figure 1.1   Leading IH-producing locations 1990–2004

by the early 1990s. American (for example Sanmina, Jabil, Flextronics and Solectron) and European (for example Infineon) firms also began to participate strongly in these contract operations. Strong deepening in the high-tech infrastructure in Taiwan, Korea and Singapore has also helped attract innovation offshoring by MNCs to these countries (see Prasada, 2000; Ernst, 2006). China has become a particularly attractive location for original equipment manufacturing (OEM) and contract electronic manufacturing (CEM) from the USA, Europe and Japan, due in part to price competitiveness but significantly because of institutional reforms that raised productivity and provided the platform for a move from simple assembly to packaging, testing and design. The Chinese computer hardware industry has through this convergence of factors risen from being a peripheral actor to being a global producer and exporter from the early 1990s. As shown in Figure 1.1, IH production value increased from $645 million in 1990 to $81 billion in 2004, outstripping US production for the first time.

The accelerated growth of Chinese production started a decade earlier and in the process outpaced forerunners such Japan, Taiwan and Singapore (see Figure 1.1). Chinese hardware production tripled starting in 2000.

Table 1.2   *Domestic export value rankings of world-leading IH producer nations*

	2000	2001	2002	2003	03 Growth (%)
US	85772	69605	61268	62511	2.0
PRC	25535	28174	35225	49075	39.3
Japan	52153	39204	27673	22371	−19.2
Taiwan	23081	20124	17291	11864	−31.4
Singapore	16395	11173	11352	11646	2.6
South Korea	11856	9720	11449	11501	0.5
UK	12121	10725	10121	9946	−1.7
Germany	8657	7430	6549	6430	−1.8
Mexico	9400	8211	8246	8297	0.6
Malaysia	7236	6974	6576	6861	4.3
Ireland	6470	5670	5460	5583	2.3
France	5618	4732	4334	4313	−0.5

Notes:
1 'IT Hardware' includes only the shipment value of computers and peripherals.
2 As some of the national data in the *Yearbook* is based on customs statistics, in some cases it includes transshipment trade.
3 The data in this table has been adjusted according to the revised product definitions and national data included in the latest edition of the *Yearbook*.

Source: JEITA, *The Yearbook of World Economics Data*, EIAK, KISDI; ITIS Project, MIC (2003.11).

China is producing a wide range of IH products including personal computers, servers, desktop PCs and laptop PCs, but excluding mini/micro-computers and workstations.

Significantly, there has been a progressive rise in the share of Asia in IH production and export with an increasing emphasis on a mix of low and high value-added products. While the US remains the top exporter of computer hardware (CH) and also the destination of most exports, there have been changes in the trends. Tables 1.2 and 1.3 show the ranking of the global national leaders in IH production and export.

Although the United States has retained export leadership of IT hardware, China has continued to record the highest growth rate – at almost 40 per cent (see Table 1.2). China's manufacturing production capacity continues to rise and IH export increased from US$35.2 billion in 2002 to US$49 billion in 2003, and with this China became the second-largest exporter to displace Japan and Taiwan to third and fourth places. What is most significant is that while China continues to gain, Japan and Taiwan's shipments

Uneven paths of development

Table 1.3   Exports of IH hardware by regions

Export Year	Global	Asia Pacific (excluding Japan)		Japan		Rest of the world*	
	$M	$M	%	$M	%	$M	%
1999	454646	43685	10.63	59806	15.15	46412	11.37
2000	502594	59190	13.37	70745	16.41	54021	12.06
2001	440394	57787	15.10	59957	15.76	50881	13.06
2002	401908	58132	16.88	52142	14.88	48039	13.55
2003	413114	63171	18.05	53488	14.87	50714	13.99

Notes: * 'Rest of the world' stands for the rest of the developing world, excluding the US and Western Europe.

Source: Calculated from IDC, November 2004.

fell by 19.2 and 31.4 per cent respectively, a significant decline that has widened the gap between them and China. Table 1.3 and Figure 1.2 show the rise of exports by the Asia-Pacific area and the falling trend in the share of Japanese shipments. The rest of the developing world has also been catching up in high-tech exports, but Africa is not an important beneficiary.

Table 1.4 shows exports of computers and electronics components. For instance in both the Standard International Trade Classification Categories (United Nations) 752 and 75997, the share of Taiwan and China in 2000 equalled or surpassed that of a number of Western European countries, and this started in the early 1980s. By 2000 East Asian economies accounted for around 50 per cent of computer exports. The label of 'simple' assembling and 'mere copying' is increasingly no more appropriate a description of products and processes of some developing world. In other words, developing countries are increasingly in mastering IH production.

Currently, China has assumed leadership in global notebook production; the output is shared between domestic and foreign multinationals, notably by firms that migrated from Taiwan or are managed by Taiwanese. Domestic actors have concentrated productive efforts on the local markets and they have been quite successful at adapting imported technology to satisfy local demands. Due to the huge Chinese domestic demand, there is a significantly high share of foreign and joint-venture firms of close to 75 per cent in China's exports (see Chapter 2).

The prominence of Taiwanese firms in China's IH sector is a result of declining profit margins[5] in Taiwan (see Figure 1.3). However, the locational shift was also aided by a change in the legal constraints that

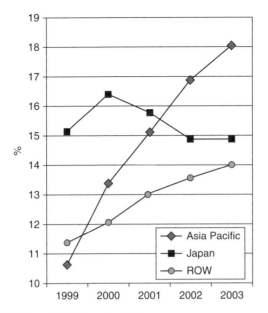

Source: Calculated from IDC, November 2004.

*Figure 1.2   Growth of export value of Asia Pacific, Japan and ROW
          regions*

prevented notebook production by Taiwanese firms in China (Foster et al., 2006). Again much of the OEM contracts were being moved to China by foreign vendors putting pressure on Taiwanese firms to begin to design their own design capability and additionally look for new markets. From production of peripherals they moved on to PC production. A significant part of the output came out of mainland China, and has risen over 1993–2000 (see Table 1.5). Taiwanese firms produced 78–95 per cent of components and peripherals offshore in 2000 of which 60–90 per cent were produced in mainland China. Taiwanese firms manufactured over 80 and 47 per cent respectively of desktops and motherboards offshore. Taiwanese firms produced 45 per cent of desktops and motherboards in mainland China (MIC, 2001).

Among African economies South Africa is the only economy that shows significant numbers of PC exports, but even there the numbers provide scant comparison with East Asia. In South Africa PC shipment totalled 774 784 units during 2002, reflecting a year-on-year growth of 1.5 per cent. During 2002, South African PC market revenues decreased 0.6 per cent year on year, to reach R7774.4 million (BMI-Tech, 2003).

Table 1.4   Country shares in world IH hardware exports

| | Shares of world exports | | | |
| | SITC 752 computers | | SITC 75997 elec. components | |
	1992	2000	1992	2000
Europe				
France	0.05	0.04	0.04	0.02
Germany	0.07	0.05	0.05	0.04
Ireland	0.02	0.05	0.05	0.06
Italy	0.03	0.01	0.03	0.01
Netherlands	0.04	0.08	0.05	0.05
United Kingdom	0.09	0.08	0.07	0.04
Hungary	0.00	0.01	0.00	0.01
Asia				
Japan	0.21	0.08	0.16	0.09
Taiwan	0.07	0.09	0.04	0.09
Hong Kong	0.02	0.02	0.06	0.07
Korea Rep.	0.03	0.05	0.02	0.07
China	0.00	0.06	0.01	0.04
Singapore	0.13	0.11	0.06	0.08
Thailand	0.01	0.01	0.03	0.05
Malaysia	0.00	0.04	0.04	0.00
Philippines	0.00	0.03	0.00	0.02
Americas				
USA	0.23	0.17	0.23	0.18
Canada	0.02	0.01	0.04	0.02
Mexico	0.01	0.04	0.01	0.02
Costa Rica	0.00	0.00	0.00	0.01

Source: UN Trade Statistics.

The strength of educational and public sector PC spending, as well as a stable small and medium-sized business (SMB) sector, have been cited as the primary drivers of IT production in South Africa. SMB shipments were up 57.4 per cent year on year in 2002 (BMI-Tech, 2005).

In 2004, the top ten vendors together accounted for a 74.5 per cent share of the total PC sales in South Africa. This is up from 72.6 per cent reported in 2003. In revenue terms the top ten held a 79.8 per cent share of the market, slightly down from 80.1 per cent reported in 2003. The top five vendors on the South African PC market in 2004 respectively were: HP, Mustek, Dell, Proline and IBM (BMI-Tech, 2005).

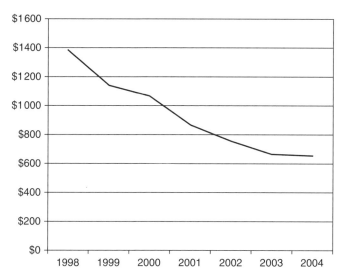

Source: Created from MIC (2005).

Figure 1.3   Average sales prices for notebook sales in Taiwan

1.3   INNOVATION POLICIES AND INFORMATION HARDWARE

Innovation policy differs from orthodox science and technology policy in two main respects. First, it seeks above all to promote systemic dynamics within the national economy rather than focusing on one set of actors. Second, it encompasses a wide array of policies that are rooted in the social system in which the policy is operational. The overall objective of innovation policy is to generate systemic efficiency, though lead sectors are often targeted owing to scarce resources, synergistic potential and initial conditions. The sectoral systems of learning approach helps examine the evolution and dynamics of learning by doing, learning to learn and learning to innovate by confining the focus to specific knowledge bases. The East Asian late followers that are under study here have attained high levels of per capita income and have succeeded in moving into high-value manufactured export goods such as information hardware. Economies that targeted IH and built the requisite institutions and links to upgrade into higher value-added activities such as Korea, Taiwan, Singapore and now China have managed to drive learning and innovation. Economies that targeted IH to generate investment and employment such as Malaysia,

Table 1.5   Taiwan firm production in China

Type of product	Offshore production as % of total[a]			China production 1998	
	1995	1998	2000	1998	2000
All products	25.0	43.0	51.7	NA	NA
Components					
Power supplies		91	95	64	90
Keyboards		91	95	59	86
Mice		89	95	74	95
Cases		75	80	45	71
Monitors		71	81	35	60
Sound cards		67	NA	68	NA
Mapping cards		64	NA	64	NA
CD-ROM/DVD/RW		59	78	43	69
Scanners		38	86	32	85
UPS		25	NA	25	60
Graphics/video cards		18	NA	18	20
Motherboards		36	47	34	45
PC systems					
Desktops		89	84	8	45
Laptops		0.01	7	0	7

Notes:
[a]   Total production includes production in Taiwan, China, and all other overseas locations
     (e.g., the Americas, Europe, etc).
     NA – Information not available.

Source: MIC (1999, 2001).

Thailand, the Philippines and Indonesia have expanded operations largely in low value-added operations.

These countries have employed a number of systemic instruments including enterprise clustering policies, collaborative R&D and science parks (Rasiah, 2005; Rasiah and Lin, 2005; Mathews and Cho, 2000; Lall, 2001; Amsden, 1989; Amsden and Chu, 2003; and in Africa see Oyelaran-Oyeyinka and McCormick, 2007). There are other instruments including: the use of science parks in China, Malaysia and Taiwan; R&D alliances (Taiwan is a notable case); informal networks of scientists and engineers in Taiwan (Rasiah, 2007); and the formation of intellectual networks through old school relationships.[6] African countries have been slower in recognizing the need to address the systemic aspects of policies.

The economic performance of successful latecomers therefore rests in part on their policy-induced efficient, high-quality technology institutions, highly skilled engineers and professionally managed enterprises (Fransman, 1985; Amsden, 1989; Kim, 1997; Chang, 1994; Chang, 2003; Amsden and Chu, 2003; Rasiah and Lin, 2005). On the other hand, the major weakness of the innovation policies of African states has been the neglect of the evolutionary character of technological advance in long-run economic development (Oyelaran-Oyeyinka, 2006). While governments have established ministries of science and technology (S&T), most have little interaction with other economic policy ministries and R&D agencies that are in turn isolated from the private sector. This was the situation in communist-era China until deep-seated institutional reforms helped changed the situation. This pattern of development inadvertently alienates the innovation and science policy-making machinery from mainstream economic policy-making. Again the supply side of knowledge and policy is largely disconnected from the demand side. Governments for instance have set little store on using procurement and demand policy to stimulate demand for innovation. The formulation and implementing of industrial policy is also quite separate from the S&T policy-making process. In effect, national technological infrastructure tends to give little support to domestic firms that would benefit from the evolutionary process of technological deepening through learning that is the hallmark of dynamic latecomers. In sum, the legacy of past practices of doing S&T policy, rather than an emphasis on innovation policies, and the weak bureaucratic capacity to manage a modern system of innovation, have combined to severely limit the administrative and institutional capabilities of the African state.

The key innovation policies that are responsible for the rapid growth of the IH industry include fundamental elements such as policies on education as well as the steps taken to remove institutional impediments to research–industry collaboration. For instance, in China, firstly, governments at the central and provincial levels have used demand policies to stimulate growth. Secondly, the Ninth Five-Year National Development Plan, 1996–2000 focused on increasing the proportion of domestic content in Chinese-assembled computers (for example peripherals such as monitors, printers, disk drives and add-on cards among others). Thirdly, the government aggressively pursued joint ventures with large MNCs in order to gain desired technological capabilities. Concomitantly, China imposed high tariffs and taxes on imported computers to promote local manufacturing.[7]

Two policy reforms are akin to major institutional shifts. The first is the transformation of the previous state-owned enterprises to a hybrid of market-like business organizations affiliated to national institutions such as the Chinese Academy of Sciences (CAS) and key ministries such as the Ministry of Electronics. The well-known 'three capital' enterprises

(Great Wall, Legend and Founder) continue to grow and contribute to a dynamic sector. The second is the institutional shift in the rules governing the academic–industry relationship.

Another industrial organizational model that has led to a dynamic IH sector is the emergence of hi-tech clusters in the triangle of cities in the Yangtze River Delta near Shanghai. They include Suzhou (Asus, Uniwill), Shanghai (Quanta located in Songjiang, and Inventec); Wuhan (Compal); Kunshan (Compal, Wistron, Elite (ECS), Twinhead, Mitac and Clevo), and Wujiang (Arima and FIC). Zhujiang Delta and Changjiang Delta are the principal regions for export of IH products in China and have played very important roles in export for the whole industry.

1.4   LEARNING AND INNOVATION: MEANING AND MECHANISMS

Given that this book seeks to explain the evolution of a particular sectoral system through the mediation of institutions (including policies and instruments) and the link between them and firms, it is important to establish at the outset the meaning and mechanisms latecomers have utilized to learn and innovate. Despite its growing application by policy-makers in developed and in a number of developing countries, considerable obfuscation exists on what innovation might mean in everyday life, and its applicability to solving the problems associated with underdevelopment such as disease burden and poor nutrition.

Apart from the need to distinguish clearly between inventions and innovation, the accent on the source and point of origin of innovation is crucial. An innovation process can be triggered in many ways and not always by a deliberate formulation of a scientific research programme in a laboratory. Bottlenecks in production within a firm, changes in technology, competitive conditions, international rules or domestic regulations, environmental or health crises and even wars have been known to stimulate a process of innovation. From the mid 1970s, a number of changes in the pattern of production and competition have put pressure on firms everywhere to engage in a continuous process of learning and innovation. Two of these stand out in particular: the growing knowledge intensity of production and its extension beyond the high-technology sectors to reshape a broad spectrum of traditional industries, and the emergence of innovation-based competition. As traditional barriers to trade and investment are being dismantled, innovation-based competition diffuses around the globe, intensifying the pressure on firms in developing countries to master imported technology and to innovate. These changes have challenged governments to introduce policies that stimulate and support learning, and innovation policies to drive upgrading. Boxes 1.1 and 1.2 show what innovation is in development, and the distinct differences in the nature of science, technology and innovation respectively.

Related to the new conception of innovation are challenges of economic structures in a development context that are very different from those of industrialized environments, such as poorly developed educational and knowledge infrastructure, and underdeveloped financial and skills markets. Coordination and information externalities are at the heart of these discussions but they take on new and urgent notes in situations of underdevelopment. In fact, far from being a peripheral matter, innovation policies should be an urgent and immediate concern of overall economic policy in developing countries. The reason is that these societies are characterized by poor coordination and negative externalities that cannot be redressed by policies that tend to promote atomistic behaviour by national agencies or a distancing of the public and private agents.

Lundvall's (1992) explication of user–producer relations being central to coordinating the interface of innovation exchange remains central to driving innovation-driven development – the shift from asymmetric to horizontal and interdependent links in value chains is symptomatic of the successful transition of Taiwanese, Korean and Chinese firms in global IH value chains. The failure of Thai, Malaysian and Indonesian firms to make this transition explains why IH manufacturing in these economies has not progressed beyond low value-added operations.

BOX 1.1   INNOVATION AND DEVELOPMENT

- Innovation in a developing context includes continuous improvement in product design and quality.
- Changes in organization and management routines, creativity in marketing and modifications to production processes that drive costs down.
- Increase efficiency and environmental sustainability.
- The ability to manage a portfolio of partnerships, to form linkages and to learn through them.
- As opposed to the focus on novelty that is central to the concept of invention and a key criterion for patenting, innovation is a broader concept.
- In the mind of policy-makers, this distinction is often difficult to make.

BOX 1.2   SCIENCE, TECHNOLOGY AND INNOVATION POLICIES

Science Policy: Objective is the Production of Scientific Knowledge

- To manage and fund the accumulation of knowledge in relation to natural phenomena by creation and support of appropriate organizations, research labs and universities.

Technology Policy: Objective is the Commercialization of Technical Knowledge

- To manage and fund the accumulation and application of practical knowledge needed for particular productive activities, including transfer of technology from overseas and the transfer of scientific knowledge into wealth creation. Organizations are: research laboratories, universities and firms.

Innovation Policy: Objective is Improvements in the Overall Performance of the Economy

- To foster the transfer of science and technology (S&T) knowledge into application by ensuring that necessary complementary resources (capital finance) are available, by supporting entrepreneurship and by protecting intellectual property rights (IPR). The focus of innovation policy emphasizes the interaction between actions within specific institutional and policy contexts that influences their innovative behaviour and performance.

Source: Lundvall (1992).

1.5   INNOVATION IN LATECOMER DEVELOPMENT

There is little doubt that knowledge by itself and embodied in different mediums (as human agents, codified information, new machinery and equipment) particularly with the advent of the Internet has been spreading at an unprecedented rate, but it is equally true that large swathes of the globe are being left behind. While knowledge bridges are occurring, so also are knowledge divides. The spread of the Internet across countries as well as the adoption of related artefacts such as computers and the telephone gives an indication of the skewed growth of human knowledge. But what lies behind the uneven generation and diffusion of knowledge, and with it unequal development, is the diverging development of knowledge appropriating and creating capabilities. Put differently, what factors separate the countries that made rapid progress in 'catching up' and those that 'fell behind'? This question has remained central to economists for decades (Marx, 1860; Mill, 1844; List, 1885; Veblen, 1919; Young, 1928; Schumpeter, 1934; Kaldor, 1957; Lewis, 1956; Myrdal, 1957; Gerschenkron, 1962; Amsden, 1989).[8] There are three broad identifiable historical catch-up paths (clearly there will be others) following from Veblen's account of Germany's industrialization, Gerschenkron's institutional historical approach and the more recent account of Japan's and other East Asian countries' successful industrialization (Johnson, 1982; Freeman, 1987; Fransman, 1985; Amsden, 1989; Amsden and Chu, 2003; Mathews, 2002; Wade, 1990; Chang, 1994, 2003; Reinert, 1994; Rasiah, 2007b). The stylized facts of the catch-up stories are as follows:

- The occurrence of earlier industrialization of forerunners provides an opportunity for latecomers to initiate their own processes of industrialization through learning; not just to imitate the technological process but also to configure new and context-relevant 'institutional instruments' (this is the term used by Gerschenkron).
- This process of catching up demands an institutional arrangement that is peculiar to the endowment of the particular country. The institutional instruments include financial incentives[9] to overcome the scale effects of increasingly complex industrial plants and, notably, instruments to remove the barriers imposed by the state of education of society. As Abramovitz (1956) puts it: 'The state of education embodied in a nation's population and its existing institutional arrangements constrains it in its choice of technology.' Institutions exert a pervasive influence in a country's catch-up process, by defining its past and future.
- The catch-up strategy has almost always succeeded through the targeting of rapidly growing sectors, advice that was taken seriously in East Asia, starting with Japan.[10]
- Catch-up involves an activist state; however the role of the state will differ in style and content across countries and time. In Japan for example, and later South Korea, the use of financial instruments of the state ('directed credit') was deep and pervasive. In Taiwan the

rise of the country's semiconductor industry was spearheaded by a combination of state-promoted policies. The Industrial Technology Research Institute (ITRI) was a key actor while public–private research consortia proved to be effective institutional instruments in developing laptop PCs (Matthews, 2002).

- The nature of demand has also been critical in catch-up strategies (Malerba, 2006). Domestic demand was critical in driving scale-based industries in large economies such as the United States, Germany, Japan and Korea. However, export-oriented industries were central to all successful industries in Taiwan.

1.6 LEARNING AND INNOVATION CAPABILITY BUILDING

Learning and innovation are now considered the *sine qua non* for driving long-term competitiveness even in poor least-developed economies. Increasing integration in global networks of investment, production and trade has made it inevitable that firms seeking to compete in global markets must acquire the requisite knowledge – embodied in humans, processes and products – to compete. Whilst essentially it is the firms that compete, the term 'competitiveness' as a concept goes far beyond the firm. The embedding institutions and the systemic relationships that show connections between economic agents, and the pulse of coordination between them, are central to the competitive advantage of firms. Hence, firms embedded in superior systemic surroundings such as Silicon Valley, Emilia Romagna, Kei Hin District, Bavaria and Taiwan enjoy significantly more high-tech synergies to compete in electronics and automobiles than firms located in underdeveloped systemic surroundings such as the Athi River Valley (Kenya), Pnom Penh (Cambodia), Cicarong (Indonesia) and Johor (Malaysia).

An extensive body of literature exists on the critical role that systems of innovation play in driving learning, innovation and competitiveness in firms (for example Nelson and Winter, 1982; Lundvall, 1992; Freeman, 1987; Edquist, 2004). Much of this literature, however, relates to national systems of innovation with a broad focus on an interpretative link between institutions and firms. Malerba (1992, 2004, 2006) has offered a lucid synthesis of the significance of sectoral systems of innovation by identifying all of their critical elements. Inasmuch as the specificity of certain institutions and relationships is valued when examining firms in particular industries, few if any have actually examined these relationships from the lenses of firms across a wide range of economies in two continents.[11]

Exceptions to this include the work of Rasiah (2003a, 2004, 2007) and Oyeyinka (2003). Using the electronics industry as the sector-specific empirical base, this book seeks to add to this literature, as well as to offer potential contributions to understand better the peculiarities of systemic and institutional elements in the learning and innovation taking place in electronics firms.

1.7 SECTORAL SYSTEMS OF INNOVATION

Although sector- and industry-specific studies have long existed, initiatives to understand the dynamics of learning and innovation took on a new dimension following the evolutionary dynamics of knowledge flows – since the work of Schumpeter (1934, 1942) and subsequently that of Nelson and Winter (1982) and Lundvall (1988), and the articulation of the concepts of taxonomy and trajectory by Dosi (1982) and Pavitt (1984), the effects of particular industry-specific knowledge base as a critical driver of new knowledge – innovation success driving new innovations (both first-movers and latecomers) is discussed well by Malerba and Orsenigo (1997), and Malerba et al. (2001). Although the knowledge bases of particular industries have increasingly penetrated other industries, as Malerba (1992) has argued, the industry-specific boundaries of know-how have remained essential to sustain learning and innovations. Hence, information hardware with its engine in microchips is examined in the book to understand systemically the processes of learning and innovation in a range of disparately developed economies in Africa and Asia.

Following the work of Nelson and Winter (1982), Lall (1992) built the foundations to use firm-level capabilities as the central pillar to understand learning and innovation in the development process, and in the process also pioneered a framework for estimating it. Ernst et al. (1998), Figeiredo (2002) and Rasiah (2004) advanced these concepts further by differentiating technological capabilities. Rasiah (2004, 2007) tested and established a highly significant positive link between the host site's embedding national innovation system (NIS) and technological capabilities in firms. Separating technology – both already embodied (for example technical qualifications, machinery and equipment, products) and tasks developing them (for example training, and process organization and R&D programmes) – by human resources, process technology and R&D, Rasiah (2007b) showed that correlations differ considerably. In automotive and electronics component firms in the underdeveloped locations of East Asia where significant ownership differences existed, foreign firms enjoyed higher human resources and process technology practices than local firms owing to the access they enjoy from superior parent plants. These differences gradually differed as the embedding host-site environment became stronger. The taxonomic features of these firms seem to require similar human resources and process technology practices for them eventually to compete in open markets. Stark differences appear in R&D technology: (1) R&D activity is positively and strongly correlated with the embedding strength in R&D support (for example R&D human capital and expenditure, and the requisite high infrastructure); (2) local firms lacking access to foreign plants show higher reliance on national innovation systems to undertake R&D; and (3) where the high-tech support at the host site is strong, even foreign firms show incidence of offshoring innovation activities (see also Ernst, 2006).

This volume starts by specifying common building blocks of the sectoral system of innovation. While knowledge systems are universal – cutting across economies and industries – sector specificities demand the development and diffusion of specialized knowledge. A sectoral innovation system (SIS) has its own knowledge base and learning processes, it has specific technologies, systems boundaries, firms, institutions and interactive activities, and yet it is connected indirectly with institutions, firms and other systemic elements outside its own sector boundaries. Some institutions and firms connect wholly with particular sectors, while others interact directly with two or more sectors. Some institutions (for example basic service and utility organizations such as security, customs, water and electricity boards, and high-tech organizations such as universities) connect with all sectors. The sectoral system of innovation allows the capture of all elements that firms – as the most dynamic elements – connect with for driving learning and innovation directly or indirectly, consciously or unconsciously, and destructively or constructively.

The argument for the application of the sectoral system of innovation framework is that it is able to address the evolutionary problem of how capacities can be developed to help firms, sectors and countries to cope and compete in dynamic, ever-changing technical, economic and institutional environments. Furthermore the capacity to innovate will involve a system of diverse organizations or actors, notably the private sector, but also others outside the state, whose actions are shaped by a variety of institutional, policy, market and technological signals. The framework is therefore particularly suited to exploring emerging, dynamic sectors where the private sector and other non-governmental actors are playing leading roles and where firms, sectors and countries have to cope with shocks and deal with competitive pressures.

The emergence of a new species of firms to start new sub-sectors is symptomatic of a vibrant region or economy where new knowledge drives differentiation and division of labour. Structural change of this kind stimulates diversification of economic activities arising from the appropriation of knowledge, and provides new opportunities for growth that could be inclusive of small and medium-sized firms as primary producers, as employees and as consumers of intermediate products. Vibrant regions thrive on new species of industries and new firms, so that the old and inefficient firms are replaced continuously with the efficient and competitive ones (Schumpeter, 1942; Best, 2001; Rasiah, 2002). An understanding of sectorally significant technological trajectories helps in tracing the paths of learning and innovation in firms (Nelson and Winter, 1982; Malerba, 1992, 2006).

To provide a level of analysis with sufficient depth to illustrate and exploit the explanatory powers of the sectoral systems of innovation framework, information hardware is chosen as our case study sector. Seven countries were selected for comparative study in Africa and Asia. These are: China, Malaysia, Taiwan, Indonesia, Nigeria, South Africa and Mauritius (see Appendix Table A1.1). Time and financial resources prevented the inclusion of Korea. To this end two themes provide the necessary scope for in-depth analysis of specific cases and comparisons across product groups (information hardware), sectors and country experiences are considered in different national policy environments. The themes are export competitiveness and domestic structural change in a new technological area, that is, information hardware.

Central to the cases in the first theme is the question of how countries build their capacity to compete locally with imports, and how this can be done in ways that have employment generation outcomes as well as build the technological capability of domestic firms. An issue in all these cases is the question of how exporting countries deal (or may need to deal) with the fallacy of composition, that is, the problem of many players entering for instance the computer component market, and the need to innovate continuously to avoid the effects of falling prices.

The second theme will look at both the emergence and growth of computer hardware and associated technologies in their use of (or switch to) products that were previously mainly for local markets, as well those developments surrounding the greater value added of manufactured products. This is a theme that is driven by factors such as the industrialization of the high-tech sectors, clustering and innovation.

These cases deal with the issues of how to cope with rapid transformation at the global level by building innovation capacities to promote industrialization with emphasis on sectors and SMEs where domestic competition is key and in which non-state actors such as industry associations and chambers of commerce are central.

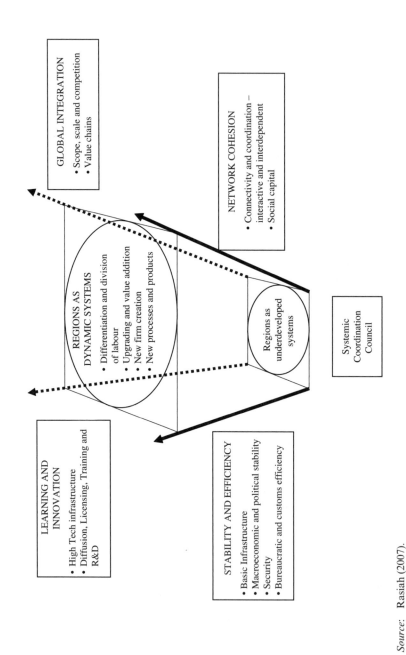

Source: Rasiah (2007).

Figure 1.4   Systemic quad for driving long-term growth

1.8 A MODEL FOR EXAMINING LEARNING AND INNOVATION

Instead of simply separating and assessing the state of all the elements which Malerba (2006) identified as critical in the sectoral systems of innovation, this book uses the systemic quad (see Figure 1.4). By defining four critical pillars the systemic quad not only provides an easier, systematic and coherent assessment of related elements, but also helps distinguish policy and institutional matters from atomized economic agents. In addition, regions or economies at the bottom of the technology ladder often face demand constraints, missing institutions and industries, so much so that unless a Keynesian–Schumpeterian push is initiated laggards cannot be drawn onto the learning and innovation train. Firms remain the active agents and their roles in defining the movement of a region gradually rise as regions evolve from importing and imitating knowledge duplicatively to imitating creatively and eventually innovation knowledge (Kim, 1997).

The key elements of a sectoral system of innovation are the economic agents (actors) and institutions (including instruments and organizations). The four pillars identified in Figure 1.4 are necessary to drive learning and innovation synergies in particular regions and economies. All four pillars must evolve with interdependent and interactive participation from the critical economic agents. There also needs to be interdependence between the four pillars, that is, the four pillars must evolve simultaneously with strong coordination between them.

Actors or Agents

They include individuals, firms and organizations. Individuals include enterprise owners, and engineers and scientists; organizations include enterprises, universities and firms, R&D departments and financial institutions such as development banks. Special attention should be paid to ownership structures (foreign versus local, and if they show transnational ownership patterns). Ownership structures create different sorts of incentives with regard to innovation. The size of enterprise is equally important for its relationship to choices of products, techniques of production and ability to generate capital for investment, and is usually also related to the level of education of owners and the opportunities available to them for learning on their own if a good extension system is not in place.

One of the features of effective innovation systems is the way organizations beyond the state are playing a proactive role in the creation and development of opportunities. In addition, flexibility is also important, as highly compartmentalized and rigidly defined roles do not allow organizations to reconfigure and respond flexibly to changing circumstances. For example, is the public sector concentrating too much on technology development and not enough on its role in providing supporting structures for innovation such as credit and training?

The key questions in analysing sector actors include: Who are the sector actors? Are they from the public or private sectors? What role are SMEs and other sector organizations playing in planning and policy? To what extent is there role compartmentalization in relevant public agencies? How rigid is their mandate? Has this evolved to deal with contemporary development questions? Are intermediary organizations beyond the state starting to emerge in importance, and how are public agencies and public policy trying to deal with this?

Institutions and Organizations

In this book we define institutions differently from organizations. We adopt the definition of an institution suggested by North (1990: 3):

> Institutions are the rules of the game of a society or more formally the humanly-devised constraints that structure human interaction. They include formal and informal dimensions and the latter in very insidious ways tend to control and modify the former in profound ways. They are composed of formal rules (statute law, common law, and regulations), informal constraints . . . and the enforcement characteristics of both.

There are a host of institutions for standards, regulations, labour markets, testing and quality. It is important to understand what they do, how they do it, when they were established and how effectively they perform their assignment. Institutions are defined as rules and laws as well as the norms and habits that shape interactions. Institutions are important because they affect the transformational and transportation costs of production and exchange.

What habits and practices do organizations have which restrict interaction, knowledge sharing, learning, investing and inclusiveness of actors? What types of habits and practices should be developed and in which organizations? Are there policies designed to support innovation that are being negated by existing habits and practices? What measures could be put in place to account for this?

Institutions and organizations in an innovation system are one of the defining factors determining the propensity to innovate continuously. Institutions affect innovation in a number of ways. There are institutions that affect the critical processes of interacting, knowledge sharing and learning. There are institutions that affect risk-taking and which determine whether an organization will invest in training, new equipment or technology that will be needed to innovate. And there are institutions that govern the inclusiveness of organizations and systems of the agenda of all relevant stakeholders, but particularly poorly developed ones. Inclusiveness is important to innovation because it is often a source of demand. Also non-market mechanisms such as collaboration and linkage are important even where market mechanisms are developed.

These sorts of institutions can be very subtle. It is often useful to think about broad habits first. For example is there a tradition of organizations from the private sector working with the public sector? Do research organizations work with enterprise or industry associations? What has characterized the relationship between sectors? Relationships within groups of similar organizations also need to be understood. For example is there a tradition of small-scale firms working collectively and sharing information?

It is useful to explore how organizations interact with others. Using the typology above, what sort of linkages do they mainly have? Is there a tradition of actively seeking new links and partners? Or is the partnership base static? This is important because it determines an organization's ability to reconfigure linkages in the face of changing circumstances. It is part of the dynamic capability to innovate.

Understanding how the habits and practices of an organization affect risk-taking can also be difficult. Long-established family businesses that have followed the same line of business for many years are probably less likely to take risks. Strong hierarchies in public organizations tend to stifle risk-taking. Professional incentives such as criteria for promotion can also affect risk-taking. It is important to recognize the existence of these sorts of habits and practices as cushioning policies can then be devised to account for these and make it easier for organizations to respond to other incentives, policies and stimuli to invest, interact or be inclusive.

Systemic Coordination

In a coherently networked economy or region systemic, stakeholder or public–private partnership councils partisan to shaping learning and innovation representing economic agents – pursuing their own self-interest as well as the region, cluster or economy as a whole – as well as organizations play an important role in coordinating the development of the four critical pillars that constitute the systemic quad.

Typically governments play a pivotal role when the four pillars are underdeveloped, as the elements that are necessary for an innovation system to function at the bottom of the technology ladder will either be non-existent or weak. Government was central in the formative years of take-off in Japan, Korea, Taiwan and Singapore. the role of the Ministry of International Trade and Industry (MITI) in Japan, the Korean Development Institute (KDI) in Korea, the Industrial Technical Research Institute (ITRI) and its sectoral unit, the Electronic Research and Service Organization (ERSO) in Taiwan, and the Economic Development Board (EDB) in Singapore played major roles in the early years to drive acquisition, learning and innovation.

As the economic agents and markets evolve, their roles increase in the coordination of the region, cluster or economy so that the focus on learning and innovation reflects their collective interests – firms, employees (managers, professionals and workers) and the people that embed them. Hence, systemic governance and coordination – whether reflecting the collective interests of all agents or just a few – provides the direction for guiding the four critical pillars of the systemic quad. These developments appear strongly in the development of Japan, Korea, Taiwan and Singapore.

Stability and Efficiency

The first pillar of the systemic quad focuses on the provision of efficient basic infrastructure, political and macroeconomic stability, bureaucratic efficiency and security. Indeed the proliferation of export processing zones at Shannon International Airport (Ireland) and in the developing economies began with the provision of these services as transnational corporations sought to relocate low value-added activities that only required a literate, disciplined, easy to train and docile (to enable easy hiring and firing) labour force in light assembly activities gripped by high volatility in demand (Rasiah, 1987).

This pillar is essential for economic agents operating in any of the sectors. The focus on this pillar is also important for driving learning and innovation as frontier clusters, regions and economies must provide the lowest transaction costs for their economic agents to be competitive. Institutional change – including in infrastructure management – absorbing cutting-edge information technology and swift handling of cargo are paramount to drive logistics operations.

Political instability, customs tardiness and bureaucratic inefficiencies can severely undermine the capacity of IH firms seeking to participate in high value-added activities. Indeed, the Philippines – which competed well with Singapore and Malaysia to attract semiconductor firms in the early 1970s – lost out two decades after that owing to political instability, recovering only when stability was restored in the 1990s. Tied to political stability is macroeconomic stability, as the capacity of poor economies to invest in the innovation infrastructure will be limited by strong pressures to address poverty and stability problems. For African economies this is a major problem.

Network Cohesion

The second pillar drives coordination and strengthens connectivity between economic agents and institutions. Regions with a dynamic set of economic agents and institutions use these to effectively coordinate and connect firms and organizations. These include provision of utilities such as power, water, telecommunications; education and training institutions; and R&D laboratories. These sets of institutions drive innovation and competitiveness through flows of circular and cumulative causation. What Young (1928), Kaldor (1957) and Cripps and Tarling (1973) argued at a structural level can be presented in network terms through the concept of clusters.

The focal point of innovation in a dynamic cluster is essentially the interdependent and interactive flow of knowledge and information among people, enterprises and institutions (Rasiah, 2002). It must obviously include coordination between the critical economic and technological agents across value chains who are needed in order to turn an idea into a process, product or service in the marketplace. In dynamic clusters such as Silicon Valley and Route 128, innovations evolve from a complex set of interrelationships among actors located in a range of enterprises, universities and research institutes. The execution and appropriation of these innovations *inter alia* expand further actors in dynamic clusters to intermediary organizations such as suppliers, venture capitalists, property rights lawyers and marketing specialists.

The government is a major player providing a significant share of the funding for public goods, though the National Science Foundation (NSF, 2003) has warned about a decline in funding from the early 1990s. Government funding comes in the form of research supported within the military, as well as support of research undertaken in firms and other laboratories. The military was the prime move of transistor technology in semiconductors and became the basis for the opening of the first private semiconductor firm. The transistor was invented in the Bell Laboratory (US military) and Fairchild became the first semiconductor firm (see Rasiah, 1987 [1993]).

Most industrial estates and export processing zones in the past generally only focused on basic infrastructure. The long-term objective of government policy in these economies has been to ensure sustained increase in labour force participation and wages so that the broader objectives of poverty alleviation and human development are met. In some export processing zones the broad recommendation by the World Bank is for a limited role of government in the provision of basic infrastructure. This policy, wherever it was taken on board as the only policy action, proved to be highly inadequate as a strategy to drive upgrading (see Rasiah, 2007). Without the right set of policies to promote learning and innovation, increased integration in the global economy undermined the capacity of these regions to compete against rising wages, and the emergence of new sites such as China. Also, it limits the capacity to meet the rising technological deepening requirements in the key sectors (for example electronics) with deleterious consequences such as unemployment, underemployment, poverty and poor human resources. Lall (2001) observed that economies that failed to develop their technological capabilities became losers in the globalization process.

Learning and Innovation

The third pillar of the systemic quad emphasizes the participation of economic agents (individuals, firms and institutions) in learning and innovation. High-tech infrastructure provides the environment where the institutions coordinating learning and innovation evolve effectively to stimulate technology acquisition through learning by doing, licensing, adaptation, training, standards appraisal mechanisms, and a strong intellectual property rights (IPR) framework to prevent moral hazard problems facing innovators and R&D.

The innovation system framework recognizes that learning can take a number of forms: learning by interacting, learning by doing, learning by imitating (in order to master process or technology), learning by searching (for sources of information) and learning by training. Again, while all these forms are important, successful innovation systems are characterized by a high degree of interactive learning.

In addition, one of the reasons for differences in innovative capacities between regions and nations is the gap in their knowledge bases – both internally generated and from external sources. Economic agents that complement firms with knowledge differ in their scientific and technological skills and experiences. The habits and practices of the actors differ regarding how and what they learn, for instance, diversification into new peripherals clones, services and so on.

It is the failure of export processing zones in several developing economies to engender the critical high-tech institutions (to support upgrading and R&D operations) that has restricted learning and innovation in firms. Hence, the requisite IPR and incentive (including matching grants) framework, and training, R&D (including through universities), venture capital and standards organizations are vital to drive the movement of regions, clusters and economies from underdeveloped status to a mature status, as shown in Figure 1.4.

Global Integration

The fourth systemic pillar requires that clusters, regions or economies are globally connected – through markets and value chains. Global markets provide the economies of scale and scope and the competitive pressure to innovate. While the accumulation of knowledge learning and innovation opens the path for further learning and innovation (creative accumulation), exposure in global markets drives the continuous replacement of obsolete technologies and firms with new ones.

In addition, global integration also facilitates the integration of economic agents in a cluster, region or economy into global value chains. In tradable sectors such as IH and garments the processes of insertion and integration and reintegration in global value chains is central to participation in export markets (see Gerrefi, 2002; Gerrefi et al., 2005). Examples of such changes include the introduction of cutting-edge just-in-time and flexible specialization techniques in electronics, and the proliferation of software technology in the use of CAD and CAM machines and the interface between firms' assembly activities and the major markets abroad. In Indonesia for example, Texmaco which is located in an EPZ (export processing zone) in the outskirts of Jakarta responded to the changing nature of global value chains in the garment industry by integration assembly, fashion design, packaging and logistics to supply brand name holders. Lacking in institutional support – both basic and high-tech infrastructure – Texmaco has managed to compete globally despite facing tremendous transactions costs in Indonesia.

Government policy in the promotion of clusters must be defined by a cluster coordination council comprising representatives from all the critical economic agents – firms and institutions in the cluster, including the four pillars. The cluster council should also act as a vehicle to stimulate the simultaneous and interdependent interaction of markets and government in driving the four pillars to prevent failures in all three.

Economies that managed to strengthen the four systemic pillars have managed to sustain several decades of rapid growth and employment absorption, value addition and sustained exports (for example Singapore, Taiwan Province of China, Hong Kong, Ireland and Israel). Economies that simply focused on providing basic infrastructure, political stability and security, at least in EPZs and industrial estates, have failed to enjoy sustained growth and employment absorption, value addition and sustained exports (for example Brazil, Indonesia and the Philippines).

Whereas sustained value addition, differentiation and division of labour, and wage increases have helped sharply raise standards of living and human development in the successful economies noted, their lack has denied the latter economies this experience.

Finally, the boundary of offshoring is shifting as MNCs build specialized facilities for R&D in developing countries. Evidence provides two major drivers of the offshoring of R&D activities in developing economies, viz., access capabilities located at host sites (for example software in India and resources in South Africa), incentives providing access to domestic markets (for example Brazil) and grants and tax breaks (for example Singapore and Ireland) (see Rasiah, 2004; UNCTAD, 2005). Taiwan and Korea provide a different experience as knowledge from MNCs – especially product know-how – was accessed through licensing agreements (see Edquist and Jacobssen, 1987; Rasiah and Lin, 2005; UNCTAD, 2005).

1.9   OUTLINE OF THE BOOK

This detailed theoretical chapter starts the book by setting out the two broad themes and a general proposition. It outlines the key factors that explain the wide and divergent paths of development between East Asia and sub-Saharan Africa. It looks at the processes of technological capability accumulation through learning which is now widely accepted as a central force in historical economic catch-up. We provide some justification for the country and sector comparative perspective and sum up our basic hypothesis. We assume that the paths of development of nations are uneven in the sense that countries chart unequal trajectories depending on where they came from, the processes they adopted (path-dependence), the natural endowment they possess and its consequences for sectoral specialization patterns.

We take the position that 'nothing just happens' and states have strong and unique roles to play in the catch-up process. Explicit investment in technological capability acquisition, an activity that is central to modern economic development, is underpinned by a unique and nationally distinct set of institutions and organizations. In other words, industrialization is not simply about the purchase of machinery or simply increasing investment in research and development (R&D). The uneven paths of development are rather complex and akin to running a gauntlet. However, analysts do have a few areas of agreement, namely: that knowledge, not just technology alone in its narrow sense, is critical; that certain leading sectors are able to propel economies in the direction of high-growth dynamics; that learning through diversity generation (this is triggered in economic systems through innovation) fosters economic development; and that diversities of institutions and systems of production (and innovation) explain the persistent differences in the path of development and ultimately the economic outcomes of national efforts.

Chapter 2 relates the fascinating evolution of the Chinese computer industry which demonstrates that innovation policies, as well as the institutions supporting the system, must co-evolve with different stages of development. The study shows that innovation policies designed for the computer industry showed sensitivity not only to the particular context of Chinese traditional habits but also were flexible enough to accommodate external factors and actors. Again specific institutions may lead to the creation of unintended conflicts and systemic disharmony that require greater coordination that can only be provided by an equally sophisticated policy regime.

Chapter 3 examines IH in Indonesia and shows that while foreign firms competing in export markets show higher human and process technology capabilities, the weak high-tech infrastructure facing all firms in Indonesia has foreclosed a speedy accumulation of capabilities in local firms. Local firms are engaged in activities with low value added. The underdeveloped systemic and institutional environment has also affected the ability of small and medium-sized firms from effective access to collective action support services.

In contrast Malaysia (Chapter 4) shows much superior infrastructure and as such has been able to attract global IH firms to clusters such as Penang and Johor, although the outcome is clearly differentiated on the basis of the commitment of governments to invest in cluster infrastructure and coordination. For this for reason, firms in Penang are better integrated in global markets and value chains than firms in Johor. The superiority of systemic coordination in Penang over Johor is reflected in the incidence and depth of participation of firms in learning, innovation and labour productivity. In addition to higher capabilities, IH firms in Penang – irrespective of ownership – showed higher technological intensities (process and product) than for firms in Johor. The skills-intensity levels of firms in Penang were also higher than for firms in Johor. Firms in Penang also seem to be paying higher wages to support higher technological and skills intensities than firms in Johor. This strategy has also enabled firms in Penang to enjoy higher labour productivity than firms in Johor. The evidence underscores the book's evolutionary argument that institutional and systemic support are critical to the process of learning, innovation and competitiveness in firms.

Chapter 5 examines the case of the computer assembly sector in an African country, Mauritius. The chapter concludes that the IH sector is in a nascent stage and actors are involved largely in assembling rather than in core manufacturing activities. The main actors are domestic small and medium-sized firms for which the government has provided a relatively stable macroeconomic environment but little in terms of specific sectoral policies except for the establishment of an ICT incubator.

Similar to the Mauritius and Indonesian cases, the Nigerian case study in Chapter 6 illustrates how lags in policy regimes as well as poor institutions and infrastructure constrain what could otherwise be a dynamic sector. The chapter comes to the conclusion that innovation systems grow on the strength of available physical infrastructure, which for this cluster has been a severe constraint. Human capital, represented by the educational qualifications of the workforce, is a distinct attribute of the sector and has proved to be an important factor in determining the growth and innovation propensity of all groups of firms.

Support from governments has been found inadequate on many counts as confirmed by all instruments of analysis employed. From the findings of this study, it becomes clear that the government has not paid attention to the specificity of sectoral innovation systems, and 'functional' policies have suffered from a lack of enforcement and resources.

In Chapter 7, we see the case of incipient evolution of a sector due in large part to lags in policy action in spite of a relatively superior infrastructure regime. The IH sector began to grow only in the early 1980s (whereas the Malaysian sector had been receiving intense attention and support more than two decades earlier) from a relatively immature market to a significant growth sector in South Africa. Both hardware and software activities have developed largely in the absence of national coordinated strategies specifically to promote these sectors. IT activities in South Africa are very heterogeneous and unevenly distributed across regions. The firms are concentrated in the large metropolitan areas where hardware reselling and assembling represent the largest sub-sector, comprising over 40 per cent of the total IT revenues. Also, much of the sector's revenues are distributed among a few large indigenous companies and foreign MNCs. In both hardware and software activities, the sector is increasingly populated by SMEs.

The last case study chapter (Chapter 8) examines the state of the four pillars of the systemic quad that helped drive learning and innovation in the computer and components industry in Taiwan, arguably the most successful, with China. All four pillars – basic infrastructure, high-tech infrastructure, global integration and network cohesion – have been so well developed that they not only enjoyed high empirical ranking scores but also produced few differences by ownership and size. The effective coordination of government and markets helped drive the development of the systemic pillars effectively so that small and medium-sized firms were able to avoid the typical barriers they face in other developing economies to compete successfully with large firms. Institutionally it is only in collaboration with R&D and course curriculums of universities that local large firms enjoy statistically significant stronger links than foreign and small and medium-sized firms.

Finally, Chapter 9 concludes by returning to our central proposition. We propose a model for examining the role of a sector in economic development within a setting of a diverse set of polities that define learning and innovation. Clearly, individual countries follow imperfect and uneven paths of industrial and technological evolution defined by variations in initial conditions and policy support. To understand fully how the different countries' experiences help explain the importance of institutions and institutional change, we created a taxonomy of systems with its critical drivers comprising learning, innovation and competitiveness. The chapter ends with a broad set of proposals for advancing learning and development in late development.

NOTES

1. This book takes as given the fact that policies and institutions are context specific and may be relevant only for a specific time. For instance institutions that East Asian countries employed in early stages of catch-up to achieve unprecedented export success may be irrelevant at another time. Global rules of the game have changed and new actors have emerged to change the dynamics of trade and other exchange relations.
2. For instance, and increasingly, the so-called 'low-tech' sectors (salmon in Chile for instance) revolutionalized by new technologies, are increasingly being used as sources of wealth generation.
3. See World Bank (1989) for the former and Easterly (1989) for the latter.
4. The BII is a component value of Internet User Index (Int. User/1000), Personal Computer/1000 (PC Density) and Telephone User/1000. The index was calculated by normalizing the values and the compound annual growth rate found over the 1995–2004 period.
5. It is the nature of 'technological revolutions' that there is a gradual lowering of costs over time.
6. In China, a large percentage of the pool of engineers came out of Tsing Hua and formed the core of the pioneers of one of the biggest computer hardware companies in China.
7. In course of time as China joined the World Trade Organization (WTO) in 1995, the tariff levels have gradually been reduced from 82 per cent in the early 1990s to 15 per cent.
8. The catch-up challenge has recently occupied the attention of leading economists working on innovation and technological change. Through the Globelics and 'Catch-up' groups, the latter initiated by Richard Nelson, several research projects are currently being carried out across regions.
9. Gerschenkron's famous example is Germany's use of investment banking as an institutional instrument to foster industrialization. He alluded to the forms of state support in Russia as another. In recent times, East Asian countries have deployed an array of institutional instruments that co-evolved with targeted industries. As Mathews and

Cho (2000: 187) put the case of Taiwan: 'The Taiwanese approach to the upgrading of technological capabilities within industry has been pursued using innovative institutional frameworks over the course of three decades. These frameworks have co-evolved with the industries they fostered. The major sources for leverage have been training and engineering development; multinational investments and joint ventures; institutional support infrastructure such as the Hsinchu Science-based Industry Park ... innovation alliances; and government coordination'.

10. The latecomer history of East Asia is replete with successful stories of how in relatively quick succession South Korea and Taiwan followed the leader, Japan in electronics and automotive production. For details of the East Asian experience, see Amsden (1989); Amsden and Chu (2003); Mathews and Cho (2000) among others.

11. Malerba (2006) seeks to put together a volume on Pharmaceuticals, Agro-food, Software, Telecommunications and Automobiles. This interesting volume, however, only seeks to examine three or four countries in each of the industries involved. In addition, Malerba's (2008) volume is expected to be submitted well after this book.

APPENDIX

Table A1.1   Country and sectors

Country	Indicators
South Africa	Computer hardware
Nigeria	Computer assembly
Mauritius	IH
Taiwan	IH
Malaysia	IH
Indonesia	IH
China	Computer hardware

2. The rapid rise of China

2.1 INTRODUCTION

The Chinese computer industry started relatively late compared to the much longer history of this sector in the West, but the sector has been developing very rapidly since the 1980s. Currently, China, including Taiwan, has become the number three global computer manufacturing country. After China joined the World Trade Organization (WTO), it took advantage of its provision and the benefits, and now the electronics industry in China has risen to number one among all the industries in the national economy ranked by growth rate, industrial size and the growth rate and size of its exports.

In 2004 China's IH products registered a manufactured value added of RMB1880 billion, which was an increase of 34 per cent over the preceding year. Added value of the industry increased at the same rate and reached RMB400 billion. The value of IT exports totalled US$141 billion, an increase of 53 per cent over the 2003 figure, which was considerably higher than China's overall increase in exports. Among all the sub-sectors of the electronics industry, the computer industry has been growing very rapidly in recent years as the scope of national informatics is enlarged and the demand for computers rises. In 2007, it constituted the largest proportion of the Chinese electronics products manufacturing industry. In 2003, the production and sales size of the computer industry in China was 33.6 per cent of the total information technology (IT) industry. The Chinese computer industry structure is composed mainly of computer hardware, which constitutes 80 per cent of the total industry. Computer software manufacturing and services respectively comprised 9 per cent and 11 per cent of industry. This chapter will focus mainly on the computer hardware manufacturing sector, although the two segments, computer hardware and computer software, are often linked in ways that make statistical distinction difficult.

There are three main segments in the computer manufacturing chain, namely: computer clones including PC laptops, work stations, servers, embedded systems and so on; peripherals including printers, scanners, digital equipment, CD drivers, outside machine memory equipment; and components including CPU (central processing unit), hard disks, memory and microprocessor chips, main boards and so on. According to the Chinese national economy industry categories and codes (GB/T4754-2002), the computer manufacturing industry is made up of the computer clones manufacturing industry, the computer Internet equipment manufacturing industry and the computer peripherals manufacturing industry. However, the computer Internet equipment segment has a very small proportion of production value and sales, though it has experienced a very rapid growth rate.

The computer industry is a global industry, and is characterized by well-known global value chains. Multinational corporations like Dell, HP, Fujitsu-Siemens and Acer control over one-third of the global personal computer (PC) market, especially the core technologies of the industry. These firms are located at the high value-added end of the industrial chain, while countries and firms with lower levels of technological capabilities engage mainly in processing and assembling. Overall the Chinese computer industry is still located in the latter stage. However, the industry has experienced a considerable process of learning with initiatives coming from both firms and the government.[1] The process of learning has seen many Chinese firms taking a step-by-step catching-up strategy due to the distance between them and global players.[2] Another feature of the strategy is that firms have been learning to innovate through collaboration. Chinese firms have gradually realized that 'know-who' to collaborate with is critical for them to upgrade their technological and innovation capabilities. Some firms have established a variety of collaboration arrangements with multinational corporations (MNCs), research institutes and universities. During the process of firm-level learning, the government has equally experienced considerable policy learning. At the initial stage, policies mainly focused on the creation of a stable environment, and also devised a number of measures to promote industrial development. In the 1990s, as domestic demand increased, the target of the policies shifted to raising production capability, and in the process firm size and technology level grew. From mid-2000, structural changes based on indigenous innovation within the industry are the focus of national innovation strategies and policies.

Although Chinese computer firms are moving up the technological ladder, most still lack innovation capabilities; they tend to compete largely in low-price goods. Hence, the growth in the size of the computer industry has been accompanied by falling profit rates (see Figure 2.1), and this has influenced the profitability of the entire high-technology industry in China.

In this chapter, we describe the historical development of the Chinese computer industry, and analyse the sources of its fast growth and technology innovation capabilities, especially the role of government in the catching-up process. We try to answer the questions: What are the

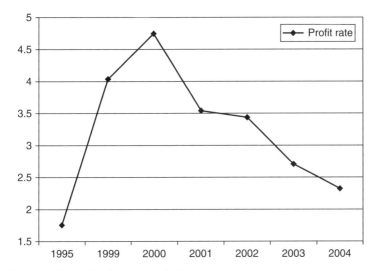

Note: Indicator: Profit rate = profits/sales revenue.

Source: Calculated according to data from the National Statistics Bureau, National Development and Reform Committee and Ministry of Science and Technology edited, China Statistics Yearbook on High Technology Industry 2005.

Figure 2.1   Profit rate of the computer and office equipment industry in China

determinants of the Chinese computer industry catching up? How influential are institutions and innovation polices in shaping China's computer sectoral innovation system?

2.2   HISTORICAL BACKDROP

The origin of the computer industry in China can be traced to certain events in 1956.[3] The Institute of Computing Technologies of the Chinese Academy of Sciences was set up on 25 August 1956, the first computer technology research institute in China. However, it was not until the late 1970s and 1980s that policies on the industry took effect. In 1979, the Bureau of National Computer was set up by the State Council, the first national-level administrative organization of the computer industry. In 1985 the first PC, Great Wall 0520, which could be applied to large-scale industrial production was developed in the public state research institute. In effect, the computer industry in China formally developed from the science and research sector moving gradually to the market. At this time, computer users in China were very few, and the computer was used mainly for basic calculations; a mass domestic market has yet to evolve. The trajectory of the sector is best traced through its phase-wise development.

Stage 1:   Science and Technology Plan and Development Fund, 1980s

In 1986, the former Ministry of Electronics Industry, inspired by the development of the electronics industry in the USA, spelled out the key policies and listed four priority categories of electronics products for development: integrated circuits, computers, software and switching boards. The policies contained various tax incentives which include production taxes, half of income taxes, tariffs on key equipment and machinery which constituted 10 per cent of R&D expenses of turnover, and exemption of import taxes of significant imported projects. In order to recruit highly qualified personnel, engineers and scientists were given incentives such as high salaries while new policies were put in place for fostering small-scale ventures. For example, the government allocated RMB100 million every year to set up the Electronics Industry Development Fund. The fund was used to set up over 2000 research and development experimental and production assemblies. There were 235 enterprises and organizations that benefited from the above policies. The most significant outcome, arguably, is the emergence of certain computer firms, namely, the China Great Wall Computer Group Corporation, Lenova (formerly known as Legend) China, the Inspur Group and Taiji Computer Corporation Limited.

The companies originated from the deep changes to institutions and policies related to the industrialization and commercialization of science that involved both technology personnel and the research organizations. Central to this new institutional arrangement was the 1988 reform of the national science and technology system, the Torch Plan, which was formulated to push the process, mainly to encourage the emergence of science and technology-based firms, and to set up high- and new-technology parks.

Stage 2:   Market Competition, Development and Concentration (The Early 1990s)

Since the 1990s, the computer industry experienced a strong competitive pressure on prices. There is evidence that as the industry grew, prices of products declined very rapidly. Table 2.1 shows the case of notebook PC production in China.

The price war led to a high level of concentration of the computer industry. In 1997, the market share of sales of the top four companies was 31.8

Table 2.1   Notebook PC production in China

	2000	2001	2002	2003	2004
Production (Ten thousand items)	3.0	8.0	39.0	646.3	2750.0
Sales (RMB billion)	7.54	9.53	12.46	17.31	27.443
Sales (Ten thousand items)	4.19	5.76	8.05	12.60	21.864
Price on average (RMB)	17995	16545	15478	13738	12552

Source: Editing Committee, China Economy BOOMING Supervision Centre (edited), China Industrial Maps: IT 2004–2005, Social Sciences Academic Press, 2005.

Table 2.2   Notebook PC market share in 2004 (%)

	Dell	IBM	HP	Toshiba	Fujitsu Siemens	Acer	Lenova	Others
Global	17.9	5.9	15.8	–	4.0	3.6	19.8	52.8
China	12.9	18.2	9.9	6.8	–	–	19.8	32.4

Source: Editing Committee, China Economy BOOMING Supervision Centre edited, China Industrial Maps: IT 2004–2005, Social Sciences Academic Press, 2005.

per cent; in 1998 it rose to 34.1 per cent. In 2004, the figure had reached 60.8 per cent (see Table 2.2). In 2001, the Lenova Group became the number one computer company and controlled the lion's share of the total market which it still maintained in 2007. In 2004, its market share reached 19.8 per cent. By the end of the 1990s, the market share of domestic PC manufacturers had increased significantly, especially after Lenova acquired the PC business of IBM in 2005, an event that further boosted the market share of domestic PC manufacturers.

Stage 3:   Learning from the International Market: from Imitation to Innovation (Late 1990s)

China has become a very important global player by building a strong production base for both domestic and export markets. In many product categories, it has become the number one producer in the world. However, the Chinese computer industry is still relatively unsophisticated and is located at the end of the industrial value chain.

The industry has evolved from simple imitations, as firms accumulate capabilities through active participation in international computer industrial technology. Firms have adapted and through this process made plenty of profits through the integration and development of Chinese character processing technologies into new models of computers. One of the keys to their success is mastering the core components, namely, integrated circuits, chip design and software moulds. The international market played a very important demonstrating role at the initial stage of development. Chinese firms learn by responding to international consumers' needs and making changes to old computer models through the supply, service and sales of imported computers. During the 1980s, the learning modes of firms did not involve the mastering of core technology and the knowledge of key fields. Since the 1990s, more and more multinational corporations have entered into China, and many world-class PC producers like Compaq, Dell, HP and IBM have set up factories in China. As the domestic market became more competitive, multinational corporations gradually accelerated the modes and speed of technology diffusion. The flow of technology increased as more and more multinational computer corporations set up R&D centres in China.

2.3   CHINESE COMPUTER SECTORAL INNOVATION SYSTEM

Along with the National Economy Informatics in China, the computer industry developed very rapidly. In 1986, there were only 42 000 PC items in China. In 2004, the number of PC items had increased tremendously to 45 120 thousand, and the number of PC sales items reached 3,083 thousand in 2003 (see Figure 2.2).

The sector comprises a wide variety of firms involved in the manufacturing of both clones and computers. Both the production value and sales of computer clones manufacturing were higher than those of computer peripherals (see Figure 2.3 and Table 2.3). In 2004, the production value and sales of the clones industry were RMB411.39 billion and RMB461.95 billion, while sales of the peripherals industry were RMB351.02 billion.

However, the profits of the two sub-sectors moved in opposite directions. In 2004, the profits of the clones industry were RMB7.97 billion, while those of peripherals industry were RMB9.24 billion, which was higher than those of the clones industry (see Table 2.3). The contrasting sales and profits figures reflect structural problems in the process of Chinese computer industry development. With increasing globalization,

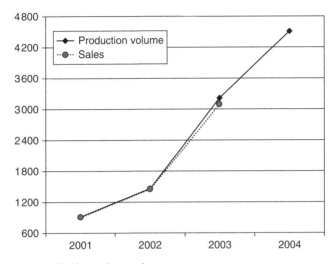

Note: Values provided in ten thousand.

Sources: Editing Committee, China Economy BOOMING Supervision Centre edited, China Industrial Maps: IT 2004–2005, Social Sciences Academic Press, 2005.

Figure 2.2   Production volume and sales of personal computers

many domestic firms had accepted the outsourcing business of MNCs' processing and assembling activities due to lack of key technologies in the field. These activities have over time been shifted to the low value-added end of the industrial value chains.

Concerning the size of firms in the industry, large firms obviously have much higher leverage than small firms that specialize in peripherals, both in production value and in profits earning (see Table 2.4). As mentioned before, market competition has directly caused the concentration of the industry. In addition, a very important factor is the 'Large Firm Strategy Document' issued by the government, by which the government tries to cultivate and support the industry champions.[4]

An important and notable characteristic of the Chinese computer industry development is that it has very significant regional differences. The manufacturing bases are mainly concentrated in the Guangdong, Jiangsu and Fujian provinces and Shanghai and Beijing main cities (see Table 2.5, Table 2.6). In these regions production is mainly concentrated in three locations including the Yangzi River Delta, Pearl River Delta and Loop Bo Sea Region, which have formed the computer manufacturing industrial clusters in those regions. The three regions have different features: for

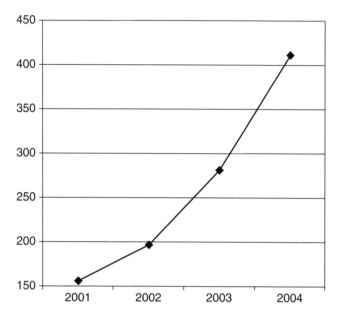

Sources: Editing Committee, China Economy BOOMING Supervision Centre edited, China Industrial Maps: IT 2004–2005, Social Sciences Academic Press, 2005.

Figure 2.3   Production value of computer clones manufacturing industry 2001–04 (RMB billion)

Table 2.3   Computer manufacturing industry sales and profits, 2004 (RMB billion)

Items	Sales	Profits
Clones	461.95	7.97
Peripherals	351.02	9.24
Total	826.44	17.83

Sources: Editing Committee, China Economy BOOMING Supervision Centre edited, China Industrial Maps: IT 2004–2005, Social Sciences Academic Press, 2005.

instance, the Pearl River Delta has a very strong costal manufacturing base with importation processing; the Loop Bo Sea Region is the most highly knowledge-intensive region with a large number of low-cost science and technology personnel; and the Yangzi River Delta has combined the above two factors, though it does not have such a concentrated knowledge base as the Loop Bo Sea Region.

*Table 2.4 Industrial production value and profits by size, computer
manufacturing firms, 2004 (RMB billion)*

	Large firms	Medium firms	Small firms
Total production value clones	291.489	68.133	51.763
Total production value peripherals	161.04	147.84	51.86
Subtotal	452.529	215.97	103.62
Profits clones	7.058	0.76	0.152
Profits peripherals	3.25	3.94	2.07
Subtotal	10.308	4.7	2.22

Sources: Editing Committee, China Economy BOOMING Supervision Centre edited,
China Industrial Maps: IT 2004–2005, Social Sciences Academic Press, 2005.

*Table 2.5 Turnover of computer clones manufacturing industry at selected
provinces/cities in 2004 (RMB billion)*

	Guangdong	Shanghai	Jiangsu	Fujian	Beijing	Shandong	Liaoning
Turnover	169.83	162.24	56.99	31.18	26.81	6.20	5.41
Proportion of Total	36.76%	35.12%	12.34%	6.75%	5.80%	1.34%	1.17%
Number	32	18	31	9	21	9	8

Sources: Editing Committee, China Economy BOOMING Supervision Centre edited,
China Industrial Maps: IT 2004–2005, Social Sciences Academic Press, 2005.

2.4 KNOWLEDGE BASE OF THE SECTORAL SYSTEM

R&D personnel and investment are among the most important inputs
for industrial innovation, and in this section we review the changes over
time as a proxy of innovation capacity of the computer sectoral system.
In addition to the engineers and scientists that make up production design
and services, R&D personnel assume an important role as key actors in
the knowledge base and sources of innovation as firm capabilities deepen.
There has been sustained R&D investment by firms since the middle of
the 1990s, as other inputs in the Chinese computer manufacturing industry
continue to increase. In 1995, the number of the science and technology
(S&T) personnel was 8422, and it increased to 16 411 in 2002. The number

Table 2.6   Innovation-relevant personnel and expenses, 1995–2002 (RMB ten thousand)

Indicators	1995	1997	1998	1999	2000	2001	2002
R&D personnel	1 355	7 660	4 028	6 139	3 941	66 83	6 589
R&D expenses	5 473	72 611	44 911	76 554	115 541	107 124	248 386
S&T personnel	8 422	13 884	12 386	11 960	14 886	18 143	16 411
Scientists and engineers	4 745	10 436	8 180	8 301	11 347	14 275	13 310

Sources: National Statistics Bureau, National Development and Reform Committee and Ministry of Science and Technology edited, *China Statistics Yearbook on High Technology Industry 2003.*

Table 2.7   S&T organizations, computer industry, 1995–2002

Indicators	1995	1997	1998	1999	2000	2001	2002
S&T Organizations	123	93	92	103	63	80	72
S&T personnel in S&T Organizations	4750	5631	4399	5893	6715	5722	6434

Sources: National Statistics Bureau, National Development and Reform Committee and Ministry of Science and Technology edited, *China Statistics Yearbook on High Technology Industry 2003.*

of R&D personnel of the industry increased from only 1355 in 1995 to 3589 in 2002. The number of scientists and engineers has equally increased from 4745 in 1995 to 13 310 in 2002, while R&D investment increased from RMB54.73 million in 1995 to RMB2.48 billion in 2002 (see Table 2.6).

Compared with the rapid increases of R&D personnel and investment input of the computer industry, the number of S&T organizations in this important knowledge creating sector in the industry has been decreasing overall since the middle of the 1990s (see Table 2.7).

Innovation inputs have been disaggregated into different components as the indicators in Table 2.8 show. Over the period, investment for

Table 2.8   S&T expense structure of the computer industry (RMB ten thousand)

Indicators	1995	1997	1998	1999	2000	2001	2002
Technology adaptation expenses	16335	39518	38952	35929	28852	28770	45302
Technology import expenses	2467	28788	24007	52744	77839	117165	192875
Absorption expenses	297	6968	1952	3548	6136	7625	1976
Purchasing domestic technology	142	714	143	190	251	934	330

Sources: National Statistics Bureau, National Development and Reform Committee and Ministry of Science and Technology edited, *China Statistics Yearbook on High Technology Industry 2003.*

technology imports and adaptation have increased steadily. Before 1999, the main innovation input was for technology adaptation, which was higher than the expenses for importation. In particular, since 1999, expenses for technology importation have increased significantly. It rose from RMB527.44 million in 1999 to RMB1.93 billion in 2002. In the same period, investment for technology adaptation increased from RMB359.29 million to RMB453.02 million. This means that the main technology sources of Chinese computer firms are from abroad and not the results of domestic R&D efforts. Moreover, with the rise in high-technology importation input, only a very small amount of investment is spent for assimilation and absorption. In 2002, industry investment on absorption was only RMB19.76 million. Investment in firms for purchase of domestic technologies was lower than the absorption expenses, which was RMB3.3 million in 2002 (see Table 2.8). During the catching-up process by industries in developing countries, a variety of other absorption capabilities beyond R&D are critical for the firms.[5]

Therefore in analysing the capability of the sector as well as the flow of knowledge into it we employ indicators relevant to new products and patents to describe the innovation output of the sectoral system. All innovation outputs have been increasing gradually since the middle of the 1990s (see Table 2.9).

Table 2.9   Innovation outputs of the computer industry (RMB ten thousand)

Indicators	1995	1997	1998	1999	2000	2001	2002
New product project	555	370	303	441	376	536	464
New product expenses	14946	68773	52492	155353	133132	165469	233161
Prod value of new products	–	1302417	2191763	3663980	5600311	6138917	7758901
Sales of new products	366412	1149145	2255762	3564635	5369985	6293591	7527523
Profits of new products	28283	67818	191210	211125	393457	263025	408558
Patent application	12	34	81	139	263	558	953
Patent granted	9	13	47	69	131	115	38

Sources: National Statistics Bureau, National Development and Reform Committee and Ministry of Science and Technology edited, *China Statistics Yearbook on High Technology Industry 2003.*

2.5   INNOVATION NETWORK AND INDUSTRY–UNIVERSITY LINKAGES

The computer hardware industry is a knowledge-intensive sector, which means that firms must have rather strong knowledge creation and technology development bases. For many Chinese computer firms a large part of the necessary knowledge cannot be domiciled within the firm and it is therefore important to learn to collaborate and learn to innovate through collaboration. Different types of collaboration have been formed between different actors and organizations. In order to show system linkages we illustrate with five different case studies of interactive learning promoted by several important Chinese computer firms: see Boxes 2.1–2.5. From our research, Chinese computer firms have developed a relatively strong capacity to collaborate and have established different types of industrial academia linkages. The case studies also illustrate the unique institutional arrangements that the state made to foster the growth of the computer hardware sector.

BOX 2.1 INSPUR GROUP

Origin of the Company

Inspur Group is one of the earliest enterprises engaged in the IT industry in China, and also the largest provider of application and resolution of the IT industry in China. It was established in 1990. Inspur Group has two stock companies, Inspur Information and Inspur Software, and many other subsidiaries. Its business covers such industries and fields as PCs, servers, tax controlling machines, communication products, information security, software outsourcing, as well as service, application software for large industry, finance and ERP, e-government, tobacco and circulation.

Partnerships and Industrial Academia Linkages

In the early phase of the company's development, the Inspur Group established close collaborative relationships with Shan Dong University, Xi'an JiaoTong University, Beijing University of Posts and Telecommunications (BUPT), National University of Defense Technology, Haerbin Institute of Technology, Huazhong University of Science and Technology, Beihang University (BUAA), Beijing Institute of Technology, and the Institute of Software of Chinese Academy of Sciences. The collaborative modes include taking part in the national S&T plan projects to develop the new Internet servers, high-performance computers and ERP, CRM, SCM management software; and the setting up of the collaborative laboratory and human resources base. For instance, there is a considerable potential for developing software in China, an activity which relies largely on computer and engineering knowledge. Compared with India for instance, China's software industry lacks international competitive capacity. For this reason the group established special software classes in Qilu Software School, in cooperation with some foreign enterprises and Shandong University, to train specialized international IT talents. The school, along with the training of special software outsourcing engineers, plans to become a training base for domestic IT talents with the introduction of advanced training systems and cooperation with international multinational companies to meet the demand of the domestic market that is expanding rapidly. The objective of the founders is for the school to develop the present infrastructure of software and hardware into a global centre of excellence to service the IT industry. Shandong University Qilu Software School is one of the schools listed in the first group of national demonstrating software schools, while Inspur Worldwide Services (LCW), a subsidiary of the Inspur Group, is engaged in software development for foreign projects connected with other firms abroad, especially in Japan. In order to provide employment for students after graduation and also meet demand of the market of international software skills, particularly the requirements of software exporting enterprises, Shandong University Qilu Software School and LCW cooperated in establishing the special training class of 'International Software Talents'.

Moreover, from the beginning of the 1990s, the Inspur Group started its international cooperative business. It set up some joint ventures with Casio of Japan, Ericsson and LG, and set up business and cooperative relations with such world-famous corporations as EDS of America, Furukawa Electric of Japan, NEC, NTT Soft, SOPIA and Nucleus of India, among others. In 2004, the Inspur Group established the formal Global Strategic Partnership with Microsoft. Both sides proposed to have deep collaborations covering R&D on software products, technological training, problem-solving customization, firm management and international cooperations.

Source: Authors' field survey.

BOX 2.2 CHINA ELECTRONICS CORPORATION (CEC)

Origin of the Company

The CEC group was established in 1989, as one of the key state-owned conglomerates under the direct administration of central government. CEC currently administers 13 listed holding companies, 36 shareholding companies, 20 fully funded subsidiaries, with a registered capital of RMB5.88 billion, and total assets of RMB58.3 billion. In 2005, the revenue of CEC reached to RMB53 billion, and the exports reached RMB1.6 billion.

The Main Divisions of the Company

Shanghai Huahong Group Co. Ltd., Great Wall Technology, China Huada Integrated Circuit Design Group, China National Software

& Services Co. Ltd. (CS&S), Shenzhen SED Group, China National Electronics Import & Export Corporation (CEIEC), CEC Corecast, Amoi Electronics, and CEC Holding among others. CEC has 4 national-level enterprise technology centres, 1 national engineering research centre, 10 provincial technology centres. It has in total almost 30 professional enterprises R&D centres, 5 post-doctoral stations and 1 station for master cultivation.

CEC Technological Innovation System

As one of the key state-owned groups, CEC has characterized its corporate governance as the strategic investment controlling shareholders. It enables CEC initially to establish and operate its technological innovation system. The firm has a research institute which is responsible for the organization and coordination of key cross-cutting generic technologies among its subsidiaries. In addition it has a number of R&D centres in the different subsidiaries which are coordinated from the centre from where demand-induced new products research is formulated. Those R&D centres cover fields including integrated circuits, software, telecommunications, digital home appliances, system engineering and apparatus and instruments.

Main Partnerships and Strategic Alliances Locally

Chinese Academy of Siences (CAS), Tsinghua University, Peiking University, Zhejiang University, Xi'an Electroncis Science and Technology University.

Main Partnerships and Strategic Alliances with other Foreign Companies and Institutions

IBM, ST, Microsoft, NEC, Toshiba, Fujitsu, Philips, Belgium IMEC.

Main Products and Services

CEC is engaged mainly in four business fields: semiconductors; computer software/hardware and system integration; telecommunication network and terminals; and digital home appliances. Its business activities cover the complete value chain of the industry, including R&D, design, manufacturing, application, marketing and distribution, and technical service. It is also involved in the manufacture of semiconductors, computer software and hardware, telecommunication engineering and mobile handsets.

Details of the Products Designed by the Company

The 'Panda' integrated circuit design instrument is one of the products designed through the company's research and development. This product makes China one of the few countries with intellectual property rights in the field. The company has also designed a second-generation household identity card through its internal research and development capacity. It has developed a full industrial value chain containing chip design, manufacturing and assembling, and has become the biggest domestic supplier of the second-generation identity card. The company also designed a 32 USB/KEY capacity card designed through in-house research and development, which is the first and only domestic security chip type based on a 32 CPU core.

Source: Authors' field survey.

BOX 2.3   HAIER GROUP

Origin of the Company

Haier Group was named in 1991, and its former company was Qingdao Refrigerator Factory, which was a collective company established in 1984. By the end of 2005, the revenue of Haier Group had increased from RMB3.48 million to RMB103 billion, and exportation had reached $1.31 billion.

Main Partnership and Strategic Alliances with other Chinese Companies and Institutions

Strategic alliance with Suning and Gome chain stores.

Main Partnerships and Strategic Alliances with other Foreign Companies and Institutions

America: cooperation with top ten retailers, for example SEARS, Lowe's, Home Depot, Best Buy, PC-Richard, Wal-Mart, Sam's, Costco, BrandsMart and Target.

Japan: cooperation with top ten retailers, for example Yamada, Kojima and Jusco.

Europe: cooperation with Kesa, Media Market and Carrefour.

Main Products and Services

Haier's product categories include refrigerators, refrigerating cabinets, air conditioners, washing machines, televisions, mobile phones, home theatre systems, computers, water heaters, DVD players and integrated furniture, among which are ranked market leaders in China, and three are ranked among the top three worldwide in their respective industries. Haier is also a world leader in the technology domains of intelligent integrated home furniture, networked home appliances, digitalization and large-scale integrated circuits.

Main Divisions of the Company

Haier has over 240 subsidiary companies, over 110 design centres, plants and trading companies and over 50 000 employees throughout the world. Haier's industrial focus includes technology research, manufacturing, trade and financial services. The global revenue of Haier for 2005 was RMB103.4 billion. Haier Electronics Group Co. Ltd. (HKG:1169), a subsidiary of Haier Group, is listed on the main board of the Stock Exchange of Hong Kong. Qingdao Haier Co. Ltd. (SHA: 600690), also a Haier subsidiary, is listed on the Shanghai Stock Exchange.

Haier Central Research Institute was established on 26 December in 1998. It is the core technological organization within group, and the all-around science and research base through which the company carries out technological cooperation. It is located in Qingdao, Shandong province in China. The institute has collaborated with 28 world-class companies from the USA, Japan, Germany and the rest of the world, and established 48 research and development units both in China and abroad.

Source: Authors' field survey.

BOX 2.4   LENOVA CHINA

Origin of the Company

Spin-out from state-owned R&D institute. In 1984, with an initial capital outlay of only RMB200 000 (US$25 000) former Legend's founding chairman Liu Chuanzhi, together with ten like-minded colleagues, launched the New Technology Developer Inc. (the predecessor of the Legend Group) funded by the Chinese Academy of Sciences. In 1989, the company was renamed Legend. It realized the IPO (initial public offer) in 1994 in Hong Kong. In 2003, it shifted the label successfully from Legend to Lenova. By the end of 2004, Lenova Group aquired the PC business of IBM, to become the number three PC manufacturer in the world. By the end of 2005, the revenue of Levova China had reached RMB19.69 billion, and exports had reached $8.3 billion.

Main Products and Services

PCs, notebooks, servers, printers, projectors, mobile phones.

Main Partnerships and Strategic Alliances with other Chinese Companies and Institutions

Institute of Computer, Chinese Academy of Sciences (CAS), Graduate School of Chinese Academy of Sciences (CAS), Tsinghua University, Beihang University and so on.

Main Partnerships and Strategic Alliances with other Chinese Companies and Institutions

IBM, Microsoft, Intel and so on.

Lenovo Corporate Research & Development was established in January 1999, which was the central research and development organization belonging to the group level. It has focused mainly on applied research and development which promotes innovation. With the core of Lenovo Corporate Research & Development, Lenova Group has established the Global R&D system with sub-institutes in Shanghai, Chengdu, and R&D centres in China Shenzhen, USA and Japan.

Source: Authors' field survey.

BOX 2.5   HISENSE GROUP

Origin of the Company

In September 1969, the predecessor of Hisense, Qingdao No. 2 Radio Factory, was established to produce transistor radios. At that time, the factory only employed ten-plus staff. In February 1979, Qingdao Television Factory was established and the factory became a state-designated TV manufacturer. In 1992, Mr Zhou Houjian was appointed the director of Qingdao Television Factory. He was 35 years of age at the time. Soon after, the factory took off and entered a period of rapid growth. In March 1993, Hisense invested RMB20 million to produce POS and soon became the largest POS manufacturer in China. In 1994, Hisense Company Limited was established. By the end of 2005, the revenue of Hisense Group has increased from RMB412 million to RMB33 billion. In the same year, exports of the Group reached 462.7 million dollars.

Main Partnerships and Strategic Alliances with other Foreign Companies and Institutions

IBM, HP, GM, HITACHI, PHILIPS, TOSHIBA, LG, ORACLE, SHARP, SONY, ELECTROLUX, SANYO, SIMENS, PANASONIC/NATIONAL, SUMSUNG and GFK.

Main Products and Services

TVs, refrigerators, air-conditioners, computers, communications, network technology, POS, and network security.

Hisense Group Technological Innovation System

It has three layers of innovation organizations. At the peak of the organization is the Hisense R&D Centre, which is responsible for strategic forsight research, new technology incubating and human resources training. It was established on the basis of the previous Hisense Group headquarters, which integrated R&D, production and administration. Hisense R&D Centre is a state-level enterprise tech centre, an industrialization base for State Project 863 and a state centre for the demonstration and promotion. As a research entity combining industry, academia and research, Hisense R&D established the Hisense Research Institute of Shandong University, a platform on which Hisense cooperates with renowned higher education institutes. Hisense R&D employs over 1500 engineers and scientists of various disciplines with more than half of them holding medium and senior technical titles. Out of more than 1500 staff, there are nearly 50 senior experts and Doctoral degree holders, 300-plus Masters and 90 per cent of the R&D staff are young men below the age of 40. The second layer of innovation organization is the different types of technology institutes belonging to the subsidiary companies, which are mainly responsible for new product development. The third level is the technique teams of different workshops within the subsidiary companies.

Source: Authors' field survey.

Table 2.10   Import and export, computer products, 1999–2003 (billion dollars)

Items	1999	2000	2001	2003
Total values	19.51	28.06	35.04	97.8
Export	12.29	17.53	22.29	63.34
Import	7.22	10.55	12.75	34.46
Balance	5.07	6.98	9.54	27.88

Sources: *Chinese Electronics Industry Yearbook 2004.*

2.6   EXPORT SPUR

International trade shares of the Chinese computer industry have increased significantly in recent years. China's production capacities for computer peripherals such as printers, display and other computer components and materials have increased rapidly and it is now number one in the world in many respects. The USA is still the largest destination of Chinese computer industry exports. In 2003, exports to the USA were 27.2 per cent of total exports, generating revenue of over $66 billion. The next two destinations are Hong Kong and Japan. The above countries and region have 65 per cent of the total market share of China's exports. Meanwhile sales of Chinese computer products in Germany, France, South Korea and Ireland have also been increasing very rapidly. Table 2.10 shows the import and export values in the 1999–2003 period.

However, the effects of 'learning from exportation' are limited due to the industrial features and the status of the Chinese computer industry in the global computer industrial chain. Firstly, this is because the products exported are mainly low-technology oriented, and exports are low value-added products, while imported products are mainly high value-added products. The key advantage of Chinese computer products is their low price and this factor has been the main export competitive force. In 2000, the average export price of a microcomputer was $391.55 per unit, while the import price was $1782.5 per unit. The export price of printers was $73, while the import price was $184. In 2003, the subtotal of export values of computer components, keyboards, CD drivers, mice and soft disk drivers was $19.837 billion. Secondly, the main export trade mode is process trade with imported materials, which accounts for 82.6 per cent of the export market. In 2003, it reached $54.78 billion. In the same year, processing assembly trade was 14 per cent of export share. Thirdly, foreign firms are still the dominant players in Chinese computer industry exports. Their export size exceeded $50 billion in 2003. Moreover, export of joint ventures exceeded $9 billion with more than 90 per cent of Chinese computer products export relating to foreign investments.

2.7 SYSTEMIC INTEGRATION

FDI has played a very important role in the Chinese computer manufacturing industry. In 2007, foreign firms including joint ventures are the leading actors in the industry in terms of both production value and profits. According to official data, in 2004 the total production value and profits of the clones industry created by foreign firms were RMB382.55 billion and RMB7.58 billion, much higher than for other groups of firms in the industry (see Table 2.11).

In the same year, the total production value of the peripherals industry created by foreign firms was RMB341.82 billion, which is much higher than for other groups of firms within the industry; the number of foreign firms was much larger than that of other types of firms (see Table 2.12).

In geographic terms, there are three main computer manufacturing bases in China which are the Pearl River Delta, Yangzi River Delta and Loop Bo Sea Region. These regions are also where foreign direct investment (FDI) is concentrated. The Pearl River Delta is the largest computer and components manufacturing base. In one region alone, that is DongGuan, the production volumes of head plates, boxes, divers, scanners, keyboards and main boards have respectively about 15 per cent to 40 per cent of global market share. The Yangzi River Delta has gradually become a very important region because it is where the foreign market and the mainland market are connected. Suzhou of Jiangsu province has become one of the global computer hardware manufacturing centres. The main computer companies, including the top four scanner companies, number one battery factory, number one linker factory, number one mouse factory and some circuit board printing companies from Taiwan have all started to invest

Table 2.11   Industrial production value and profits, computer clones manufacturing firms, 2004 (RMB billion)

Economy Types	Total Production Value	Total Profits
State-owned	1.556	0.011
Collective	0.238	0.005
Joint collaboration	0.068	0.0008
Joint-stock	9.716	0.282
Private	2.832	0.056
Foreign firms/JV	382.552	7.582
Others	14.423	0.056

Sources: Editing Committee, China Economy BOOMING Supervision Centre edited, China Industrial Maps: IT 2004–2005, Social Sciences Academic Press, 2005.

Table 2.12   Industrial production value and profits, computer manufacturing and peripheral firms, 2004 (RMB billion)

Economy Types	Total Production Value	Number of Firms
Foreign firms/JV	341.816	378
Joint-stock	11.768	61
Private	3.693	40
Other firms	2.367	23
State-own and collective	0.827	18
Joint stock collaboration	0.303	4

Sources: Editing Committee, China Economy BOOMING Supervision Centre edited, China Industrial Maps: IT 2004–2005, Social Sciences Academic Press, 2005.

in this region. Suzhou has created the base for research and development, manufacturing and sales in-phase development with the leadership of large corporations. The top five global laptop original equipment manufacturing (OEM) factories have set up factories in or around Shanghai. Since 2001, the main laptop companies of Taiwan have moved into Suzhou and Shanghai, and with them came companies that provided necessary upstream support. The concentration of global OEM firms in this area has pushed the centre of the global laptop industry to the Yangzi River Delta, and in the process created a sectoral system of laptop manufacturing and R&D in this cluster. The Yangzi River Delta is becoming the new global laptop manufacturing base. Compared with other clusters, the Delta Loop Bohai region has not become the large-scale computer manufacturing base that was envisaged. However, most of the large and famous computer companies have established R&D and operating bases, like Lenova, the Founder Group, Tsinghua TongFang and IBM. Here the key advantages relate to the science, technology and knowledge capacities.

2.8 INNOVATION POLICIES FOSTERING THE COMPUTER HARDWARE SYSTEM

In the beginning, the primary role of government had been to ensure macroeconomic stability, rather than to intervene in support of specific firms or sectors. Although the state has promoted a wide array of policy initiatives, there is a lack of concrete data to show the effectiveness of direct government intervention in technology acquisition and on the relationship between firm-level performance and government technology plans. However, taking a comparative institutional approach as we have done in this book, there are major differences in industrial structure, patterns of ownership and the effectiveness of governments in stimulating technological progress compared with other countries. Differences are due partly to historical reasons (compare South Korea and Taiwan), others are due to strategic and political choices made (Malaysia and Thailand) (Hobday et al., 2001). Concerning the development of a high-technology industry, the initial condition of a country, such as the pool of scientists and engineers and the presence of knowledge infrastructure, is an important variable. However, from the Chinese and other East Asian experiences the competitive advantages of a high-technology industry could be created through strategic policy initiatives (Wang Yuan et al., 2002). For instance, government and government agencies have been central to the process of creating and nurturing a semiconductor industry in East Asia. The relationship of government and business is 'governed interdependence', a kind of productive and complementary relationship: government agencies need the private sector for implementation of policies, while the private sector needs public agencies for coordination of catch-up activities, particularly in financial allocation, risk-sharing and technological upgrading. The relationship between public and private sectors is not fixed, but co-evolves with the industry that is being created (Mathews and Cho, 2000). The two specific functions of innovation policies are to deal with the problems of market failure, and in strategic terms, to change the factor conditions that create competitive advantages.

During the 1950s to 1970s, there were no specific departments responsible for the computer industry development in China. The basic institutional framework was made up of the science and technology 'sections' and electronics 'sections' which were responsible for research, development and production. Given the relatively weak technological environment of the time, the Chinese government took measures to support the development of the computer industry against the backdrop of a planned economy. The famous Founder Chinese characters typesetting system evolved from a collaborative development project supported by governmental allocation to the Department of Computer Science of Peking University and the Shandong Weifang Computer factory (renamed Shandong Huaguang Company) in 1974. There were three main phases in the evolution of innovation policies which we now discuss in turn.

Institutional Reform since the Late 1970s: from Planned Economy to Market Economy

Since the late 1970s, the macroeconomic conditions were gradually changed from the planned economy to a market economy. The environment within which the Chinese electronics industry developed also changed significantly. First, market deregulation increased competition. Second, along with the reform of the research system, institutes began to provide services for economic activities rather than being limited to research. Third, the reform also included a move to a more open economy which involved importation of technology and exchanging technology (for Chinese firms) with market access (for MNCs). Fourth, the development of the electronics industry experienced a transformation from military application to civil application and technology imitation and adoption. Meanwhile, the government enacted policies to develop the electronics industry such as pushing for firms' collaboration, and selectively supporting some sub-sectors of the electronics industry as policy priorities such as IC (integrated circuit), computers, software and switching boards.

Concerning the institutions and polices specific to the computer industry, the Electronics Computer Bureau, which was responsible for computer industrial polices and planning, was first established in 1979.[6] Detailed polices were enunciated to promote the development of the Chinese computer industry. Although China was promoting an open door policy, the government took some protectionist policies to support the initial stage of the Chinese computer industry such as import regulation and tariff protection. Thus, many national firms including Legend (later Lenova), Start and Founder were able to develop rather rapidly at the beginning. From the middle of the 1980s, the government took a number of measures to support the development of the domestic computer industry including tax policies, setting up the Development Fund, purchasing technology licenses, sub sidies as well as emphasizing national production. Many measures were

Table 2.13 Main policy instruments to promote Chinese computer sector in the 1980s

Policy	Contents	Application time period
Tax policy	Four electronics products including integrated circuits, computers, and software and switching boards, exempt from production taxes, exempt from half of the income taxes, exempt from the tariffs of key equipments and apparatus; pick up 10 per cent R&D expenses of turnover and exempt from importation taxes of significant imported projects.	1986–94
Development Fund	Government allocates RMB100 million per year to support the technology alteration, technology commercialization of the above four products. Since the 1990s, it has also been used to start up significant projects.	1986–2007
Subsidies	Government allocated RMB200 million as loan subsidies to support the application of computers.	Cancelled
Licenses	Importation licenses management on computer and components	Cancelled in early 1990s
National production	Computer production must reach the certain rate of national production.	Cancelled in early 1990s

Source: Compiled by Xin Xin, 2007.

abandoned as the economic environment changed, but the Development Fund has been retained (see Table 2.13).

National Economy Informatics in the Promotion of the Computer Industry in the 1990s

A very important pillar of the Chinese computer industry development is the project on national economy informatics which started in 1993. In addition, the 'golden bridge', 'golden custom' and 'golden card' projects were implemented, all of which tremendously inspired and created domestic market demand and pushed the application of computers. The Ministry of Electronics Industry formally put forward a strategy to set up a 'national champion company'. The reform of the telecommunication industry started in 1994 while the transformation of research institutes started in the late 1990s.

FDI policies on the computer industry were changed from 'limited open', the protection of domestic industry, to 'enlarge open'. The licenses management was cancelled, and tariffs have been gradually reduced. The government consistently encouraged FDI in the Chinese computer industry. In 1997, the National Council produced a catalogue of products involved in promoting FDI which include the large and medium computer, and the newly developed typewriter.

Globalization and Innovation of the Electronics Industry Since 2000

Since 2000, the policy environment has changed radically. On the one hand, after China joined the WTO there have been different influences on the different sub-sectors of the electronics industry. In 2003, the decision to reform the export drawback mechanism was issued. In accordance with WTO rules, by 1 January 2003 the overall level of electronics and information products tariff was reduced to 9.9 per cent; the information technology products tariff was reduced to 1.5 per cent, which translated to a 57 per cent reduction. There are 90 tax items on which the tariff was reduced to zero, and the tax items with zero tariffs constitute 83.2 per cent of the whole information technology products tax items. The computer industry has become a much more open and competitive industry than before, and the government has not been directly involved in this development. The market entry regulation has been phased out, and it is now relatively very easy for computer products producers to enter the industry. As long as the technology they adopt meets a certain standard, they can be given a production license.

On the other hand, since 1990, Chinese computer manufacturing has become the largest sub-sector within the whole electronics manufacturing industry. But it still thrives largely on low value-added products and technologically lags behind in several areas in the global computer industrial chain due to a lack of innovation capabilities, especially in core technologies and components. The Chinese government has tried to redress the situation by promoting a more dynamic industrial development environment. It does this by promoting the transformation of purely domestic computer firms from being production-driven to being innovation-driven. The government decided to support the development of integrated circuits, newly typed electronics components and 3C products.[7] Notably, integrated circuit (IC) and newly typed electronics components are related to the computer core software manufacturing, which directly influence computer products added values. By this, incentives are being used to force technology upgrading.

In June 2000, State Circular Number 18 was issued: 'State council declaration on policies to promote the development of software industry and IC industry'. China's State Council announced that all integrated circuits manufactured in China would receive a rebate of the value-added tax (VAT) in excess of 6 per cent. Normally China applies a VAT of 17 per cent on sales of imported and domestically produced semiconductors, and in this direction a number of relevant policies were announced. In the period of 2000 to 2003, several policies promoting the software industry were announced by the Chinese government. They include a circular on finance and taxes to promote IC and software (2000, 2003) and a circular on regulation on key issues on income tax polices of software and new high technology companies. Finally in the same year, another administrative circular that made it easy for IC Design companies to enjoy certain tax incentives was issued.

The government also in the same vein set up IT industry bases and IT industry parks. Enterprises in these industrial bases and parks are eligible for support based on certain criteria including fixed assets as well as the nature of their development model from schemes such as 'the electronic information industry development fund'. Local governments were also mandated to provide different forms of assistance to firms to the tune of no less than RMB50 million annually. Some of the important projects include: technology standards, IC and software, information safety, electronics government affairs and electronics finance.

Moreover, the government adopted active internationalization strategies in order to take full advantage of international resources to develop the industry. On one hand, the government tries to encourage MNCs to set up R&D centres in China. Multinational corporations were encouraged to adjust their strategies and relocate to China as part of their global strategy, and more specifically to shift production and R&D to China. On the other hand, the government in 1999 had announced its export strategy based on the 'science and technology promotion trade'. In 2006, the government also announced a strategy that clearly sought to encourage firms, especially high-technology firms, to enter into the international market.

From our analysis of the evolution of policies and the institutional supporting system that sought to develop the computer industry, it is evident that a process of co-evolution and policy learning had been taking place. In the early years of China's development of the electronic industry, policies were targeted at creating the right environment; the government tried to protect domestic industrial firms in the 1980s through a battery of policies. In the 1990s, the targets of policies shifted to increasing production capacity, industry and firm size, and more crucially to raising sectoral innovation capacity in order to meet the rapid growing demands of national economy informatics. Since 2000, the industrial structure has reached a new and certainly a high level, with indicators showing growth in size and world market share, but it still faces many challenges and bottlenecks. Due to lack of core technologies and key components, domestic firms still rate on the low value-added stage of the industrial value chain, and profitability has been even decreasing as industrial size has been enlarging. Improvements to indigenous innovation capabilities of the domestic firms have become the insistent demands of industrial development. Thus, the policies have shifted to reflect these new targets of industrial innovation capabilities since 2000.

2.9 SUMMING UP

This chapter demonstrates that Chinese computer firms are moving up the technological ladder through learning in order to catch up with global leaders. This process has seen firms searching different sources to accumulate capabilities. One notable source is to set up linkages with research institutes and universities. Another is to establish collaboration with technologically advanced MNCs, depending on specific needs which might include building research and development capacity, training engineers, setting up industrial standards, and importing machinery and equipment.

The selection of firms' innovation strategies have co-evolved very closely with the changes to the institutional support environment. Innovation policies have been designed in response to different economic and technological regimes. The evolution of the Chinese computer industry has demonstrated that innovation policies, as well as the institutions supporting the system, must consider the features of different stages. We find that innovation policies designed for the computer industry not only showed sensitivity to the particular context of Chinese traditional habits, but were also flexible enough to accommodate external factors and actors. However, it is still too early to conclude on how well these policies will sustain long-term performance. There are at least two points that need to be emphasized here. One is that the sectoral innovation system is still evolving. This is because a number of policies originate from different organizations and lack necessary coordination. The other is that a number of specific institutional supports at the sectoral level create unintended conflicts and systemic disharmony. Given that each sector has its own knowledge base, the innovation policies require more sophisticated coordination.

NOTES

1. Both central and local governments have played very important roles in pushing the development of the computer industry. In this report, we mainly focus on the behaviour of the central government. Some actions of local governments in the report will be

specified. On the one hand, the strategies and behaviour of local governments are much diversified due to the regional diversities. On the other hand, most of the efficient strategies and policies taken and tested by the local governments have been upgraded to be national ones issued by the central government, which a typifies bottom up policy learning. This testifies to the success of the Chinese economic reform programme.
2. For instance, the president of one top computer firm said that the company normally makes R&D plans that last two or three years depending on what the market demands; the firm's technology capabilities have been accumulated incrementally, but concurrently adopt new relevant technologies.
3. In 1956, the former Prime Minister Zhou Enlai organized a team to formulate the Guidelines of the National Twelve Years Science and Technology Development. In the guidelines, the government selected four sub-sectors as priorities which include emergency measures including computers, electronics, semiconductors and automation. In the judgement of the Chinese government, the computer industry was on the path of development already.
4. Examples of government promotion efforts include support to the four large firms mentioned earlier.
5. R&D is not only the key source of innovation, but also determines a firm's absorptive capability to internalize external knowledge as a prerequisite for successful innovation in the longer run (see Cohen and Levinthal, 1990). Much research has shown that absorption capability has been the critical and key factor for countries to realize catch-up.
6. It is the Department of Computer, Ministry of Information Industry nowadays.
7. 3C refers to newly developed telecommunications and digital IT products that require high capabilities to manufacture computers, servers, routers and switching boards.

APPENDIX

Table A2.1   Evolution of organizations in the Chinese computer industry

Period	Organizations
1979	Bureau of National Electronics Computer Industry, Ministry of Electronics Industry.
1986	Reorganization of the Bureau of National Electronics Computer Industry. The bureau did not respond adequately to the needs of firms. The bureau has been divided into three parts: the Bureau of Computer and Information, the Research Centre for Computer and Information Development, and the China Computer Development Corporation, which was the base of the Great Wall Corporation later.
1988	Department of Computer, Ministry of Electronics Industry.
1993	Department of Computer, Ministry of Electronics Industry.
1998	Department of Computer, Ministry of Information Industry.

Source: Compiled by the authors.

3. Low value-added operations in Indonesia

3.1 INTRODUCTION

Indonesia managed to stimulate information hardware (IH) manufacturing on a significant scale from the late 1980s following the spillover effects of the Plaza Accord when the Northeast Asian firms began a wave of relocation to the whole of developing Southeast Asia.[1] Although this wave slowed down owing to overheating and a lack of institutional support for upgrading in Malaysia and Thailand, and the emergence of China as an attractive site, IH manufacturing has continued to grow in economies such as the Philippines, Vietnam and Indonesia. Indonesia's huge labour force, especially the concentration in Java and the coordination offered by Temasik Holdings, which enjoys the lease of the export processing zone in Batam, has helped attract labour-intensive assembly activities such as printed circuit boards, component assembly and consumer electronics to Indonesia. In addition, a handful of local Indonesian firms have also emerged to assemble brand-less cheap computers for the local market.

Indonesian regulations on foreign direct investment (FDI) were for many years restrictive (see Panglaykim, 1983; Hill, 1995, 1996; Sjoholm, 1999, 2002; Blomstrom and Sjoholm, 1999; Dhanani, 2000; Okamoto and Sjoholm, 2003). Indonesia has become more liberal following the financial crisis of 1997–98, albeit at a time when the political risks have risen. Total foreign ownership was prohibited until the inclusion of Batam in the Singapore–Johor–Rhiau (SIJORI) growth triangle in 1989. Foreign ownership regulations in the rest of Indonesia became more liberal following the 1997–98 financial crisis. Basic infrastructure coordination – access to shipping outlets, orderly labour mobilization and security – offered at export processing zones have been reported as critical for IH firms to operate in Indonesia. Most high-tech institutions are underdeveloped in Indonesia but the importance of training and retraining, even in low value-added assembly activities where firms are forced to reduce defects and delivery times, is expected to generate demand-driven training centres at proximate locations. Although the exports of IH products have expanded, Indonesia's highly underdeveloped infrastructure threatens to discourage upgrading in the industry. With the exception of a few export processing zones, problems with customs, security, and power and water suppliers were cited in a previous study as seriously debilitating (see Thee and Pangestu, 1998; Rasiah, 2005). Indeed severe basic infrastructure weaknesses were cited by some firms as a major reason for the leasing of the export processing zone in Batam to Singapore-owned Temasik Holdings.[2]

Although protection was extended to several sectors (including automobiles), industrial policy in Indonesia had largely been restricted to the heavy industries of steel, aeroplanes and petrochemical products (see Rasiah, 2003b). The production of military transport planes was abandoned by the Habibie administration following the financial crisis, and the production of steel and petrochemicals have also since stagnated. Severe government failure has been reflected in poor coordination of customs, immigration, security, transport and telecommunication services in most parts of Indonesia (see Hill, 1996, 1999; Vedi, 1997; Prawiro, 1998; Booth, 1998, 1999; Thee, 2000). Although export-oriented IH firms have evolved largely in export processing zones where these basic infrastructure institutions have been sufficiently efficient, the lack of sector-specific institutional support has stifled learning and innovation in the electronics industry (see Rasiah, 2005). Indonesia hence presents a case of an economy facing an infant systemic quad without institutional support for driving learning and innovation, and hence firms in the country are expected to show very low technological intensities and complexities.

Using the framework advanced in the introductory chapter, this chapter attempts to examine the four pillars of the systemic quad that explain the expansion of IH manufacturing in Indonesia. The rest of the chapter is organized as follows. Section 3.2 presents the methodology and data used in the chapter. Section 3.3 evaluates the state of the four systemic pillars from the lenses of firms. Section 3.4 examines the knowledge depth and technological intensity of the firms using taxonomic and trajectory categories. Section 3.5 presents the conclusions.

3.2   METHODOLOGY AND DATA

As advanced in the introduction chapter, the strength of development of the four pillars advanced in the systemic quad, that is, basic infrastructure (BI), high-tech (HT) infrastructure, nature of global integration (GI) in value chains and markets, and network cohesion (NC) will have a strong impact on firm-level technological intensities and complexities (see also

Table 3.1   Technological intensities, IH firms, Indonesia sample 2001

Variable	Proxies	Specification
HR	Training expenditure in payroll, cutting-edge HR practices, scale of HR operation (training centre (4), department (3), staff with training responsibility (2) and training undertaken externally (1)	Normalized using formula: $(x_i - x_{min})/(x_{max} - x_{min})$
Process Technology	Age of machinery and equipment, cutting-edge process (inventory and quality) technology (TPM, TQM, JIT, MRPI, MRPII), expenditure on physical reorganization of the firm as a share in sales	Normalized using formula: $(x_i - x_{min})/(x_{max} - x_{min})$
Process R&D	Process R&D expenditure	Actual percentage in sales
Product R&D	Product R&D expenditure	Actual percentage in sales

Notes: TPM – total preventive maintenance; TQM – total quality management; JIT – just in time; MRPI – materials resource planning; MRPII – integrated materials resource planning.

Source: Rasiah (2008).

Rasiah, 2005). Hence, the methodology used in this chapter first examines firms' assessment of the four pillars defining the embedding environment in Taiwan, before the evaluation of technological intensities and complexities is carried out.

The chapter uses two-tailed t-tests to compare statistical differences of firms' assessment of institutional and systemic instruments facing them, as well as technological intensities of foreign and local firms in Indonesia. Likert scale scores ranging from 1 to 5 were used to score firms' rating of use and quality, and connections and coordination of the critical institutions. A score of zero was given when firms reported non-existence of connections (either directly or indirectly) with any particular institution. The estimation of the technological variables is shown in Table 3.1. Trajectories and taxonomies were used to differentiate technology, and technological intensities were captured by normalizing related proxies (see Table 3.2). Given the underdeveloped status of firms in Indonesia the sixth category, of knowledge depth detailing firms' participation in R&D that is geared towards the development of

Table 3.2   Technological complexity, IH firms, Indonesia sample 2001

Knowledge depth	HR	Process	Product
(1) Simple activities	On-the-job and in-house training	Dated machinery with simple inventory control techniques	Assembly or processing of low value added components
(2) Minor improvements	In-house training and performance rewards	Advanced machinery and problem-solving	Precision engineering and CKD assembly
(3) Major improvements	Extensive focus on training and retraining	Cutting-edge inventory control techniques, SPC, TQM, TPM	Cutting edge quality control systems (QCC and TQC)
(4) Engineering	Hiring engineers	Process adaptation: layouts, equipment and techniques	Product adaptation
(5) Development-related R&D	Hiring R&D personnel and devising new modes of HR development	Process R&D: layouts, machinery and equipment and processes	Product development (e.g. ODM and OBM)

Notes: SPC – statistical process control; QCC – quality control circles; TQM – total quality management; TPM – total preventive maintenance; TQC – total quality control; ODM – original design manufacturing; OBM – own brand manufacturing.

Source: Developed from Rasiah (1992).

processes and products new to the universe with firms showing take-up of patents, is excluded.

The chapter draws from a three-industry survey conducted in 2002 on the garments, electronics and auto-parts industry in Indonesia. Information on IH firms was extracted from this survey. The national survey used a sampling frame supplied by the national statistics department to select for study.[3] Of the 150 firms that were selected 67 responded (see Table 3.3). In addition to the Asian Development Bank (ADB) survey conducted in 2002, also accessed are interviews carried out by the author with general managers, engineers and chief executive officers on the participation of the firms in global value chains (see also Rasiah, 2005). Unless otherwise stated, all information presented is for the year 2001.

Table 3.3   Breakdown of sampled data, IH firms, Indonesia 2001

	Ownership		Size	
	Foreign	Local	Large	SM
Selected sample	50	100	50	100
Mailed	50	100	50	100
Full response	22	45	24	43
Interviewed	4	10	5	9

Note: Firms were classified as foreign once foreign ownership reached 50 per cent of overall equity; Firms were classified as large when employment size exceeded 500 and the remaining firms were classified as small and medium-sized (SM).

Source: ADB Survey, 2002.

3.3   SYSTEMIC DEVELOPMENT

The four pillars of the systemic quad are used to examine the state of Indonesia's embedding environment from the lenses of computer and component firms. Unlike Malaysia and Taiwan where deliberate state strategy targeted IH among the high-tech industries, the IH industry in Indonesia did not enjoy strong government push. The only set of institutions where attempts were made to promote low value-added activities related to the provision of basic infrastructure through the approval of export-oriented incentives and better supply of power, water and transport networks in export processing zones.

Basic Infrastructure

Indonesia's basic infrastructure institutions have remained weak but the provision of these services at export processing zones has been sufficiently good to attract foreign firms engaged in high-volume low-margin activities where low defects and short delivery times are important.

Using Likert scale scores (1–5 with rising strength) firms were asked to rate the quality of each of the institutions stated in the questionnaire. The mean scores were evaluated using two-tailed tests by ownership and size. An initial pilot interview with four foreign and ten local, five large and nine small and medium-sized firms showed that there were no industry-specific basic infrastructure services sought by IH firms in Indonesia.

The mean scores recorded on all the basic infrastructure (BI) institutions were low irrespective of ownership and size (see Table 3.4). Nonetheless,

Table 3.4   Basic infrastructure, Indonesia sample 2001

	Ownership			Size		
	Foreign	Local	t	Large	SM	t
Secondary school graduates	1.448	2.12	−1.679	1.767	1.978	−1.057
Communication skills of workforce	1.751	1.943	−1.037	1.901	1.855	0.69
Healthcare	2.113	2.002	0.069	2.313	1.875	1.67
Roads	2.575	2.227	2.312**	2.325	2.385	0.055
Air and sea transport	1.757	2.015	−1.375	2.011	1.895	0.658
Telecommunications	2.064	1.737	1.998**	2.479	1.497	2.603*

Note: * and ** refer to statistical significance at 1 per cent and 5 per cent respectively.

Source: Compiled by ADB survey (2002).

the two-tailed t-tests produced statistically meaningful results for road transport and telecommunications. Special privileges enjoyed particularly by foreign firms located in export processing zones over local firms may explain these differences. The evaluation of BI by the three foreign firms located in Batam was higher than that of the remaining firms located in Java, suggesting that the coordination offered by Temasik Holdings has helped better the supply of these services.

Size of firms produced a statistically significant difference only with telecommunication firms (see Table 3.4). It appears that the embedding basic infrastructure environment is too poor to remove biases against small firms. It could also be that large firms have the capacity to install more expensive equipment to coordinate better with Indonesian telecommunication systems.

High-Tech Infrastructure

The pilot study only picked up interest among local firms to upgrade and participate in high-tech activities. However, the one local firm that has attempted to introduce research and development (R&D) reported facing excessive costs owing to a lack of human capital and R&D labs in Indonesia. Foreign firms reported having no plans to upgrade to higher value-added activities in Indonesia owing to a lack of high-tech institutions and political stability. Given that most IH firms in Indonesia do not participate in R&D activities it is difficult to expect any statistical

Table 3.5   High-tech infrastructure, Indonesia sample 2001

	Foreign	Local	t	Large	SM	t
University R&D collaboration	0.567	0.545	0.157	0.765	0.433	1.156
University courses	1.461	1.223	1.014	1.745	1.056	1.763
Government R&D labs*	0	0	0	0	0	0
Training institutions	1.113	1.325	−0.679	1.633	1.045	1.785
Quality of human capital	1.587	1.876	−1.536	2.217	1.545	1.672

Note: * no link was reported.

Source: Compiled by ADB survey (2002).

difference by ownership and size. Also, the lack of strong sector-specific training institutions, which is important even in labour-intensive computer and component assembly to reduce defects and meet quick delivery times, has forced firms to invest more in training and retraining. This demand is expected to be higher in foreign firms that export either directly to final markets or to more developed economies such as Johor in Malaysia for further assembly.

As explained in the previous section, Likert scale scores (1–5 with rising strength) were used to rate the importance (frequency of use and quality of service offered) of each of the institutions stated in the questionnaire. The mean scores were tested using two-tailed t-tests by ownership and size. An initial pilot interview with three foreign and seven local, four large and six small and medium-sized firms showed that there were industry-specific high infrastructure services sought by IH firms.

Although simple means varied as expected, none of the t-test results were statistically significant (see Table 3.5). The low and insignificant score is likely to be a consequence of a short period of existence of large-scale IH production in Indonesia. The lack of any link whatsoever with R&D labs suggests that IH firms in Indonesia may not be ready for participation in such activities. However, given that one firm is engaged in a level 5 knowledge activity it is likely that neither government nor privately owned R&D labs focusing on IH technology existed in Indonesia in 2001.

Table 3.6   Specialization, IH firms, Penang and Johor 2004

	Ownership		Size	
	Foreign	Local	Large	SM
PCB assembly	3	9	3	9
Telephone components	2	7	2	7
Telephones	3	5	3	5
Computers	0	7	0	7
Computer components	2	9	2	9
Computer monitors	1	5	1	5
Television sets	2	1	3	0
Stereo, VCD and DVD sets	9	2	10	1
N	22	45	24	43

Source: Compiled from UNU-MERIT, World Bank and DFID Survey (2004).

Global Integration

Integration in the East and Southeast Asian trade networks along with strong trade ties with the United States offered firms in Indonesia strong export and FDI prospects, competition and knowledge flow opportunities. Restrictions on FDI especially until 1998, however, limited the amount of FDI flows to Indonesia. Hence, whereas Malaysia enjoyed large waves of export-oriented IH firms relocating to the country from 1971, Indonesia's first major influx only came in the 1990s. The short period and shallow integration means that IH firms in Indonesia lack the depth in global value chains to support long-term growth and deepening of the industry in the country.

The case studies show that Indonesian IH firms reported enjoying export linkages with Japan, the United States, Europe, Singapore, Malaysia, India and Africa. However, none of the firms in the survey reported participation in the starting up of firms in other countries – both local and foreign. Expertise on the ramping up of operations in Indonesia is reported to have come from Japan, the United States, Europe, Korea, Taiwan, Singapore and Malaysia. Hence, Indonesian firms without any driving abilities in IH value chains lack the leveraging power to extract value addition.

None of the foreign firms reported engaging in assembly of the high value-added products such as semiconductor chips and computers, and support of precision tooling services for these industries. The only computer firms in the sample are small, and assemble them for the domestic market using local labels (see Table 3.6). The Taiwanese-owned foreign

computer monitor firm reported relocating operations from Malaysia
because of lower wages in Indonesia.

Network Cohesion

Weak high-tech institutions and global integration have left firms located
even in export processing zones in Indonesia unattractive for firms to
consider upgrading strategies. The short production experience and dev-
astation from the financial crisis means that IH firms in Indonesia are not
expected to enjoy strong network cohesion.

The overall mean intensities involving logistics firms, training organizations and local government were higher than for the other organizations
in the sample, suggesting that connections and coordination with these
organizations and firms is critical to drive low value-added operations in
the IH industry. Two-tailed t-tests of firms' responses on network cohesion
by ownership only produced statistically significant differences on ownership involving logistics companies (see Table 3.7). Otherwise connections
and coordination between the economic agents in the IH industry appear
weak irrespective of ownership.

Large firms enjoyed a statistically significant advantage over small and
medium-sized firms in accessing training institutions and local government. Large firms also enjoyed a higher mean with training organizations
but it was statistically insignificant (see Table 3.7).

Interviews from the pilot study of four foreign and 11 local firms (five
large and nine small) suggest that foreign firms located in export processing

Table 3.7   Network cohesion, Indonesia sample 2001

	Foreign	Local	t	Large	SM	t
Universities	0.913	0.985	–0.001	1.117	0.872	0.889
Buyer and ancillary firms	0.995	1.233	–0.659	1.547	0.935	1.756
Chambers of commerce	1.013	1.957	–1.257	1.467	1.755	–0.635
R&D labs#	0	0	0	0		
Logistics companies	2.227	1.875	2.113**	2.457	1.732	2.577*
Training institutions	1.595	1.497	0.069	1.892	1.335	1.533
Local government	2.113	1.957	0.534	2.317	1.826	2.013**

Notes: * and ** refer to 1 per cent and 5 per cent level of statistical significance.
no link was reported.

Source: Computed from ADB (2002) survey.

zones enjoy strong support from local government, training organizations and logistics firms to drive down defects and delivery times. Severe infrastructure weaknesses also appear to explain why small and medium-sized firms enjoy less access to local government and logistics firms.

3.4 TECHNOLOGICAL INTENSITY AND COMPLEXITY

The weak embedding environment examined in the previous section is expected to be reflected in low human resources (HR), process technology (PT) and R&D intensities in the IH firms in the Indonesian sample. As in the previous section the empirical evidence is examined here by ownership and size.

Technological Intensities

Ownership and size differences were only statistically significant in HR and process technology (see Table 3.8). Foreign firms enjoyed higher HR and PT means than local firms, and the results were significant at 1 and 5 per cent respectively. The breakdown by size was even more statistically significant with large firms enjoying higher HR and PT means.

The results suggest that foreign and large IH firms internalize as well as instal the requisite technological capabilities to compete in export markets. It is necessary for export-oriented IH firms to continuously train and retrain their workers, and instal cutting-edge inventory and quality control methods to reduce defects and delivery times. The case studies show that most small and medium-sized firms are engaged either in supplier activities to large firms in the country, or simply in the assembly of brand-less computers and consumer electronics sets for the domestic market, and

Table 3.8   Technological intensities, Indonesia sample 2001

	Foreign	Local	t	Large	SM	t
HR	0.670	0.442	3.589*	0.714	0.407	5.700*
PT	0.420	0.328	2.055**	0.448	0.308	3.430*
Process R&D	0.169	0.180	−0.159	0.206	0.159	0.703
Product R&D	0.052	0.043	0.458	0.065	0.035	1.438

Note: * and ** refer to 1 per cent and 5 per cent level of statistical significance.

Source: Computed from ADB (2002) survey.

hence face less competitive pressure to utilize cutting-edge HR and process technologies.

Technological Complexities

The strong development of the systemic quad discussed in section 3.3 is reflected in an impressive depth of participation in complex knowledge activities in Taiwan. All firms, irrespective of size and ownership, reported participation in at least level 4 activities where engineers are important to their activities, frequent layout and other process changes, and product adaptation are carried out (see Table 3.9).

Differences by ownership and size appear in the levels between 2 and 5 (see Table 3.9). Adequate coordination of basic infrastructure in export processing zones is likely to allow some foreign firms to use level 2 technological complexity to improve efficiency and the quality of the products assembled in Indonesia. Access to superior technology from parent plants is likely to mitigate the privileges offered in export processing zones for foreign firms in Indonesia. Foreign firms enjoyed a slight lead in incidence over local firms only in level 2 technological complexity: in HR and process technology 15 (68.2 per cent) foreign and 27 (60 per cent) local firms respectively, and in product technology 11 (50 per cent) foreign and 21 (46.7 per cent) local firms. Local firms enjoyed a slight lead in the incidence of participation in level 3. In HR and process technology the breakdown was 3 (13.6 per cent) foreign and 9 (20 per cent) local firms respectively, and in product technology it was 3 (13.6 per cent) foreign and 11 (24.4 per cent) local firms. Foreign firms were not engaged at all in levels 4 and 5. Only local firms participated in level 4: 3 (6.7 per cent) in HR and process technology respectively, and 1 (4.2 per cent) in product technology.

Only one firm reported participation in the level 5 category of HR, process technology and R&D activities. None of the foreign and small and

Table 3.9   Technological complexity, IH firms, Indonesia sample 2001

	HR				Process Technology				Product Technology			
	Foreign	Local	Large	SM	Foreign	Local	Large	SM	Foreign	Local	Large	SM
1	22	45	24	43	22	45	24	43	22	45	24	43
2	15	27	24	15	15	27	24	15	11	21	23	7
3	3	9	11	1	3	9	11	1	3	11	11	1
4	0	3	3	0	0	3	3	0	0	1	1	0
5	0	1	1	0	0	1	1	0	0	1	1	0

Source: Computed from ADB (2002) survey.

medium-sized firms were engaged in this activity. All the computer firms in the sample simply assembled brandless computers by reverse engineering them. The one firm engaged in level 5 technological complexity was a local conglomerate firm with activities stretching to air-jet looms, textile manufacturing and truck assembly. The firm had surface mount technology in the assembly of precision components. The firm also reported having reverse-engineered most of the CNC machinery it was using in the tooling undertaken in truck assembly.

Given that the supporting infrastructure in Indonesia is poorly developed, it is expected that large firms will be able to internalize some of the services to participate in technologically more complex activities than small and medium-sized firms. The survey results confirm this, as incidence of participation in technologically more complex activities was higher in large than in small and medium-sized firms. In HR and process technology all large firms and 15 small and medium-sized firms were engaged in level 2 activities (see Table 3.9). The breakdown in product technology in level 2 activities was 23 (95.8 per cent) large and 9 (20.9 per cent) small and medium-sized firms. In level 3 activities 11 (45.8 per cent) large and 1 (2.3 per cent) small and medium-sized firms were engaged in HR, process technology and product technology respectively. Only large local firms participated in levels 4 and 5: 3 (12.5 per cent) in level 4 and 1 (4.2 per cent) in level 5.

Overall it can be seen that a weak systemic and institutional environment has discouraged learning and innovation in IH firms. Small and medium-sized firms in particular face severe institutional support problems. Although foreign firms showed higher HR and process technology intensities, local firms showed higher incidence of participation in technologically complex level 3, 4 and 5 activities.

3.5 SUMMING UP

This chapter has examined the state of the four pillars of the systemic quad facing IH firms in Indonesia. All the four pillars – basic infrastructure, high-tech infrastructure, global integration and network cohesion – remain underdeveloped so that only labour-intensive low value-added assembly activities dominate electronics production in the country. The provision of sufficient basic infrastructure support at export processing zones, including customs, has been instrumental in attracting high-volume low-margin assembly by foreign firms.

Foreign firms competing in export markets show higher HR and process technology intensities than local firms because they need to use cutting-edge HR practices, inventory control and quality-control practices to keep defects and delivery times low. However, given the weak high-tech infrastructure facing firms in Indonesia and the access they enjoy from their parent plants, foreign firms in Indonesia participate very little in the technologically complex activities of 3 and none at all in 4 and 5. Local firms are engaged in activities 4 and 5, albeit that the weak high-tech environment has restricted the incidence to extremely low figures.

The underdeveloped systemic and institutional environment has also restricted small and medium-sized firms from accessing support services effectively where collective-action problems are involved. Hence, large firms enjoy higher HR and PT intensities than small and medium-sized firms.

Although the Indonesian example does not provide information on the emergence of strong links between institutions and firms, it offers strong lessons on what industrial policy can do to quicken learning and innovation in firms located in underdeveloped structures. The low levels of development in the country obviously limit the options available, but government policy must still focus on creating and connecting simultaneously the four systemic pillars so that the simultaneous promotion of basic and high-tech infrastructure institutions, integration in global value chains and markets, and network cohesion helps drive learning and innovation. A sectoral focus on IH technology in the development of high-tech infrastructure is also critical to stimulate upgrading in the lone local firm, and to attract other firms to participate in R&D activities.

NOTES

1. Apart from Brunei, Myanmar, Cambodia, Laos and East Timor, Singapore is the only other exception. Electronics manufacturing has faced considerable restructuring and upgrading in Singapore without a growth in firm numbers, owing to its small size and the successful policies launched by the government to attract higher value-added activities. The others have yet to enjoy significant agglomeration of electronics firms.
2. Interview carried out on 20 August 2006 in Johor Bharu.
3. Ari Kuncoro carried out much of the fieldwork in Indonesia. The author interviewed three electronics firms and received 17 questionnaires (additional to the 50 received by Ari Kuncoro).

4. Rapid expansion with slow upgrading in Malaysia

4.1 INTRODUCTION

Malaysia provides an interesting case for assessing the state of learning and innovation in computer and component firms in an economy endowed with good basic infrastructure but weak high-tech infrastructure. Computer components and peripherals production has expanded since the first major wave of foreign export-oriented electronics firms relocated operations to Malaysia from 1971 (Rasiah, 1988). After the introduction of a series of passive technology instruments such as the opening of the technology transfer unit (TTU) in 1975 and the first Industrial Master Plan (IMP) in 1986, the government attempted to focus on learning and innovation as the driver for upgrading and structural change in a range of strategic industries identified in the Action Plan for Industrial Technology Development (APITD) in 1990. Information hardware (IH) was among the key sub-industries identified in this list, which became even more important following the adoption of the cluster approach in the second Industrial Master Plan (IMP2) launched in 1996. Despite blueprints contained in the IMP2 to drive learning and innovation, problems of coordination and the lack of human capital have stifled firms' participation in R&D activities in Malaysia.

This chapter examines the link between the systemic pillars, and technological intensities and productivity in the IH industry in Malaysia. The prime manufacturing locations in Malaysia where IH manufacturing operations are carried out are Penang, the Kelang Valley, Senawang, Melaka and Johor. Kulim and Sama Jaya are the other locations with significant manufacturing of these items. Penang and Johor were chosen for the purposes of this chapter because they are the two largest conurbations of IH firms in Malaysia. The only wafer fabrication plants in 2006 in Malaysia were located in Kulim (local-owned Siltera and German-owned Infineon) and Sama Jaya (local-owned First Silicon). Infineon was the most sophisticated of these plants engaged in power chip fabrication, but it was still ramping up operations at the time of the fieldwork. The selection of the two states also allows the assessment of institutional support faced by firms with similar federal policies but different state-level coordination.

The rest of the chapter is organized as follows. Section 4.2 presents the methodology used and breakdown of data collected from Penang and Johor. Section 4.3 examines the state of development of the four pillars that drive systemic synergies in the two states. Section 4.4 assesses the impact of these developments on technological capabilities and productivity in these states. Section 4.7 finishes with the conclusions.

4.2 METHODOLOGY AND DATA

The chapter uses comparisons of simple two-tailed t-tests to examine statistical differences of firms' assessment of institutional and systemic instruments facing them in the two states, as well as technology, wages and productivity of foreign and local firms in the two states. Likert scale scores ranging from 0 to 5 were used to score firms' rating of connections and coordination quality with critical institutions. The estimation of the technological, productivity and export-intensity variables is shown in Table 4.1. Trajectories and taxonomies were used to differentiate technology, and technological intensities were captured by normalizing related proxies (see Table 4.2).

The chapter draws from a larger survey conducted in 2004–05 on the electronics industry. IH firms in Penang and Johor were extracted from this survey. The national consultants engaged in the survey used a sampling frame supplied by the national statistics department to select for study. The data collected came from the responses obtained and are shown in Table 4.3. The response rate was around three times higher for local firms than foreign firms in both states. Unless otherwise stated all information presented is for the year 2004.

4.3 SYSTEMIC DEVELOPMENT IN PENANG AND JOHOR

This section uses the systemic quad introduced in Chapter 1 to examine the development of the IH industry in Penang and Johor. Although very few firms assemble computers in Malaysia, the number of firms engaged in computer components (for example capacitors, resistors, printed circuit boards (PCBs), diodes and semiconductor chips) and completely knocked down (CKD) parts (for example monitors, keyboards and LCD screens) manufacturing is large. The focus in the section is to examine how strongly developed are the four pillars of the systemic quad facing these firms in Penang and Johor.

Table 4.1   Variables, proxies and measurement formulas, IH firms in Johor and Penang 2004

Variable	Proxies	Specification
Labour productivity		VA divided by workforce
Export intensity		Exports in output
Skills intensity		Skilled, technical and professional personnel in workforce
Wages		Actual monthly wages in ringgit
HR	Training expenditure in payroll, cutting-edge HR practices, scale of HR operation (training centre (4), department (3), staff with training responsibility (2) and training undertaken externally (1)	Normalized using formula: $(x_i - x_{min})/(x_{max} - x_{min})$
Process technology	Age of machinery and equipment, cutting-edge process (inventory and quality) technology (TPM, TQM, JIT, MRPI, MRPII), expenditure on physical reorganization of the firm as a share in sales.	Normalized using formula: $(x_i - x_{min})/(x_{max} - x_{min})$
Product R&D	Product R&D expenditure in sales	Actual percentage
	Product R&D expenditure in sales, Product R&D personnel in workforce	Normalized using formula: $(x_i - x_{min})/(x_{max} - x_{min})$

Notes: TPM – total preventive maintenance; TQM – total quality management; JIT – just in time; MRPI – materials resource planning; MRPII – integrated materials resource planning.

Source: Rasiah (2008).

Basic Infrastructure

Both Penang and Johor enjoy fairly good basic physical infrastructure with strong links to the modern North–South Highway. Johor is in addition located just across the causeway from Singapore where a vibrant industrial region has emerged (see Best, 2001). Yet, basic infrastructure coordination in the more congested Penang is superior to that in Johor (see Table 4.4).

Table 4.2　Technological capabilities, IH firms 2004

Knowledge depth	HR	Process	Product
(1) Simple activities	On-the-job and in-house training	Dated machinery with simple inventory control techniques	Assembly or processing of low value-added components
(2) Minor improvements	In-house training and performance rewards	Advanced machinery and problem solving	Precision engineering and CKD assembly
(3) Major improvements	Extensive focus on training and retraining	Cutting-edge inventory control techniques, SPC, TQM, TPM	Cutting-edge quality control systems (QCC and TQC)
(4) Engineering	Hiring engineers	Process adaptation: layouts, equipment and techniques	Product adaptation
(5) R&D	Hiring R&D personnel and devising new modes of HR development	Process R&D: layouts, machinery and equipment and processes	Product Development (e.g. ODM and OBM)

Notes:　SPC – statistical process control; TQM – total quality management; TPM – total preventive maintenance; CKD – completely knocked down; QCC – quality control circles; TQC – total quality control.

Source:　Developed from Rasiah (1992).

Table 4.3　Breakdown of sampled data, IH firms, Johor and Penang 2004

	Johor		Penang	
	Foreign	Local	Foreign	Local
Population of firms	401	100	362	90
Mailed	301	75	271	68
Full response	33	39	28	37
Response rate	10.3	32.0	11.0	31.1

Source:　UNU-MERIT, World Bank and DFID Survey.

Table 4.4   Basic infrastructure, IH firms, Johor and Penang 2004

	Foreign		t	Local		t
	Johor	Penang		Johor	Penang	
Water	3.12	3.11	−0.02	3.14	3.01	−0.31
Electricity	3.18	3.97	2.44**	3.25	3.04	−0.65
Primary and secondary schools	3.57	3.68	0.01	3.45	3.23	−0.10
Health care	3.11	3.19	0.07	3.17	3.12	−0.04
Customs	3.45	3.98	1.45	2.95	3.27	1.37
Security	2.75	3.12	2.01**	2.98	3.25	1.45
Transport	2.21	3.87	2.52**	2.11	3.45	2.72*
Telecommunications	3.55	3.67	0.45	3.12	3.55	0.91
N	33	28	39	37		

Notes: Likert scale score of firms (0–5 with from none to highest possible rating)
* and ** – statistically significant at 1 per cent and 5 per cent respectively.

Source: UNU-MERIT, World Bank and DFID Survey (2004).

Smooth coordination between the state's Penang Development Corporation (PDC) and firms was the basis behind rapid improvements in the provision of basic infrastructure in Penang. Indeed, the coordination of the Free Trade Zone Penang Companies Association (FREPENCA) with the PDC led to the Penang government expanding its airport to world-class status in 1978. Similarly, the PDC also helped strengthen links between the power supply, waterworks, customs, police, housing, transport and immigration departments to ensure that firms located in Penang faced minimal logistics problems.

The role of the Penang government and its influential development corporation were instrumental in attracting assembly operations by flagship IH firms from the early 1970s. The now defunct local-owned Penang Electronics was Penang's first electronics firm, which was started in 1970. Whereas by 1975 giant firms such as Intel, Motorola, Advanced Micro Devices, Hewlett-Packard, National Semiconductor, Hitachi and Clarion had all relocated operations into Penang, electronics firms only began to move in strongly to Johor from the 1980s.

Whereas Penang enjoys a world-class airport to undertake quick cargo transport, the Johor airport lacks the capacity to provide such service. Because state government officials did not proactively target and attract flagship firms engaged in quick cargo flights to relocate in Johor, the airport does have the demand to support world-class flight facilities.

Hence, with the exception of ST Electronics (located in Muar) no other semiconductor firms have relocated in Johor, while there are more than ten semiconductor firms in Penang.

Network Cohesion

Strong systemic coordination initiated by the Penang Gerakan government under the leadership of Lim Chong Eu and closely networked with support from the chambers of commerce, FREPENCA and coordinated by the PDC (led by its founding general manager Chet Singh), helped raise connections and coordination of relationships between firms and institutions in Penang. Although it was only in 1990 that the Penang Industrial Coordination Council was created, informal links between these bodies was already being organized from 1970 when the Penang government sought to industrialize the state. Although these institutions and the links between them were promoted by the federal government across the country after the introduction of the Second Industrial Master Plan (IMP11), the strength of connections and coordination between them and firms, and inter-firm links, have been fairly weak in Johor.

The empirical evidence shows that Penang firms are better networked than Johor firms (see Table 4.5). Using Likert scale scores, firms were asked to rate the strength of connections and coordination between them and critical institutions, and other firms. Firms located in Penang showed superior rating than firms located in Johor in all the statistically significant two-tailed results. The results for R&D support were statistically insignificant, which is reflected by a lack of significant R&D relationships between firms (both foreign and local) and R&D institutions (for example university R&D, Malaysian Institute of Microelectronics Systems and the incubators put up in technology parks by the government). Networks between local firms and standards organizations were statistically significant (at the 5 per cent level). Interviews showed that local firms mainly sought the International Standards Organization (ISO) 9000 series certification from the Standards and Industrial Research Institute of Malaysia (SIRIM). Five foreign firms who qualified for this series in the 1990s reported no longer being interested in them.

High-Tech Infrastructure

Government policies in Malaysia identified electronics and with that *inter alia* IH as a strategic industry for promotion. Electronics figured in the first import-substitution (IS1) policy that was introduced in 1958 (just after independence in 1957) so that Matsushita Electric relocated

Table 4.5   Systemic networks, IH firms, Penang and Johor, 2004

	Foreign		t	Local		t
	Johor	Penang		Johor	Penang	
Ministries	2.75	3.05	−1.01	2.17	2.77	−0.97
Industry association	2.17	3.67	−3.15*	2.05	3.25	−2.95*
Training institutions	2.01	3.98	−3.25*	2.15	3.33	−3.02*
Universities	1.03	2.01	−3.11*			
State development corporation	2.35	3.57	−2.75*	2.11	2.63	−2.25**
R&D support units	0.1	0.3	−0.01	0.2	0.5	−0.10
Incubators	0	0	−0.00	0	0	0.00
Standards organization	2.01	2.15	−0.70	1.88	2.54	−2.45**
Horizontal inter-firm links	1.87	2.45	−2.68*	1.90	2.33	−1.88
Vertical inter-firm links	2.11	2.95	−2.45**	2.00	2.47	−2.01**
Complementary supplier links	2.21	3.13	−2.97*	2.02	2.94	−2.54**
N	332	28		39	37	

Notes: Likert scale score of firms (0–5 with from none to highest possible rating)
* and ** – statistically significant at 1 per cent and 5 per cent respectively.

Source: Compiled from UNU-MERIT, World Bank and DFID Survey (2004).

into Sham Alam to become Malaysia's first electronics industry in 1965. Electronics was again listed among the key components of the first export-oriented industrialization (EO1) drive following the Investment Incentives Act of 1968. Clarion and National Semiconductor became the earliest export-oriented electronics multinational corporations to relocate into Malaysia in 1971 (Rasiah, 1987 [1993]). Whereas the prime focus of IS1 and EO1 was on attracting FDI to create jobs and foreign exchange, government policy shifted to include upgrading and linkages since the launching of the first Industrial Plan (IMP1) in 1986. Although the Malaysian Institute of Microelectronics Systems (MIMOS) was started in 1985, it was not until the 1990s that an institutional framework was developed to stimulate learning and innovation in the industry. The Action Plan for Industrial Technology Development (APITD) of 1990 led to the founding of the Malaysian Technology Development Corporation, the Human Resource Development Council and the

Malaysia Industry Government High Tech (MIGHT) in 1993, and the corporatization of MIMOS in 1995. The government also launched the second Industrial Plan (IMP2) in 1996 and subsequently the Multimedia Super Corridor (MSC) in 1997 (Malaysia, 2001; Rasiah, 1999). The IMP2 targeted industrial diversification and deepening by adopting clustering as its key strategy. IH was earmarked as one of the strategic sub-industries for promotion by the government. Whereas the policy framework in the country promised to provide the high-tech infrastructure to drive, *inter alia*, learning and innovation in IH firms, the developments on the ground differed significantly. This section captures the strength of these institutions and the coordination relationships between them and firms in Penang and Johor.

The high-tech infrastructure in Penang is better than that in Johor but the whole country is deficient in R&D labs and R&D human capital. Technological capabilities developed in Penang's IH firms are significantly higher and more varied than in IH firms in Johor. While incoherent federal education and innovation policies denied both states the human capital and knowledge base necessary to stimulate participation in R&D activities, state-oriented institutional development provided the support essential to resolve collective-action problems and with that offer greater learning and problem-solving opportunities in Penang than in Johor. This section explains these differences.

Although federal policies on the development of high-tech infrastructure has offered a similar environment for the entire Western Corridor that includes the states of Penang and Johor, with the exception of support for R&D – resources such as incentives and grants, labs and R&D human capital – Penang still managed to provide greater high-tech synergies than Johor in some areas. The Penang Skills Development Centre in Penang was rated highly by both foreign and local firms. Indeed training institutions in Penang enjoyed a much higher and statistically significant mean Likert scale score than those in Johor (see Table 4.6). Penang also enjoyed a statistically significant and higher mean for the supply of skilled labour than Johor. In addition to losing skilled workers to Singapore, five firms also reported that the lack of skilled labour has restricted their upgrading plans.

The assessment on R&D produced extremely low scores. The supply of R&D human capital yielded very low means irrespective of location or ownership, which is a consequence of the lack of such human capital in Malaysia. Intel, AMD, Hewlett-Packard and Dell officials in Penang reported in 2004 their inability to undertake more R&D activities because of limits imposed on the import of foreign human capital. It is unclear if the government announcement in 2006 to provide Multimedia Super

Table 4.6   High-tech infrastructure, IH firms, Penang and Johor 2004

	Foreign		t	Local		t
	Johor	Penang		Johor	Penang	
Supply of skilled labour	1.67	2.25	−2.21**	1.55	2.01	−1.99**
Supply of engineers and R&D human capital	0.57	1.15	−1.35	0.35	0.55	−1.35
Industry–university collaboration	1.57	2.11	−1.88	1.63	1.71	−0.01
Standards organization	1.87	2.01	−0.60	1.57	2.31	−1.55
Training institutions	2.11	3.25	−2.97*	2.34	3.11	−2.45**
R&D incentives	2.45	2.55	−0.10	2.11	2.57	−1.55
R&D grants	0.00	0.00	−0.00	0.56	0.77	−0.99
IPR governance	1.25	1.91	−1.13	1.55	1.75	−1.05
Venture capital	1.55	1.87	−0.65	1.88	2.11	−0.33
N	33	28		39	37	

Notes: Likert scale score of firms (0–5 with from none to highest possible rating)
* and ** – statistically significant at 1 per cent and 5 per cent respectively.

Source: Compiled from UNU-MERIT, World Bank and DFID Survey (2004).

Corridor (MSC) status to Penang and Johor has effected any changes on firms' conduct on R&D activities.

4.4   INTEGRATION IN GLOBAL MARKETS AND VALUE CHAINS

All IH firms in Penang and Johor are either directly or indirectly integrated in global markets. However, IH firms in Penang are better connected to global markets than firms in Johor. The Penang government started to stimulate integration with global markets from the outset when electronics firms were targeted for promotion in 1970. Despite launching a strategic plan in 2006 to turn Johor into a globally competitive high-tech region, the government has yet to provide significant support to effect this goal. Hence, Johor looks set to remain a platform for the assembly of tail-end activities to support a regional high-tech hub in Singapore.

IH firms in Penang enjoy multinational coordination, market access and

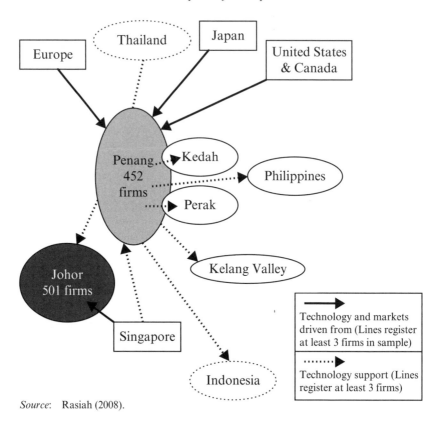

Source: Rasiah (2008).

Figure 4.1 Market and value chain links of IH firms, Penang and Johor 2004

technology support from all the major markets – that is, the United States, Europe, Japan and Canada. A few of these firms in Penang also enjoy some technology support from Singapore, for example Hewlett Packard (see Figure 4.1). IH firms in Johor largely depend on technology support from regional headquarters or parent plants in Singapore. Very few exceptions exist, the largest of which, ST Microelectronics in Muar, exports largely through Singapore.

In addition, IH firms in Penang also provide technology support to firms in Thailand, the Philippines and Indonesia, and the Malaysian states of Kedah and Perak, and the Kelang Valley region. Such support ranges from the transfer of process technologies to human resource training. Contract manu-facturers also evolved to provide support services to foreign multinationals operating in Indonesia, the Philippines and Thailand.

Table 4.7   Specialization, IH firms, Penang and Johor 2004

	Foreign		Local	
	Johor	Penang	Johor	Penang
Assembly and test	33	28	39	37
Microprocessors	0	2	0	0
Memory chips	1	5	0	1
Integrated operation	0	0	0	0
Contract manufacturer	5	13	1	5
Complementary supplier	11	7	1	4
Scale-based	18	21	7	3
Scope-based	15	7	26	34
OEM	affiliate	affiliate	7	29
Designing	0	3	0	2
OBM	affiliate	affiliate	0	0
N	33	28	39	37

Source: Compiled from UNU-MERIT, World Bank and DFID Survey (2004).

Better state-level coordination of FDI inflow by the local government and the PDC as well as high wages and a tight labour market have also driven out highly labour-intensive stages of production from Penang to Perak and Kedah. Indeed deliberate efforts to connect with high value-added firms helped Penang attract a critical mass of firms by species – from semiconductors to passive components (for example diodes, resistors and capacitors), disk drives and photonics. Intel and AMD are the only two microprocessor assembly and test plants in Malaysia and they are both located in Penang. The lack of such a focused role by the local government as well as the lack of high-tech coordination has restricted Johor to primarily low value-added activities such as printed circuit boards (PCBs), monitor assembly, and the manufacturing of ink cartridges and printers. The breakdown of type of specialization is shown in Table 4.7. Typical with the IH industry, none of the firms enjoyed integrated operations in Penang and Johor. All the firms had assembly and test activities in both states. None of the firms reported having original brand manufacturing (OBM) activities. Weaknesses in the high-tech infrastructure have obviously meant that foreign MNCs have offshored little and local firms have lacked the institutional support to expand into R&D activities.

4.5   LEARNING AND INNOVATION

Although both Penang and Johor share the same federal policies and are located in the same national economy, differences in state-level governance and systemic coordination have produced distinctly different learning and innovation capabilities in electronics firms located in these states. This section captures these differences using an adapted version of the techno-logical capability methodology approach. The approach was pioneered by Lall (1992), Bell and Pavitt (1995), Westphal et al. (1990) and Ernst et al. (1998), and extended by Figueiredo (2002), Ariffin and Figueiredo (2003) and Rasiah (2004). Two exercises are carried out in this section: (1) a taxonomy locating the depth of participation of firms by human resources (HR), process technology and product technology; and (2) comparisons of technological, skills intensity and wage means by ownership between electronics firms in Johor and Penang.

Knowledge Depth

This sub-section examines technological capabilities by the incidence of knowledge depth in the computer and peripheral firms in Penang and Johor. Only embodied technology – in humans, processes and equipment, and product – is examined here. Each of the three technology components is differentiated by knowledge depth. The results from a survey carried out in 2004 using a random sampling procedure are compiled in Table 4.8. The scores show incidence of participation of firms in the respective knowledge categories. Frontier research was not included because none of the firms in both states reported participation in this category.

The overall incidence of participation of firms in higher-technology activities is significantly higher in Penang than in Johor (see Table 4.6). Foreign firms enjoyed higher incidence of participation in the high segments of technology than local firms. Participation in product R&D was extremely low in both states, but no firms reported involvement in Johor compared to three foreign and two local firms in Penang. None of the firms in Penang were engaged in totally new product development, but the five firms that reported yes to the fifth knowledge-depth category reported that they carried out designing to meet regional tastes. A computer manufacturing firm in Penang reported carrying out designing of computers specifically to meet East Asian customers' needs. The two local firms engaged in product designing in Penang that reported having original design manufacturing capability noted that they enjoy strong interfaces with their buyers to develop product technologies jointly. Both these local

Table 4.8   Technological capabilities of IH firms, Johor and Penang 2004 (incidence)

Knowledge depth	HR				Process				Product			
	Johor		Penang		Johor		Penang		Johor		Penang	
	Foreign	Local	Foreign	Local	Foreign	Local	Foreign	Local	Foreign	Local	Foreign	Local
(1)	33	28	39	37	33	28	39	37	33	28	39	37
(2)	33	28	39	37	29	20	39	37	21	12	39	31
(3)	33	19	39	36	23	12	39	33	17	9	39	25
(4)	27	12	39	33	17	7	39	29	3	3	21	9
(5)	1	0	11	5	1	0	11	5	0	0	3	2
Total	33	28	39	37	33	28	39	37	33	28	39	37

Source: Compiled from UNU-MERIT, World Bank and DFID Survey (2004).

firms are also multinationals, with manufacturing plants located in over four countries.

4.6   TECHNOLOGICAL INTENSITIES, WAGES AND PRODUCTIVITY

Two-tailed t-tests comparing the means of Johor and Penang firms by ownership are shown in Table 4.9. It can be seen that the HR and process technology means were not statistically significant. Foreign firms, in all of which foreign MNCs owned at least 50 per cent equity, consistently enjoyed higher means than local firms in both states. Whilst foreign electronics firms in Penang also enjoyed higher means than foreign electronics firms in Johor, the commensurate comparison was also the same with local electronics firms.

The statistical differences by ownership between Penang and Johor involving skills intensity (SI), wages and labour productivity were highly significant (see Table 4.9). Given that the labour market in Malaysia has been tightening since the early 1990s despite massive imports of unskilled labour from Indonesia and Bangladesh, managers, professionals (including engineers), technicians, production superintendents and machinists continue to enjoy a wage premium. While higher wages have made Penang more attractive to skilled workers than Johor, the work atmosphere in

Table 4.9   Technological capabilities of IH firms, two-tailed t-tests, Penang and Johor 2004

	Foreign		t	Local		t
	Johor	Penang		Johor	Penang	
SI	0.28	0.43	−2.67*	0.19	0.33	−2.59*
HR	0.42	0.52	−0.96	0.37	0.44	−0.53
Process	0.53	0.69	−1.78	0.31	0.43	−0.45
Product	0.03	0.15	−2.01**	0.01	0.09	−2.11**
RDExp (%)	0.02	0.19	−2.43**	0.01	0.13	−2.21**
VA/L (MYR)	117,201	185,377	−3.17*	33,777	63,421	−3.77*
W (MYR)	1567	2881	−3.43*	901	1363	−2.97*
N	33	39		28	37	

Notes: * and ** – statistically significant at 1 per cent and 5 per cent respectively
VA/L are in annual figures while W are in monthly figures.

Source: Compiled from UNU-INTECH, World Bank and DFID Survey (2004).

Penang has changed to value motivational elements, so much so that workers are also unwilling to relocate back to their hometowns in Malaysia even when firms offered comparable wages. Indeed, an official from Flextronics located in Johor reported on 15 March 2006 that the firm failed to attract Johor-born engineers, technicians and machinists from Penang despite offering them slightly better wages then what they were getting in Penang.

Higher skills intensities and wages have also translated into higher labour productivity in firms in Penang compared to firms in Johor. The statistical results from the two-tailed t-tests (at 1 per cent) by ownership were highly significant (see Table 4.9). Foreign firms were more productive than local firms even when the observations from both states were pooled. Local firms in Penang were also significantly more productive than their counterparts in Johor. Hence, the stronger embedding environment in Penang compared to Johor – especially the role of the local government and intermediary institutions (for example the PDC and the industry associations) – has attracted higher technological and skills intensities, which in turn has manifested in higher wages and labour productivity in the former compared to the latter.

Singapore continues to attract skilled Malaysian workers with salaries reaching no less than three times what IH firms pay in Johor. All 15 firms interviewed in Johor in March 2006 reported losing skilled workers to Singapore for wages exceeding three times more.[1] Although the numbers are much less, firms in Penang also reported losing engineers to Singapore: a number of foreign-educated Malaysian R&D engineers are engaged in designing activities in Singapore. Interviews with officials from Intel, AMD, National Semiconductor, Hewlett Packard and Dell in July 2004 in Penang suggest that the supply of R&D engineers and technicians is too small for these firms to upgrade further into R&D activities. Singapore managed to ameliorate this problem by opening policy to the world to attract high-tech human capital. Until 2006 Malaysia limited this benefit to areas classified under the Multimedia Super Corridor (MSC), initially involving only an area stretching from Kuala Lumpur to the Kuala Lumpur International Airport (KLIA) located in Sepang.

4.7   SUMMING UP

This chapter has examined institutional and systemic features to compare learning and innovation in IH firms in the states of Penang and Johor in Malaysia. The results of the subsequent empirical investigation showed that all four pillars of the systemic quad were better developed in Penang than in Johor, though weaknesses in the high-tech infrastructure reduced both foreign and local firms' capacity to undertake R&D activities in both states. Penang and Johor enjoyed fairly similar basic infrastructure institutions but better coordination helped firms resolve collective-action problems so that firms reported efficient delivery of these services in the former compared to the latter. Apart from R&D-related support services such as venture capital and IPR environment, firms located in Penang also evaluated the strength of training centres and supply of skilled labour in Penang much higher than in Johor. Firms in Penang also rated connections and degree of coordination between firms and institutions far higher than in Johor. The results clearly show that firms are better networked in Penang then in Johor. Lastly, firms in Penang were also better integrated in global markets and value chains than firms in Johor.

The superiority of systemic coordination in Penang over Johor is reflected in the incidence and depth of participation of firms in learning, innovation and labour productivity. Apart from HR practices, IH firms in Penang – irrespective of ownership – showed higher technological intensities (process and product) than firms in Johor. The skills-intensity levels of firms in Penang were also higher than for firms in Johor. Firms in Penang also seem to be paying higher wages to support higher technological and skills intensities than firms in Johor. This strategy has also enabled firms in Penang to enjoy higher labour productivity than firms in Johor.

The evidence reinforces the evolutionary argument that institutional and systemic support is critical to drive learning, innovation and competitiveness in firms. Stronger institutional and systemic coordination – despite both states sharing largely similar federal policies – has helped attract and subsequently drive higher technological capabilities and productivity in Penang compared to Johor. The evidence also demonstrates the importance of the systemic quad as a policy framework to understand learning and innovation synergies in developing regions.

NOTE

1.   These interviews were organized by Asokkumar Malaikolunthu.

5. Making a difficult transition in Mauritius

5.1 INTRODUCTION

Mauritius has recorded impressive economic growth since 1980. Its outward-oriented strategies have transformed this small agricultural island into a significant exporter of manufactured goods within a very short period of time. With a gross national product (GNP) per capita of Rs140 856 (US$5030) in 2004, Mauritius is categorized as an upper-middle-income economy. The two sectors that have boosted the manufacturing performance of the Mauritian economy are the sugar milling and the clothing sectors. However, the textile sector is now in decline, which means that new sectors have to be promoted. Equally, the sugar sector is facing serious constraints. This follows the recent pressures from the World Trade Organization (WTO) on the European Union (EU) to reduce sugar prices. Ultimately the EU had to agree to reduce Africa, Caribbean and Pacific's (ACP) guaranteed sugar price gradually between 2006 and 2009 by 36 per cent with an immediate drop of 5 per cent in 2006. At this reduced price level, it will be very difficult for Mauritius to compete on the world market for sugar, as the production cost will be much higher than the market price. A restructuring programme by the government of Mauritius is in place to mechanize the sugar industry.

Mauritius is strategically located off the far east coast of Madagascar and has a rich history, which has shaped the country's economic path. Once an important stopover on the Spice Route, it is has transformed into a cosmopolitan country where English is the official language while French as well as other Asian languages are widely spoken. Hindi is spoken and understood by over 60 per cent of the population and this explains the strong business links between Mauritius and India.

With a surface area of 720 square miles, Mauritius owes its first economic boom to the sugarcane industry in the 1970s. The government soon realized that the economy could not depend forever on cash crops and that there was a need for diversification. The government has promoted export-oriented enterprises with a heavy emphasis on quality. Since the 1970s, government policies have fostered a conducive environment for the private sector to be the hub of the economy. Export promotion began with the enactment of the Export Processing Zone (EPZ) Act in 1970. The EPZ was launched in 1971.[1] As part of the process of liberalizing the economy, the government implemented five successive stand-by arrangements and two structural adjustment programmes between 1980 and 1986 which established the preconditions for sustainable export-led growth. In 1983, the government established the Mauritius Export Development and Investment Authority (MEDIA, now MIDA) to undertake investment missions and export promotions to boost foreign investment and raise export values. The devaluation of the rupee helped to make exports internationally competitive. The rupee was devalued by 30 per cent in 1979 followed by a further 20 per cent readjustment in 1981. Taking advantage of the global market conditions and exchange rate conditions at that time, Mauritius devised strategies which boosted the clothing sector. The clothing sector in Mauritius has since the mid-1980s played an important socio-economic role in terms of employment, foreign exchange earnings and in wealth creation. In 2006 it accounted for 58.8 per cent of domestic exports, around 8.3 per cent of gross domestic product (GDP) and some 13.8 per cent of the labour force, making it the largest employer and source of exports earnings. This exemplifies how the Mauritian economy has been successful in learning to innovate. Clothing is a sector in which Mauritius did not have any sort of expertise and skilled labour, yet today through various organizational innovations this sector has become one of the most important in Mauritius.

The vision of the government of Mauritius is to develop the country into an information-based economy and make the telecommunications sector the fifth pillar of the economy. The objective is to have an economy that is oriented towards higher-value, knowledge-intensive products and services. Consequently, the information sector is receiving impetus for more extensive computerization at home as well as setting up cyber cities, call centres, data processing units, software development, manufacturing hardware and related services. The goal is to make Mauritius a cyber island, a regional business hub and a gateway to Africa, through the development of an information-based economy. However, despite such bold aspirations, the computer hardware sector is at an incipient phase. This chapter examines the basic elements of the sector rather than the actual systemic dynamics of learning and innovation in the industry.

5.2   THE INFORMATION TECHNOLOGY SECTOR IN MAURITIUS

The evolution of the telecommunications sector has been characterized by intense competition between private firms, continuous technological changes, and since the late-1990s privatization of most state monopolies, the emergence of new companies and the merging of global service providers specializing in specific areas around the world. The policy of the government in the past few years (the late 1990s onwards) has been to ensure that the nation is properly equipped with the necessary infrastructure put in place, a regulatory framework, and the training of a pool of professionals to take full advantage of the changing global environment. The first telephone on the island was installed in October 1883. Overseas Telecommunication Services Ltd (OTS) provided the international telecommunication services from the time the country attained independence in 1968 until 1985. In 1988 Mauritius Telecommunications Services Ltd (MTS) was established as a corporate body to manage the national telecommunication services in place of the Department of Telecommunications. In 1992 OTS and MTS merged and for the first time national and international services were provided by one firm, Mauritius Telecom, which was established as a body corporate. Following the General Agreement on Trade in Services (GATS), the 1988 Telecommunications Act, which established a legal framework catering to the needs of the telecoms services of a state-owned monopoly, was replaced by the Telecommunications Act of 1998. This Act was replaced by the Information and Communication Technologies (ICT) Act 2001. The ICT Act 2001 repealed the Telecommunications Act of 1998 and established the following:

- The ICT Authority: established as regulator replacing MTA.
- The ICT Advisory Council: The ICTAC is a ten-member council representing the government of Mauritius and members of the ICT industry. This body advises the Minister of Information Technology and Telecommunications on any matter of interest to consumers, purchasers and users of ICT services.
- The ICT Appeal Tribunal: the role of the ICT Appeal Tribunal is to hear and arbitrate on any appeal arising against a decision of Information and Communication Technology Advisory Council (ICTA) on ICT matters. The members of the tribunal include a chairperson, deputy chairperson (both must be barristers) and up to four other members with expertise in telecommunications matters.

Evolution of the IT Sector

IT hardware manufacturing was started in Mauritius in the mid-1980s with a few private firms. The first microcomputer assembled in Mauritius was the Sinclair ZX (500-byte memory working on TV), followed by the Sinclair Spectrum with 48 kilobytes again working on TV and using radio cassette as a storage device. Many other computers, similar in style, were introduced into the Mauritian market but they were mostly targeted to gaming and basic programming. IBM computers were later imported, although the prices were very high. This was then followed by IBM clone computers which brought prices down considerably. Cost reduction became the major factor that triggered the growth of computers in Mauritius.

Availability of certificated courses, such as by the Association of Computer Professionals (ACP) and the Association of Business and Computing (ABAC), were very popular but not of a high quality. Then came the British Computer Society (BCS) in 1989 and the first internationally recognized certificate course in information technology was carried out in Mauritius in 1990 through the Mauritius Examination Syndicate (MES). Prices of both hardware and software were affordable.

The provision of communication facilities through the telephone and then the South Africa Far East (SAFE) fibre-optic cable system changed the notion of computing to one by which the country could reach the world. Infotech has also contributed to creating the space to make new technologies in the hardware sector available to the Mauritian public. Leal, Blanche Birger and Harell Mallac, large firms but small importers of PCs from Singapore and Malaysia, contributed significantly to make the PC accessible to many. Most of the large firms were competent as they could afford to train their staff, but the small importers relied largely on individual skills of the Singaporean labour force who came regularly to assist Mauritian technicians.

There were no formal structural links between the main actors and the organizations in the IT sector. No provision for learning had been made until the Chamber of Commerce introduced a training school targeted at fields such as IT. The other actors and research institutes such as the University of Mauritius, the UTM and the Chamber of Commerce all generate demand for IT knowledge. However, these organizations are not engaged in supporting R&D for the IT industry. The information hardware (IH) industry in Mauritius specializes only in the assembly of computers and has not acquired the capacity for the production of IH components. Since components and software form the building blocks of computers, the lack of IH component manufacturers means a significant lacuna in the process of learning and innovation in the industry.

A survey carried out by the National Computer Board (NCB) in 1997 covering 110 companies in the IT supply sector with a response rate of 84 per cent (92 firms) showed firms in the sector engaged in sales of hardware (48 per cent). The other activities included:

- Consultancy (47 per cent).
- Training/lecturing (40 per cent).

- Service providing (38 per cent).
- Software development (38 per cent).
- Sale of software (37 per cent).
- Hardware assembly (28 per cent).

The IT supply sector had an estimated total turnover of Rs1.09 (US$ 0.061) billion in 1996,[2] made up of the following:

- Hardware (77 per cent)
- Software (10 per cent)
- Consultancy (6 per cent)
- Service providing (3 per cent)
- Typesetting/page making/multimedia (2 per cent)
- Training (2 per cent)

As shown in Table 5.1, computer manufacturers in Mauritius import all components and related equipment. The overall import value rose in the period 2003–05, though in units there was a decline in 2005. Most of these imports were inputs into the assembly of computer clones in Mauritius.

The National Computer Board[3] (NCB) was established in 1988 as a parastatal, which operates under the aegis of the Ministry of Information Technology and Telecommunications. The NCB, amongst others, advises government on the development of the ICT sector in Mauritius.

One of the missions of the NCB is to develop and promote the ICT industry. Each year the NCB organizes INFOTECH, which is an annual information and communication technology (ICT) exhibition and conferences event, during which different hardware firms exhibit components with the latest technologies to create awareness among the public, promote the growth of the ICT industry and support the recruitment process in the ICT sector.

As part of the goal of promoting Mauritius as a competitive location for ICT activities, marketing the Mauritian ICT industry abroad and assisting local operators with establishing contacts and partnerships with potential customers, joint venture partners and outsourcers, the NCB regularly participates in international events, such as the Salon Européen des Centres des Contacts et de la Relation Client (SECA) held in Paris each year, and proposes to participate in other fairs like the Birmingham Call Centre Expo in the UK, the Bangalore IT Fair, EBIT in Madagascar, Cyber in Reunion Island and COMDEX in South Africa.

In addition, the NCB has an incubator centre to support enterprise creation, which brings together specialized resources aimed at assisting companies before their setting up and or during the initial years of operation. An incubator offers an ideal environment for start-ups and techno-preneurs

Uneven paths of development

Table 5.1   Computer parts imports, Mauritius, 2003–05

Product category	2003		2004		2005	
	Quantity	FOB value (Rs)	Quantity	FOB value (Rs)	Quantity	FOB value (Rs)
Analogue or hybrid automatic data processing machines	4350	3491831	2750	728433	2555	640909
Portable digital computers weighing 10 kg	3516	2189965	573	409291	4379	3746604
Non-portable digit computer with CPU/ input/output units	5159	1830889	1436	788002	915	872319
Non-portable digit computer in the form of systems	694	598895	1354	1443189	265	479960
Digital processing units excl. 847141/49	604	856027	2782	1794502	4728	2549365
Input or output units for computers	34952	3306724	51437	4138293	62520	6271892
Storage units for computers	8473	286301	50377	445695	21095	728514
Units of computers excl. input/output/ storage units	5467	2040459	8826	2336943	13490	3413144
Other computers excl. 847110/80	34182	10186167	37511	10416277	29312	9555010
Total imports	97397	24787258	157046	22500625	139259	28257717

Note: FOB value (Rs) data provided in US dollars with conversion rates from 31 December 2005 as stated in www.oanda.com.

Source: Computed from CSO, Mauritius data.

to transform their ideas into viable business ventures. Entrepreneurs and small businesses receive backup and guidance to be able to market their business concepts concretely, operate effectively and keep up with the pace of change whilst remaining competitive. Failures encountered during the initial phase of operation of ventures are thus minimized. In its 2001–02 budget the government mandated the NCB to set up incubators to promote entrepreneurship development in ICT, create employment and encourage technology transfer through the provision of appropriate logistics and infrastructure support. The NCB ICT Incubator Centre came into operation in January 2003.

The Mauritius IT Industry Association (MITIA) has brought together IT firms – manufacturers as well as service providers – and plays an important role to help connect members to government bodies, import–export authorities and the other elements in the sectoral innovation system such as university and training centres.

The Computer Sectoral System of Innovation

This section uses a new survey of 40 firms (50 per cent of the population of computer firms) conducted in 2005–06 to capture the systemic dynamics of computer innovation systems in Mauritius. The surveyed firms were also interviewed face to face. Local firms dominated ownership in the computer hardware sector: 95 per cent of the firms were fully owned by local capital in 2006. Using the broad perspective advanced in the introductory chapter, this section examines the different elements and networks that explain learning and innovation in the computer sector in Mauritius.

Figure 5.1 gives an idea of the number of firms established within each of the five-year periods starting from 1987. The year with the highest birth of new companies is 2001. During this year alone, the number of

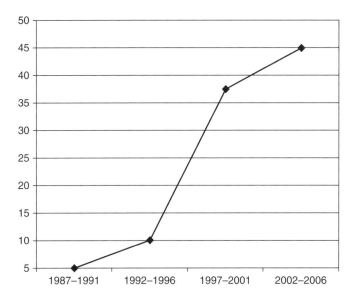

Source: Authors' survey.

Figure 5.1 Percentage of new start-up firms during the different five-year periods

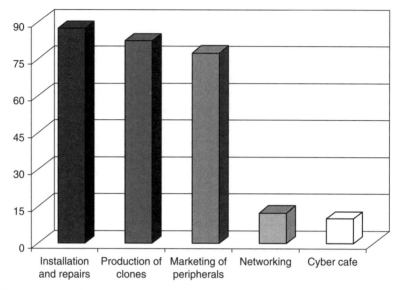

Source: Authors' survey.

Figure 5.2   Main activities of hardware firms (%)

firms established was seven, that is 17.5 per cent, and this was repeated in 2003 and 2004. The growth in number of firms led to the formation of the Mauritius IT Industry Association in 2001. The number of employees in the firms surveyed varied from 1 to 122, which shows a wide diversity of firm size in the industry.

Figure 5.2 shows the main activities of the computer firms in Mauritius: 82.5 per cent of the firms are engaged in production of clones; 77.5 per cent in marketing of peripherals; 87.5 per cent in installation and repairs; 12.5 per cent in networking; and 10 per cent of the firms also have as a side business cyber cafes. There is considerable diversification within IT-related activities in the industry; nevertheless the evidence also shows a certain degree of specialization. However, most firms are engaged in the production of clones, marketing of peripherals, and installation and repairs.

From the few firms that provided information (35 per cent of the 40 firms), profitability levels varied from 10 to 90 per cent. Among the responding firms 64.3 per cent reported profit levels of less than 25 per cent. Because of a shortage of maintenance capacity the incidence of high profitability levels is common with firms engaged in installation and repairs. Interviews with firms showed that profitability levels for almost all the firms engaged in the production of clones and marketing of peripherals has been decreasing throughout the years as more firms enter into the IT market.

The survey shows that the country has a fairly impressive educational level, reflected in that of the owners and employees of the computer hardware firms. Among owners 65 per cent of them have a university degree; 47.5 per cent have undergone technical training; with 12.5 per cent having at least a university degree and having undergone technical training. Among employees 27.5 per cent have a university degree; 67.5 per cent had technical training with 37.5 per cent to an advanced level; 15 per cent have some level of elementary education; and only 5 per cent were without any education at all.

Customs, Security and Logistics

Input sources still figure strongly in the competitiveness of low-value added operations in Mauritius. The still nascent status of the industry is reflected in the nature of sourcing with all complex and high value-added products imported. Hence, customs, security, tariffs and logistics strongly affect the conduct and performance of computer hardware firms in Mauritius

All the firms which source components from foreign markets face a number of constraints, although they vary in the relative scale of severity. Table 5.2 ranks the severity of these constraints using the mean of a Likert scale; 19.3 per cent of firms claimed that none of them are a problem while 9.6 per cent of firms reported that all of them severely affect their business. Tariffs and customs formalities were statistically significant.

Table 5.2   Firms' rating of listed constraints on imports of components

	Mean rank	t-test
High tariffs	2.86	2.6*
Customs formalities	3.12	2.6*
Finance	2.93	3.9
Information on source	2.29	7.1
Import duties other than tariffs	2.34	5.3
Multiplicity of taxes	2.64	5.8
High rates of rent	2.38	8.3
Internal transportation	3.15	4.2
Security of goods	2.60	5.5

Note: * Implies significant at 5 per cent interval.

Source: Authors' survey.

Of firms which source materials from a foreign location, 35.5 per cent do not face the problem of high tariffs. Similarly, 29 per cent of firms which source their components from a foreign location claim that custom formalities are a very severe problem for them. Although the number of documents required for imports into Mauritius is just seven, they involve a cumbersome set of processes.[4] The report prepared by the World Bank on doing business around the world puts Mauritius on the 47th position out of 176 countries regarding the number of documents required for imports. In sub-Saharan Africa, the average number of documents required is 12.2; in South Asia it is 12.5; in the Organisation for Economic Co-operation and Development (OECD) 5.9; in Latin America and the Caribbean 9.5. For the majority of the firms, the constraints listed are therefore to be interpreted in a relative sense.

This study examines Mauritius's nascent CH sector in light of global development. Firms rate quality of products differently from being world class (7.5 per cent) to date (2.5 per cent). In terms of innovation, 47.5 per cent of firms carry out product development while 3.5 per cent were engaged in service innovation. Firms obtained technology through a variety of channels including licensing, own development and foreign technical support. Much of the new products were identified by firms as new to the local market (68 per cent), while 21 per cent were adjudged new to the firms.

Unlike typical locations in a developing economy, firms reporting participation in learning and innovation activities in the sample showed high involvement. A significant proportion of firms, 36.8 and 31.5 per cent, reported participation in OBM and ODM activities. However, these figures should be interpreted with care when comparison is made with other countries, such as Taiwan for instance, as the Mauritian market is one where most of the IH products are imported, assembled and sold rather than produced and sold. In the Mauritian context, original brand upgrading activity relates to the cloning of computers with branded names. Original design would mean carrying out a design, which does not exist in the local market, still through cloning activities. In short, upgrading involves importing parts and components from different parts of the world to produce clones. The other upgrading activities are quality control (57.8 per cent), reverse engineering (10.5 per cent) and adaptive engineering (26.5 per cent).

Firms obtain technology from a wide variety of sources as shown in Table 5.3. Except for two of the sources all the channels were statistically significant at the 5 per cent level; suppliers of components and equipment, and buyers showed the highest means, followed by technology licensing. These channels are indicative of the types of activities taking place in the sector, which is mostly assembling while innovation is largely incremental in nature.

Table 5.3   Sources of technology, Mauritius, 2005

	Mean rank	t-test
Technology Licensing	1.17	2.6*
From Buyers	2.1	2.8*
Joint Venture Partner	0.8	2.4*
Component Suppliers	2.57	2.0*
Turnkey Contract	0.77	2.4*
Transfer From Parent Firm	0.8	2.6*
Hiring of Managers and Skilled Employees	1.55	3.7
Suppliers of Equipment	2.02	2.0*
Universities and Public Research Institutes	0.8	2.6*
Reverse Engineering	0.87	2.0*
Informal Sources	1.02	2.6*

Note: * Significant at 5 per cent interval.

Source: Authors' survey.

Learning and upgrading have been driven largely by competitive pressures. In an attempt to serve customers' needs better, firms constantly upgrade quality of both products and skills level of staffs. Consumers are demanding better-quality products combined with faster delivery, better packaging, products that conform to global standards, and all that at lower prices. In particular, customers since 2000 have been more demanding in terms of lower prices and better-quality products.

Given these changing demand conditions from consumers, firms have adapted continuously to the situation, whereby 47.5 per cent of firms have improved the quality of their products while 45 per cent of firms have provided more technical training to staff.

Government Support

The firms were asked about the extent to which government supported production and innovation activities, and what kinds of support they received from the government and local authorities. Only 5.2 per cent of the 47.5 per cent of firms reporting participation in product development have received assistance in the form of either grants or subsidies from the government since 2002.

Table 5.4 shows the types of support and how firms rate them. Among the range of institutional support only bank loans, subsidy for innovation and taxation policy were statistically significant. The lack of statistical

Table 5.4   Government support

Type of support	Mean rank	t-test
Available scientific/skilled manpower	2.3	3.1
Local university support for R&D	1.8	3.5
R&D institution support for technical solutions	1.9	4.2
Intellectual property protection	2.53	3.8
Quality of IT support services	2.52	4.3
Availability of venture capital	1.8	3.4
Bank loans	2.45	2.4*
Subsidy for innovation	1.72	2.9*
Taxation policy	2.12	2.4*
Science park/cluster advantage	1.77	3.2
Government procurement policy	2.02	7.4
Special support for SMEs	2.6	3.6

Note: * Implies significant at 5 per cent interval.

Source: Authors' survey.

significance in the other institutional variables suggests that critical linkages such as industry–university R&D links, R&D labs, Intellectual Property Right (IPR) framework, venture capital, science and technology parks, special support for small and medium-sized enterprises (SMEs) and government procurement instruments are either underdeveloped or non-existent in Mauritius. This contrasts sharply with the situation in the Asian countries – see Chapters 2, 4 and 8 in the book where governments have developed a wide range of instruments to support firms.

The government of Mauritius does not have any special programme directly targeted at hardware firms. However, an incubator centre was set up in April 2003 with the following objectives:

- To promote entrepreneurship in the ICT sector.
- To boost job creation in the ICT sector.
- To develop linkages with other business incubators, in order to share knowledge with incubator centres in the region.
- To promote the marketing of the incubator centre as well as its products and services.

It is too early yet to evaluate the impact of this initiative.

5.3 BASIC AND TECHNOLOGICAL INFRASTRUCTURE

Physical Infrastructure

We asked firms to rate the provision of physical infrastructure on a scale of 1 to 5 (1 = poor, 5 = very good). Five per cent of the firms have their own electrical power generators; 30 per cent their own telephone/radio facilities but none of them have their own boreholes. The firms rate transport facilities as either good or fair; 55 per cent of firms rate Internet facilities as either good or fair; 75 per cent of firms rate electricity as either good or very good; 72.5 per cent assess water facilities as either good or very good; 55 per cent of firms claim that roads are either good or fair; and more than 50 per cent of all firms claim that all the infrastructure facilities are at least good. This rating of infrastructure is far superior to what obtains in Nigeria, and comparable to that of South Africa among the African countries in this book. On a scale of 1–5, water (3.6), telephone (3.7) and electricity (3.6) were all significant at the 5 per cent level.

The study examined changes to the state of infrastructure since 2000 in order to know if there had been any improvement in provision of infrastructure. For the majority of the firms, the level of infrastructure has either remained the same or improved; in particular in the view of enterprises, water and electricity provision has remained the same over this period. However, 60 per cent of firms opined that the provision of telecommunications has certainly improved for a number of reasons. This includes the privatization of the only telecommunication service provider (Mauritius Telecom), competition in the sector (new entrants as service providers), greater competition among telephone card vendors, and the introduction of Wi-Fi Internet. All these led to a fall in the price of international calls.

Financial Support

Unlike typical sub-Saharan economies where access to capital has always been a serious problem (see Rasiah, 2004), computer hardware firms in Mauritius have managed to obtain loans fairly easily: 42.5 per cent of firms received loans for capital while 35 per cent of firms obtained loans for operational purposes, and 17.5 per cent of firms obtained loans for both capital and operations. Banks contributed 32.5 per cent of capital loans of the surveyed firms. Within this group 32.5–38 per cent of them obtained all their capital from private bank loans. Only 7.5 per cent of the firms received capital loans from development banks, and another 15 per cent received loans from friends. The loans obtained from private commercial banks are all at commercial rates and these are normally the choice of larger firms. The rates charged by commercial banks are normally higher than those by development banks. However, the development bank loans are given at preferential rates and only for certain types of borrowings, for example the setting up of small and medium-sized enterprises (SMEs). As mentioned earlier, there was no specific policy of the government towards the IH sector. Smaller firms normally opt to take loans from friends, interest free, because SMEs have no assets to give as guarantees to banks. The level of dependency on loans varied among the firms surveyed: 42.5 per cent of firms believe that they are critical for their operations, while only 7.5 per cent do not regard it as a serious problem, as this latter group of firms has never taken loans from any sources for their business. Among the surveyed firms 30 per cent of them have taken loans for starting their business and another 25 per cent have taken loans for launching new products. Fifty-five per cent of firms' rate the loans given by private banks as good, very good or excellent, while only 17.5 per cent of firms believe that the financial support given by the government is good to excellent.

Market Orientation

The domestic market remains the prime source of demand for computer hardware firms in Mauritius. Although the surveyed firms do export computer hardware to Africa the shares are extremely small: 22.5 per cent of firms reported that they export some of their products but the share of exports as a percentage to their total sales is very small (around 2–3 per cent). Out of those which export their products, 50 per cent sell in the regional market.[5] Evidently, most of the exports go to African countries, although the method of exporting differs among the firms. Among those who export, 33.3 per cent sell to overseas agents and distributors, another 33.3 per cent sell to domestic export agents and 22.2 per cent of them sell directly to customers who come to Mauritius and, in the latter case, much of the export is considered informal. Notably, 11.1 per cent of the firms agreed that export shares have increased since 2000, whereas for the others the level of exports has remained the same. The marketing support that firms receive is mainly from the private sector and government is not an important driver here. Non-governmental organizations (NGOs) provided 15.4 per cent of firms with some sort of marketing support in 2005.

5.4   COLLABORATION AND INTER-FIRM LEARNING

In this section we examine the extent, nature and depth of collaboration and coordination that has evolved among the computer hardware firms, and the institutions that have evolved to support their operations, and learning and innovation activities.

The study shows how collaboration between and among firms have changed: 50 per cent of the firms increased their collaboration as far as exchange of information and experiences are concerned. Sharing information and experience is indeed a necessary channel as it enhances learning. Since very little investment is made in R&D, all firms engaged in the exchange of information benefit. In the area of collaboration with labour, only 17 per cent of firms reported increasing their cooperation since 2000, while there is relatively poor cooperation among firms in the areas of training and marketing.

In terms of horizontal cooperation, there is above-average cooperation only in the exchange of information and experience. Only 12.5 per cent of firms, in 2005, are using industry associations more than in the past. The use of industry association as a channel of cooperation and ideas sharing is very important in this dynamic sector with a number of new high-tech, better-quality products entering the market regularly. Firms in Mauritius tend not to use industry association frequently. The main reason is that since almost all of them import their IH and parts from the same countries, they are necessarily competing with each other and for this reason collaboration is tampered by competition. However, firms collaborate more among themselves than in the past, and learn through this, although this is observed more among some small firms engaged in cloning. For instance firms sometimes rely on one another for components, although this sort of collaboration happens only among a few small firms with filial or other kinds of relationships. Also 30 per cent of firms are subcontracting more of their activities than five years ago, a significant development that might mean that some larger firms are entering into relationships with firms which specialize more in certain specific activities. Subcontracting business appears to be more intense in times of rising economic activity during which large firms, rather than employ additional labour, tend to subcontract non-core activities to smaller firms. This sort of subcontracting includes parts and component assembly. In terms of collaboration between the main firms and the subcontracted entities, quality improvement and technology upgrading are among the top areas of collaboration between them.

Evidently, changes in cooperation with suppliers are very high in the areas of exchange of information and experiences, joint marketing and speeding up delivery. This comes as a response to the higher demand of consumers in terms of better quality, quicker delivery, and so on. Information exchange between importers from Mauritius and suppliers is clearly important, since in that country investment in R&D is very

Table 5.5　Changes in cooperation with suppliers over the last 5 years (2005)

	Suppliers		Subcontractors	
	Mean rank	t-test	Mean rank	t-test
Exchange of Information and Experiences	4.1	2.0*	1.8	2.4*
Quality Improvement	4.0	2.2*	1.7	2.4*
Speeding Up Delivery	4.2	2.1*	1.7	2.0*
Joint Labour Training	3.5	2.4*	1.4	1.8*
Joint Marketing	3.5	2.5*	1.3	2.1*

Note: * Implies significant at 5 per cent interval.

Source: Authors' survey.

low in the IH sector, and also most of the products sold in this sector are imported. Information exchange between the suppliers and importers in Mauritius about new products provides the basis for trading as well as manufacturing. Another source is through trade journals by which media firms learn about new products, and the demand of customers. These types of information are fed to the suppliers so that they can better meet the needs of the Mauritian market. Table 5.5 shows the mean of collaboration with subcontractors.

Again the table shows changes in cooperation between the firms and their local and foreign buyers. Evidently firms take serious cognizance of what buyers ask for. This agrees with the findings in the literature as firms tend to be concerned more with keeping production going and maintaining market access. Firms particularly keep close watch of what their foreign buyers demand. Appendix Figure A5.1 shows changes in collaboration with local and foreign buyers.

5.5　SUMMING UP

This chapter has examined the computer assembly sector in Mauritius. We traced the evolution of the information hardware sector including that of industry associations operating in this sector, and reviewed the role of the key actors. The study concludes that the computer hardware sector is in a nascent stage and actors are involved largely in assembling rather than in core manufacturing activities. The main actors are domestic small and medium-sized firms for which the government has provided a relatively stable macroeconomic environment, but little in terms of specific sectoral policies except for the establishment of an ICT incubator. It is unlikely that much will change rapidly without some strong incentive regimes to alter the economic environment and without significant investment coming into the country. The country is experiencing a painful transition from a sugar, clothing and garment dominated economy, and there are clearly avenues to stimulate new sectors with the computer hardware sector as a promising one. How well this could be done and how quickly it takes place remains to be seen.

NOTES

1. For instance, the Act provided incentives and concessions to enterprises exporting their products, for instance ten-year tax holiday rebates.
2. US$1 = 17.948 Mauritian Rupees. Source: CIA (1999).
3. This section draws heavily from information available on the National Computer Board website, http://www.gov.mu/portal/sites/ncbnew/main.jsp
4. http://www.doingbusiness.org, accessed 24 September 2006.
5. The 11 per cent of products 'new to the global market' were essentially modifications made to adapt products to harsh tropical and humid conditions of the country.

APPENDIX

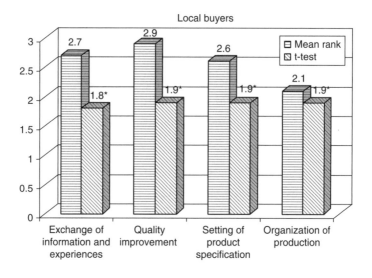

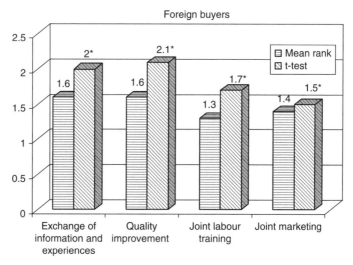

Note: *Significant at 5 per cent interval.

Source: Author's survey.

Figure A5.1   Changes in cooperation with main local and foreign buyers (2005)

6. Weak institutions constrain growth in Nigeria

6.1 INTRODUCTION

The Otigba computer hardware cluster (OCC), also known as the Lagos Computer Village, evolved from trading in imported information and communication technology (ICT) equipment, component and products since 1995. It is located within Ikeja, the industrial capital of Lagos State, the former capital of Nigeria. The geographical location of the cluster was a residential area with a handful of shops. Over time, the cluster grew to become a beehive of computer hardware and software trade and production activities. Two broad phases can be identified in the evolution of the OCC.

The Retail and Trading Phase

The cluster originated from few sales and repair outlets specializing in stationery, printers, photocopiers, branded computers and office equipment in the early 1990s within the commercial nerve centre of Ikeja. The two major streets on which the cluster developed were originally designed and approved as a residential area by the Old Ikeja local government.

Soon enough, the quiet neighbourhood turned into a major business district.[1] As the demand for computers grew in Nigeria, Otigba Street, which is the longest in the district, quickly assumed the agglomerative character of a cluster. By the year 1998, most of the residential buildings had been converted to new high-rise shopping complexes. The locational advantage encouraged the entry of new enterprises and generated employment for several unemployed university graduates.

Once the potential of the new IT business was realized, business buildings were constructed largely through private efforts as space became scarce.[2] This singular act brought the less popular computer components and accessories business in Lagos State into the national limelight, but was still insufficient to elicit positive support action from the local and state governments. This market is characterized by a wide range of computer hardware and allied products on display, which ushered in a new dispensation, the era of computer hardware assembling and allied IT business in Nigeria.

Computer Component and Assembly Phase

By the year 2002–03 the Otigba ICT cluster had about 2500 sale and repair outlets spread all over the area. With the new era in full operation, the cluster started attracting new sets of actors and the ecology of the environment changed significantly. The new actors include retailers, importers of computers and, notably, builders of computer clones. The retailers' market activities evolved quickly to include the direct importation of computer parts (which was limited to a few privileged firms before this time), components and accessories for direct sale, and repairs and servicing of computers and all sorts of office equipment. By the end of 2003, the cluster had grown in market size and undergone a major structural change, in which there are more computer shopping malls and street software vendors.

The major business activities and elements of the sector are computer cloning, reprocessing (upgrading) technology and sales of branded information hardware (IH) products. This has been made possible by the vendors and operators within the cluster who are mainly graduates of computer science, computer engineering and business administration. Remarkably, 55 per cent of respondents to our survey questionnaire are university graduates, 15 per cent are polytechnic graduates, 20 per cent are technicians while the rest, 10 per cent, are unskilled ordinary traders.

Drawing on the records collected from the main trade association there is evidence of a continuous stream of self-employed entrepreneurs coming into the cluster. Over 5000 enterprises (employing more than 10 000 workers) were recorded to be operating by the end of year 2004, and measured in terms of employee size they were mostly micro and small enterprises (MSEs). This is a huge increase (42 per cent) from the estimated 3500 MSEs that directly employed more than 6000 people in 2003. The cluster has now started to witness the arrival of bigger players from the formal sector.[3] The cluster's unique feature is the uncommon presence of highly skilled and educated graduates in electronics and computer sciences as well as related disciplines. There is considerable learning and diffusion of tacit knowledge through apprenticeship. This process has led to the emergence of trained personnel who in turn set up new businesses within the cluster, while others leave the cluster to set up outside it but with linkages to the cluster for technical support. The competition is keen and driven by pricing as a major factor.

In sum, the Otigba computer cluster has, since 2002 through individual efforts by vendors and operators, transformed into an international IH market that serves not just the Nigerian market alone, but also countries in the West African sub-region and other African nations.

A notable organizational difference when compared with traditional clusters in Africa is the level of inter-firm cooperation in evolving joint action to foster the growth of the cluster. This is attributed largely to the preponderance of educated entrepreneurs with ties from their schools, and strangers facing common threats of fierce competition and poor state support. There is an unusually surprising cooperation between small emerging enterprises and bigger players in the cluster. In this atmosphere, a new competitive market structure has emerged with free flow of price information, technological support and major market strategy information. The OCC has produced many trained personnel, some of whom are now self-employed in the cluster while others have set up businesses outside the cluster but maintain linkages with the cluster for procurement and technical support.

A major impetus for cooperation alongside market competition is the fierce threat posed by imports from Asian countries. The major sources of imports are China, Malaysia and Dubai in the Middle East. Entrepreneurs have responded to this in novel ways. One is by establishing technical and production channels with firms in these countries, which has led to informal exports and imports (trans-border trade). There are other local market strategies deployed by the operators. These include enhanced distribution networks and good customer service, and unlike the Taiwanese experience, the state has been largely absent until very recently.[4]

One of the most significant turning points fostering inter-firm collaboration was the formation in 2003 of a Computer and Allied Products Association (CAPDAN) in the cluster. CAPDAN has served and continues to serve as a protective umbrella to address the problems of the cluster in the areas of technology support, market support, security and infrastructure maintenance.[5]

With the growth of these businesses, more financial institutions and banks are locating in and around the cluster to take advantage of the high volume of money resulting from the rapid economic development of the area. The enterprises have progressively deepened their knowledge of the core technical activity of this cluster, which is computer assembling process technology. The key learning mechanism has been largely through apprenticeship and flow of tacit knowledge. There is a preponderance of knowledge and skills in trading in computers, servicing, and repairs of computers and intricate allied products (see Box 6.1).

The chapter is organized as follows: the next section outlines the methodology; section 6.3 provides the empirical findings on learning

BOX 6.1   ORIGIN AND SOURCES OF TECHNOLOGY

Origin of the Entrepreneurs

One of the remarkable things about the Lagos computer and components cluster is the presence of a large percentage of highly qualified university graduates as enterprise owners. For instance DNigL was established by an individual with both a Masters and an MBA in 1995. He had worked for several years with the NCR before he established the business. Currently the staff strength is 12 with seven university graduates and it operates from two outlets in Lagos specializing in computer systems and components as well as cloning of systems. BTL was established in 1997 and is one of the big players in the cluster with 33 staff members; the owner has a degree in engineering and a Masters degree in information technologies. He worked with NCR before establishing this business, is the president of CAPDAN, and the enterprise has offices in the United States and Ghana. GL was started in 1989 with IT Consultancy before moving into sales of hardware and components in the early 1990s. It is presently involved in sales and services of all system hardware and production of cloned systems. The founder is a graduate in mechanical engineering and a chartered accountant. He worked with International Computer Ltd (ICL) for several years as both an operations manager and the chief accountant. The enterprise has a technical partnership with Pine Technologies of Hong Kong.

The general feature of the segment is that most of the enterprises have working experience in the ICT industry. Due to the technical nature of the business it is imperative that the pioneers attain technical know-how and impart it to others through training. They are mainly engineers in hardware integration and operations. They have grown the business considerably with a large number of employees and outlets. DNL was established in 1992. The founder is a graduate of economics. The enterprise has four outlets in Lagos and one each in two other Nigerian cities. The staff strength is 23 with 18 of them in Lagos. GEL was established by a graduate with several years of experience with multinationals such as NCR in the area of computer marketing and system integration before establishing his enterprise.

The medium-sized firms are sub-distributors for HP, Dell, Intel and others, and evidently they have the largest sales outlets in the

cluster. They purchase products and goods from foreign distributors and have relatively easier access to credit and bank loans.

Origin of Technology and Products

Most of the computer hardware and components available in
the cluster are imported from foreign producers and distributors.
The products originate from countries such as China, Singapore,
Taiwan, the United Kingdom and Dubai. However, some locally
produced branded systems are in the market. The large firms are
involved in local production of casings and speakers, most of which
are used in the assembly line of the firms' production. The importation of the computer hardware, components and accessories are
sourced by the large enterprises. Firms source from where they get
the most competitive price, while ease of shipping is a critical factor
in the importation of casings, which take a lot of space. China has
established a good shipping arrangement with Nigeria coupled with
a competitive price. In the case of hard disks and other small units
which can be air freighted, price tends to be the most important factor
since air transport reduces landing time but is also more expensive.

and inter-firm collaboration. Sections 6.4 and 6.5 discuss government
actions and the econometric analysis respectively. The final section
concludes.

6.2 METHODOLOGY

The data collected were both primary and secondary data. The primary
data were obtained through questionnaires while the secondary data were
obtained through structured interview guide. The information retrieved
included: input sources, source of technology (process and product technology), availability of infrastructure, level of technical support, financial
support, market access, and the level of cluster collaboration.

A total of 450 questionnaires were administered to enterprises within
the cluster. There are over 5000 enterprises registered with the umbrella
association CAPDAN. Along with these are a legion of street operators
numbering about 1500. Therefore the questionnaires were administered
randomly ensuring that those who keep more than two or three outlets
within the cluster did not get interviewed twice. The involvement of
CAPDAN officers was crucial to the success of the survey, particularly

in encouraging its members to accept and respond which was an initial obstacle encountered from many of the enterprise owners.

The second phase of the study was the case study of selected enterprises, which were selected among the initial 450 respondents. They were selected with a view of getting a more complete picture of the operations within the cluster. They were within the micro, small and medium-sized category of enterprises, ensuring thereby that the operations, limitations and constraints of each group were captured by the study.

6.3   EMPIRICAL FINDINGS

The Otigba Computer Village (OCV) is an example of self-starting and self-sustaining agglomeration of small enterprises. The small and medium-sized enterprises (SMEs) have operated on the classic advantages of flexibility, compact management structure and low transaction costs. They rely to a large measure on their own savings and tend to access much of the information they require on products and services through informal social networks within and outside the cluster. How long this sort of organizational arrangement will be sustained is unclear, but up to now this has been a strong source of advantage for the cluster enterprises. The cluster entrepreneurs specialize in different aspects of computer production, repairs, maintenance and sales.

The composition of the cluster is presented in Table 6.1. The sample comprises 392 enterprises employing a total of 3029 workers. There are

Table 6.1   Composition of the Otigba computer hardware cluster

Type of hardware	Number of firms	Number of employees
Peripherals	7	379
Computer accessories	269	2014
Typewriters/mobile phones/camera components, parts and accessories	26	191
Maintenance and repairs	3	22
Services/marketing	17	141
Sales	16	129
Branded computer/equipment	33	313
Production and installation	2	16
Networking	6	55
Total	392	3029

Source: Authors' survey (2005).

nine main types of activities in which 71 per cent of the enterprises are involved. These enterprises are divided into micro, small and medium-sized enterprises. While 24.9 per cent of the enterprises are regarded as micro enterprises, 73.8 per cent and 1.3 per cent are small enterprises and medium-sized enterprises respectively.[6] About 95 per cent of the enterprises in the cluster were established after 1995, making them all less than ten years old. Over this period, their growth and performance have been impressive. The cluster had an average employee size of six persons in 2000 increasing to an average employee of eight per firm by 2003.

6.4   INTER-FIRM LEARNING AND SYSTEMIC COHESION

The strength of systems lies in systemic cohesion formed in part as a result of inter-firm learning and collaboration that exist between actors. This is because collaboration generates positive externalities that reduce the average transaction costs which individual enterprises may not be able to generate by themselves. In the same vein, lack of cohesiveness can limit the capacity of firms to defend their collective interests. The type of linkages, whether horizontal or vertical, determines the overall performance in the cluster and can ultimately determine how competitive the cluster becomes. Our findings reveal a high prevalence of cooperation within the cluster. More than 97 per cent of the enterprises indicated that they cooperate with other firms within the clusters while 78 per cent and 99 per cent of the enterprises collaborate on subcontracting and participation in the activities of industrial associations respectively.

We further examined the changing horizontal and vertical linkages among enterprises. Starting with the horizontal linkages, firms reported tremendous increase in the level of cooperation with other firms, as well as close collaboration within industrial associations. Industrial associations are a vehicle of unity that embeds social capital to be tapped into by members. Although 19 per cent of the firms indicated no change in this relationship since 2002, 76 per cent of the firms acknowledged an increased involvement with industrial associations (Table 6.2). Much of the horizontal linkages relate to joint marketing, quality improvement and information exchange where 87 per cent, 83 per cent and 80 per cent of the enterprises respectively indicated that relationship with other firms had increased since 2002. However a significant proportion of the enterprises had not increased collaboration with other firms in some respects. For example, in the case of joint labour training, 26.9 per cent of the enterprises indicated that the relationship had remained the same since 2002.

Table 6.2 *Perceptions of firms on changing horizontal and vertical linkages (%)*

Horizontal linkage between firms

	Strong increase	Increase	Remain the same	Decrease	Strong decrease	Total
Cooperation with other firms	41.61	50.67	7.38	0.34		100
Usage of industrial association	19.73	56.12	19.73	3.74	0.68	100
Horizontal linkage						
Exchange of info & experiences	31.37	49.02	16.99	2.61		100
Quality improvement	29.09	54.18	14.55	2.18		100
Joint labour training	18.65	43.65	26.98	8.73	1.98	100
Joint marketing	35.49	51.54	11.73	0.93		100
Backward linkage with supplier of input						
Exchange of info & experiences	32.48	53.7	13.83			100
Quality improvement	24.14	67.24	8.28		0.34	100
Speeding up delivery	30.69	51.38	14.83	3.1		100
Joint labour training	17.04	38.52	31.48	10.74	2.22	100
Joint marketing	40.26	44.73	10.86	3.83	0.32	100
Backward linkage with subcontractors						
Exchange of info & experiences	22.63	60.95	15.69	0.73		100
Technological upgrading	22.09	58.53	18.99	0.39		100
Quality improvement	20.77	59.62	18.46	0.77	0.38	100
Labour training	16.47	40.96	31.33	10.04	1.2	100
Joint marketing	35.23	46.26	13.52	2.14	2.85	100
Forward linkage with main buyers						
Exchange of info & experiences	53.27	42.68	4.05			100

Table 6.2 (continued)

Horizontal linkage between firms

	Strong increase	Increase	Remain the same	Decrease	Strong decrease	Total
Quality improvement	38.13	48.44	13.44			100
Setting up of product specification	36.24	50	10.4	3.36		100
Organization of production	23.16	46.67	26.67	3.16	0.35	100
Forward linkage with foreign buyers						
Exchange of info & experiences	31.03	58.62	10	0.34		100
Quality improvement	21.45	60.73	16.73	1.09		100
Joint labour training	23.11	30.28	33.86	8.37	4.38	100
Joint marketing	26.64	50.19	20.08	2.32	0.77	100

Source: Authors' survey.

There is evidence of considerable vertical linkages. There are two main types of vertical linkage: forward linkage and backward linkage. We find that firms in the cluster engage in two types of backward linkage, which are collaboration with suppliers and with contractors. There is considerable cooperation between the firms, suppliers and contractors in all areas of operation including information exchange and quality improvement. The same applies for collaboration with domestic and foreign buyers. More than 80 per cent of the firms indicated that cooperation since 2002 had increased between them and buyers of their products. The weakest cooperation exists in the case of joint labour training with foreign buyers and even in this case cooperation had increased by 53 per cent.

6.5   INSTITUTIONAL CONSTRAINTS

Firms source some inputs locally but rely largely on imports. Local sources account for an average of 36.5 per cent of all inputs with foreign inputs taking up the rest. The proportion of imported products depends on the nature of the business. In general, imported products are either components or finished products or both. Firms import 26 per cent of finished goods while 13 per cent import components only. The remaining 61 per cent of the firms import both component and finished products.

Since imports account for more than two-thirds of the components and finished products, the performance of firms would be dependent on systemic harmony and policies that foster trade in goods and services. Firms face severe constraints in importation.[7] The most severe constraint is the high rent paid for space and warehousing (3.7). This is followed by finance and multiplicity of taxes paid on the imported products (3.52), custom formality (3.5) and high tariffs (3.4).

6.6   TECHNOLOGY SOURCES, PRODUCT UPGRADING AND GOVERNMENT SUPPORT

More than half of the enterprises source new technology from technology suppliers while 49 per cent of the enterprises employ in-house expertise to develop new products. Where the technology has been developed through upgrading of the process, about 70 per cent of the firms do so through in-house efforts as well as with assistance from intermediary organizations and or through collaboration. The high incidence of upgrading internally suggests the existence of considerable skill among the entrepreneurs as well as technical and managerial capabilities of the enterprises. This has implication for their ability to compete as well as generate ideas to innovate within the industry.

Both groups of firms tend to be involved more in product than in services development. Even when these firms are involved in new product and service development, the sources of technology vary widely. The main sources of technology for the firms are classified by the size of the firms. The most important source for the medium-scale enterprises are component suppliers, and technology licensing for the small-scale enterprises. The least important source for both types of enterprises are the universities and public research institutes, suggesting weak collaboration with important knowledge bases, a finding that confirms what the literature says about interactive learning in the context of development.

One of the objectives of this study is to understand the nature of government support for innovation and technology development, and the assessment of government support for technology development by the enterprises is shown in Table 6.4. The table indicates that government support for technology development in the cluster has been very weak,

Table 6.3   Main sources of technology

Actors	Severity index					
	Buyers	Joint venture partner	Parent firms	Technology licensing	Equipment suppliers	Component supplier
Small	2.9	3.2	3.0	3.5	3.1	3.25
Medium	2.5	3.1	3.1	3.48	3.9	4.0

Note: Severity index: 1 = weak, 5 = strong, <2.5 = below average

Source: Authors' survey.

Table 6.4   Government support for technology development (%)

	Govt incentives	Available skilled manpower	Universities support	R & D support	Intellectual property protection	IT support	Venture capital
Weak support	85.3	71.7	76.9	77.9	54.5	45.4	75.0
Good support	9.3	19.8	9.1	12.6	22.0	19.7	13.1
Strong support	5.4	8.5	14.0	9.5	23.4	34.9	11.9
Total	100.0	100.0	100.0	100.0	100.0	100.0	100.0

Source: Authors' survey.

except for IT support for which more than half of the enterprises rate government 'good' and 'strong' support. For other innovation incentives such as skilled manpower, R&D funding and venture capital, more than 70 per cent of the enterprises indicated support from government was 'weak'.

Innovation Policy and Government Support

Government support for innovation and technology development comes in different dimensions. At the first level, there is the broad supportive environment represented by the provision of public goods such as physical infrastructure and information. At another level, there are the basic framework conditions such as available skill, support from university and intellectual property rights (IPR) protection. Firms in latecomer countries face not just the problems of resource shortage and widespread market failure, but increasingly, competitive pressures from advanced latecomers such as China and India. As several studies have shown, attenuating market failure has been a major plank of policies whether these policies are specifically coded as 'innovation policy' or not; they are formulated to support the technological and innovation capacity-building of countries. We briefly examine the two levels of support, followed in the next section by econometric analysis.

Physical Infrastructure

The poor state of physical infrastructure poses a major constraint to manufacturing and production inasmuch as the economic and social infrastructure in the country is in a state of disrepair. This has important implications for the production and innovation processes inasmuch as it profoundly raises the cost of doing business. Most enterprises, rather than rely entirely on the physical infrastructure provided by government, have resorted to private provision. For example, 90 per cent of the enterprises have electric power generators due to constant power outages in the country. In order to access safe water, 75 per cent of the enterprises have had to sink boreholes.

Other important utilities such as the Internet depend on electricity supply which has declined since 2002. In terms of quality and quantity, electricity supply is perceived to have declined by 50 per cent of respondents while telephone services have improved according to 72 per cent. In the same way, 62 per cent and 68 per cent respectively of the enterprises indicated that the quantity and quality of water supply and roads have not changed. All of these show that the state of infrastructure has not shown significant improvement between 2002 and 2007 except for telecommunication.

Technical Support

The nature of productive enterprises (small size, poor skills level) in developing countries suggests that they require substantial technical support in order for them to remain competitive. Technical support is required in the areas of information availability and accessibility, training of (skilled and unskilled) staff, quality control, and research and development services. Such technical assistance is available either from government or the private sector or both. Findings from the study reveal that government is not regarded by the enterprises as a major source of technical assistance. Most of the technical assistance comes from the private sector. The only area where government appears to have some impact is in the provision of information (28 per cent). However, an assessment of the quality of this provision shows that not only is the technical support by government meagre, but it is also perceived as very poor. In the main, enterprises tend to believe that the quality of technical support by the private sector is superior to that provided by government. In terms of the change in the provision of technical support since 2002, around 40 per cent of the enterprises indicated that support from the private sector has increased, while less than 20 per cent indicated that government support had improved. Other forms of private technical service include: quality control (61.6 per cent), training (60 per cent) and R&D services (55 per cent) (ratings by survey respondents).

Financial and Market Support

Another major constraint that small firms face in the course of production and innovation is poor access to finance either as capital outlay or as working capital. SMEs often have limited access to capital markets, locally and internationally, in part because of the perception of higher risk, informational barriers and the higher costs of intermediation. As a result, SMEs often cannot obtain long-term finance in the form of debt and equity. The government of Nigeria has established a number of specialized financial institutions and programmes to assist the firms but none of these target innovation specifically. The sources of financing for enterprises are largely from 'own sources' (55 per cent) for financing both capital and operational activities in small enterprises. A number of the enterprises have utilized funds from private banks and government sources but access is considerably limited. In other words, informal finance from own sources is regarded as the most widely used in the absence of formal finance. Clearly institutional finance is still evolving and targeted intervention as we see with Asian countries does not yet exist in Africa. Others are private banks (20.3 per cent), special government credit (31.2 per cent), while friends and relations constitute 29 per cent (sources of finance identified by respondents).

Market support for firms is similarly weak and differs little from what we observe with the other types of support. According to the firms, government support for such activity is almost non-existent and more than 70 per cent of respondents indicated that support is provided largely by the private sector.

SMEs require substantial market support (in well-functioning markets) to reach local and foreign buyers and partners. On average more than 60 per cent of the enterprises had at one time or another sought or received support for marketing activities. Out of these firms, the main source of support is the private sector which the majority of the firms indicated was the source of their support, while less than 20 per cent gave an indication of support from government.

6.7 ECONOMETRIC ANALYSIS

In what follows an econometric estimation was carried out to illuminate further the understanding of the above.

Econometric Estimate of Government Policy

The dependent variable is the ability to carry out product innovation. We investigated the effects of government policies when they are not included together with the other regressors. We found that when this is the case, none of the government policies has a significant effect on the probability to innovate. In other words, firms do not feel the impact of policies in significant enough ways to improve on product. This econometric outcome validates the low scores given by respondents to government policies.

Tables 6.5 and 6.6 report the estimation results of the probit with the sole government policy variables as explanatory variables. A likelihood ratio

Table 6.5   Probit estimates: government policies

Variable	Coefficient	Std err
Government innovation incentives	0.167	0.219
Skilled workforce available	−0.331	0.250
Technical collaboration with firms	0.169	0.231
Technical solutions availability	−0.592**	0.249
IP protection	0.612**	0.243
Quality of IT	0.902***	0.211
Venture capital	0.107	0.239
Other policies*	1.259***	0.284
Intercept	−0.316***	0.115
N	392	
Log-likelihood	−175.419	
Chi-square (8)	130.429	

Notes: Significance levels: **5 per cent and ***1 per cent.
*Other policies include public goods (infrastructure)

Source: Authors' survey.

Table 6.6 Probit estimates: government policies jointly relevant

Variable	Coefficient	Std err
Technical solutions	−0.610***	0.235
IP protection	0.592**	0.234
Quality of IT	0.887***	0.207
Other policies	1.373***	0.252
Intercept	−0.325***	0.113
N	392	
Log-likelihood	−176.529	
Chi-square (4)	128.209	

Notes: Significance levels: **5 per cent and ***1 per cent.

Source: Authors' survey.

test with $X^2_{(4)}$ = 2.22 and p-value = 0.6954 indicates that only four out of eight policies are jointly relevant, namely technical solutions, intellectual property (IP) protection, quality of IT and other policies.

In order to show how the variables, particularly government policies, influence innovation and performance, the next section examines the firm performance measured by productivity and net profit.

Empirical Results of Firm Performance

The next section examines firm performance measured by productivity and net profit. The former is proxied by the ratio of gross output over gross input in 2004 and the latter indicates whether net profit has increased, decreased or remained the same over the period 2000–04. We present estimation results only for the best specification on the grounds of a likelihood ratio test similar to what we did with the innovation variable.

Productivity: (Gross Output/Gross Input) in 2004

To analyse the determinants of firms' productivity in 2004, we estimate a tobit model suggested by the distribution of the dependent variable. A log-transformed variable is considered for the dependent variable, and as such a linear regression is not the best way of fitting the data as the dependent variable is left-censored at around –4.60.[8] The tobit estimate shows that past productivity as well as a host of factors including size, human capital and government policy were determinants of productivity.

Table 6.7   Tobit estimates for the Otigba cluster

Productivity in 2004			Marginal effects	
Variable	Coefficient	Std. Err	Coeff	SE
Productivity in 2003	1.463***	0.069	0.391***	0.030
Other gov. policies	0.552***	0.207	0.156***	0.061
Intercept	−0.548***	0.169		
Extra parameter				
σ	1.134***	0.081		
N	392			
Log-likelihood	−183.188			
Chi-square (2)	605.561			

Notes: Significance levels: **5 per cent and ***1 per cent.
* Other government policies relate to physical infrastructure such as power supply.

Source: Authors' survey.

Empirical Results

From Table 6.7 the productivity for the preceding year (2003) and physical infrastructure have significant and positive effect on productivity.

Tobit Marginal Effects

We report marginal effects for the censored dependent variable, i.e. E [ln(gross output/gross input | regressors; ln(gross output/gross input> –4.60]. For example, a 1 per cent increase in the productivity in 2003 increases the productivity in 2004 by 0:39 per cent; in the Otigba cluster, see Table 6.7 for the two variables.

Net Profit

The second performance measure we consider is net profit. It is a categorical (ordered) variable indicating whether a firm's net profit has decreased (value 0), remained the same (value 1) or increased (value 2) over the period 2000–04. The distribution of this variable suggests that an ordered probit model be used to estimate the determinants of net profit.

The estimated coefficients are reported in Table 6.8.[9] Size, skilled workforce and export activities are significant. This probability is higher for exporting firms in the cluster than their non-exporting counterparts. The role of knowledge and skill is therefore critical and this is borne out by the

Table 6.8   Ordered probit estimates for the Otigba cluster

Variable	Coefficient	Std. Err	Marginal effects	
Net Profit over 2000–04				
Size in 2004	0.243**	0.112	−0.030**	0.014
Skilled workforce	−0.448***	0.131	−0.055**	0.018
Export activities	0.507***	0.135	−0.071***	0.022
Extra parameter				
Threshold 1	−0.973***	0.242		
Threshold 2	0.543**	0.236		
N	392			
Log-likelihood	−338.694			
Chi-square (3)	22.872			

Note: Significance levels: **5 per cent and ***1 per cent.

Source: Authors' survey.

large percentage of university graduates that own businesses in this cluster. Size signifies enterprise level asset, and as our interviews show the relatively large firms are also the most active in the regional export market.

Ordered Probit Marginal Effects

There are three types of marginal effects that we can calculate, namely $P(y = 0)$; $P(y = 1)$ and $P(y = 2)$; that is, the probability that net profit has decreased, remained the same and increased. The marginal effects for the first outcome are shown to have the opposite signs of the coefficient estimates, while those of the third outcome have the same signs as the coefficient estimates. We report the relevant marginal effects in Table 6.8.

The variables in the table show a significant effect on net profit, the marginal effect (for the first outcome) associated with this variable indicating that switching from the status of non-skilled to skilled increases the probability that net profit increases by 0.055, *ceteris paribus*. The other estimated coefficients and marginal effects are interpreted alike.

6.7   SUMMING UP

The chapter comes to some concrete conclusions, namely that innovation systems grow on the strength of available physical infrastructure, and for this cluster it has been a severe constraint. Human capital, represented by educational qualifications of the workforce, is a distinct attribute of the sector and has proved to be an important factor in determining the growth and innovation propensity of all groups of firms.

Support from government has been found inadequate on many counts, as confirmed by all instruments of analysis employed. Why have the shortcomings of the state been so evident? From the findings of this study, it becomes clear that the government has not paid attention to the specificity of sectoral innovation systems, and 'functional' policies have also suffered from a lack of enforcement and resources. There is a greater variety of new and complex conditions arising from the systemic nature of innovation processes. We identify three broad features.

First, the complexity of actors, products and the heterogeneity of policy actions require that policy-making will have to move away from a focus on the supply side to managing interfaces between the supply and demand sides. This will involve a continuous balancing of autonomy and embeddedness as policy-makers seek to make innovation more widely integrated into the broader socio-economic process. This will involve not just the simple task of managing technology transfer processes, but will also involve awareness creation and stimulating demand for innovation through a variety of policy instruments (Smits and Kuhlmann, 2004; Metcalfe, 2005). It will mean redressing the organizational and institutional failures related to: (1) bridging the gap between knowledge bases and practice (for example, university–industry linkages, public research organizations (PROs) and users; (2) facilitating connections between different knowledge bases within the national economy; and (3) raising the knowledge and technological capabilities of the different organizations to perform their roles better and to become more competent in collaborative activities.

Second, far from the traditional conception of technology as a ready-made good that is easily transferred between organizations, the process of innovation is inherently complex, unpredictable and characterized by uncertainty in its outcome. Actors do not possess perfect information and, as Metcalfe points out, the adaptive policy-maker functions under the same bounded rationality as the agents that are involved in the process. The policy-maker under the evolutionary framework is not omniscient and is subjected to the same heuristic search process of trial and error as the innovating entity. Economic systems do not give one but multiple responses to a well-known problem. In other words, problem-solving is an evolutionary process, not a search for an optimal outcome. The evolutionary policy-maker is an adaptive policy-maker (Metcalfe, 1993) rather than an optimizer. Policy has to act at several levels and be conscious of the changes inherent in different phases.

The role of policy is: (1) to build institutions to attenuate uncertainty – this can be done by providing information to help firms and organizations make short- and long-term investments; (2) to provide incentives to establish organizations or strengthen existing ones where they are performing poorly – this includes intermediary organizations that mediate transfer processes and ensures pay-off to innovation, and those that take the risk element from the process such as venture capital; and (3) to provide the tools and environment for learning.

Third, systemic failure manifests itself as missing institutions and organizations, and dysfunctional connections between organizations in national systems. The implication of this is that the state has a role in: (1) building knowledge infrastructure; (2) establishing regulations and organizations to enforce the rules; and (3) formulating policies that generate networking in systems.

Knowledge infrastructure is required at the most basic level of education (training scientists and engineers), as well as at the level of public scientific research and development. These roles are fulfilled by universities and public research organizations (PROs). One of the fundamental functions of these institutions is R&D learning that creates the absorptive capacity of nations.[10] The state has historically played a leading role in both the early 'industrializers' as well as in the more recent dynamic economies such as Taiwan and South Korea (Mowery, 2005). For example, the role of universities has received considerable attention as a source of trained personnel and streams of scientific and technological knowledge, and as a facilitator, for example through the mobility of scientists between university and industry, the diffusion of new knowledge and human capital. In sum, for more than a century, states have recognized and used the institutions of universities and public research organizations (PROs) as a vehicle of catch-up in respective periods, although the roles of the institutions differ. 'Institutional differentiation' is required to generate the right kinds of knowledge and skills in an economy, by which Mowery (2005) meant the mix of tertiary but non-university establishments such as polytechnics, community colleges and other forms of technical institutes. This mix of institutional structures, and the variety of funding arrangements that support them, have contributed to the successful response of the system to labour-market demands for skills and knowledge in the developed countries.

The econometric analysis reinforces the general findings of the chapter and shows the following broad trends:

- Human capital is important and significant in the innovation models but only matters in the productivity regression when using the pooled data.
- Upgrading of products always has a positive and significant effect on product innovation, and has an impact on productivity.

- Past productivity is the most important determinant of present productivity in the cluster; this is an indication of importance of cumulative knowledge which leads to subsequent productivity growth.
- The roles of technical partners, reverse engineering, firm size and connection to outside knowledge for product innovation are all significant variables.
- Government policies have not helped to raise firms' productivity. Some of them have a positive role in product innovation (when not included with the other regressors), none of them (except 'other policies') plays a role in firms' productivity, and some of them even have negative effects on firms' net profit.

NOTES

1. Among the early comers were GAFUNK, and Balog technologies.
2. Notable among this is the Police Women Association POWA Shopping Complex with 100 office spaces at 30/31 Otigba street. This initiative stimulated the entrepreneurial spirit of the computer and allied products vendors and operators considerably.
3. 'It is the place to be now or you go under', noted an IT hardware company executive locating to the cluster from the affluent part of Lagos City.
4. The state in Taiwan played a major role in promoting electronics. This is the case with the other country experiences in this book.
5. According to the then president (2007) of CAPDAN, Mr Ibrahim Tunji Balogun of Baloq Technologies Ltd, the number of registered enterprises in the cluster under the association is over 3500 with the employees numbering between 8000 and 10 000 excluding their employers, with an estimated minimum turnover on individuals' investment over 5 million naira per annum (US$30 000). This of course is the mean for much of the small operators. There are instances where some of the enterprises realize these figures in a week.
6. We define large firms as those with 100 workers and above, medium-sized firms as those with 20–99 workers, small firms as those with 5–19 workers, and micro firms as those with less than five workers (Oyelaran-Oyeyinka 2006).
7. The constraints are measured on a Likert scale of 1 to 5, with 1 representing the least constraint and 5 representing severe constraint. Given this, a mean value of less than 2.5 means that the identified factor is not a major constraint among the others while the closer the mean value of the factor to 5 the more severe the factor is as a constraint to imported inputs.
8. As the natural logarithm function is not defined at 0, we use the rather pragmatic solution of substituting 0.01 for 0 in the calculation so that the smallest value of the transformed variable is about –4.60.
9. Stata reports J-1 thresholds as extra parameters, where J is the total number of outcomes (0.6233 in our case). The first threshold is the opposite of the intercept of the model.
10. Teubal considers two mutually reinforcing phases, namely inter-firm learning about R&D (applicable largely to the early innovation phase such as searching for markets and technical information, identifying and generating new projects, learning to screen, evaluate and choose new projects, and learning to manage the process); and collective learning, which in addition to inter-firm learning includes managerial and marketing functions that are crucial to the innovation process.

7. Information hardware at incipient phase in South Africa

7.1 INTRODUCTION

This chapter focuses on the development of the information hardware (IH) sector and the critical actors involved in the production of information technology (IT) products and services in South Africa. This has been a major preoccupation of the South African government, which for the last half decade has recognized the potential benefits of harnessing IT for resolving socio-economic challenges.

Government efforts to develop and regulate the sector under its Country Development Programme for South Africa resulted in the release of the South African ICT Sector Development Framework in November 2000. Among the objectives of this framework, are to: (1) accelerate growth of the base of information and communication technology small and medium-sized enterprises (ICT SMEs) and support their continued growth; (2) focus on developing the nascent ICT clusters, particularly in Gauteng and the Western Cape (within this latter, mainly Cape Town); and (3) leverage South Africa's strong local market for information and communication technologies (ICTs) and promote penetration in the South African regional market and global markets, particularly the emerging markets.

In what follows we first present the current state of the South African IT sector and the methodology of research. We then present both the descriptive and econometric analysis of the innovation and interactive learning behaviour of the key actors. Finally we present the productivity performance, while the last section concludes.

7.2 HARDWARE AND SOFTWARE

This chapter focuses on the development of both the hardware and software IT sectors in South Africa, although the overall thrust of the book is on the information hardware (IH) sub-sector (see Table 7.1).

Table 7.1   Activities covered by study

Manufacturing	
3000	Manufacture of office, accounting and computing machinery
3130	Manufacture of insulated wire and cable
3210	Manufacture of electronic valves and tubes and other electronic components
3220	Manufacture of television and radio transmitters and apparatus for line telephony and line telegraphy
3230	Manufacture of television and radio receivers, sound or video recording or reproducing apparatus, and associated goods
3312	Manufacture of instruments and appliances for measuring, checking, testing, navigating and other purposes, except industrial process control equipment
3313	Manufacture of industrial process control equipment
Services	
	IT professional services, software development and computer software services.

Source: Extracted from OECD (2002).

7.3   SOURCES OF DATA

Publicly available information on the sector in South Africa is limited and scattered both geographically and in time. The preparation of a past ICT Sector Development Framework was based on a number of key studies established to inform the development of an ICT strategy. The most significant study was the ICT Baseline Study, published in 2000 to establish the status and major trends in the ICT Industry in South Africa including the jobs and skills component.[1] Other major research was simultaneously done by the ICT Workforce for National Research and Technology Foresight Project sponsored by the South African Department of Arts, Culture, Sciences, Culture and Technology (DACST).[2] This later was itself informed by other previous reports.[3]

Other studies have been conducted at the national level, mainly from private sector organizations such as BMI-TechKnowledge (BMI-T) and the Gartner Group. Reports from BMI-T are very detailed and published on a regular basis, although their high price makes them generally unaffordable for small entrepreneurs in the industry.

For the study in this chapter, the following sources of information were used to set up the profile of the IT industry in South Africa:

- Major sources of statistics on population, regional economic data, employment, skills and trade were extracted from private and publicly available sources such Statistics South Africa, the International Monetary Fund (IMF), COMTRADE database and the Organisation for Economic Co-operation and Development (OECD).
- For trends and status of the ICT industry in South Africa: papers from academic and research institutions such as the University of Cape Town and the Human Science Research Council (HSRC), reports from national and sector associations such as CITI and SAVANT.
- BMI-Tech reports for the hardware and IT industry (2002, 2005).
- Detailed primary data based on sectoral innovation system questionnaire prepared by UNU-MERIT.

Survey Methodology

The survey was based on personal face-to-face interviews with directors and chief executive officers (CEOs) of 90 IT companies in the two main hubs in the country, Gauteng and the Western Cape. Such interviews are very important for understanding specific production habits and learning practices.

The number of firms included in the final sample was 90; however, for the analysis 82 firms have been included due to incomplete information. This sample comprises two sub-samples: firms receiving direct support from one of the provincial incubators mentioned above, and 'independent' companies (those that do not receive specific support).[4] The econometric analysis also uses only these 82 firms, of which 19 were computer hardware firms.

Independent firms were randomly selected (based on activity and size) from two databases:

1. In 2003, following other South African government initiatives to develop the ICT sector, the Department of Trade and Industry (DTI) in partnership with non-profit industry organizations developed a database of firms in the ICT and electronics sector. This database contains firm reports that include contact details, turnover and export markets for over 800 South African firms, making it the most up-to-date list of its kind in the country.
2. CITI (Cape IT Initiative) also has a directory of IT firms in South Africa where contact details and some basic information can be obtained.

The response rate for this survey was very high (85 per cent), partly due to the assistance of supporting institutions.

7.4   EVOLUTION OF THE SECTOR

South African IT industry has been expanding since 1995 and its growth
has been impressive. The IT market contributed R45.8 billion to the country's economy in 2005. According to estimates from BMI-Tech (2006) this
contribution will reach R60.8 billion in 2010, with an annual growth of 5.8
per cent until 2010. In this book we examine South Africa's IT sector in
relation to the growth dynamics of the other developing countries.

   Although South Africa's current share of the global IT market is small,
the sector has the potential to be a significant and growing contributor to
economic growth in domestic and export markets. Compared to its African
neighbours, South Africa is far ahead in the development of the ICT sector,
indicated by the level of exports.

   However, in many respects South Africa lags behind other developing
nations considered in this book such as Malaysia and China. The sector's
contribution to the South African gross domestic product (GDP) is relatively smaller, largely due to the fact that South Africa is a consumer, rather
than a developer or manufacturer, of computer products and services.

Key Actors in the Sectoral Innovation System

The South African IT sector is highly heterogeneous both in its composition by segment and its distribution by region. At the national level, hardware products account for most of the IT revenue, representing 40.5 per
cent followed by IT services (39.8 per cent). Package software accounted
for 19.7 per cent of the IT revenue in 2005 (Figure 7.1).

   The Gauteng Province is the leading economic region of South Africa.
Not surprisingly, Gauteng had the majority of the market share in 2005

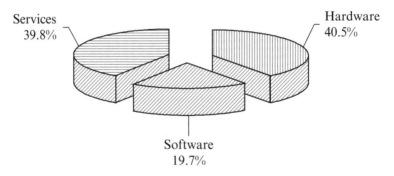

Source: Calculated from UN COMTRADE database, www.unctad.org.

Figure 7.1   South African IT market revenue proportions, 2005

with 54 per cent of the national IT market. Western Cape and KwaZulu-Natal are in second and third place respectively with 17.8 per cent and 12.2 per cent of the market.

This is because, among other requirements, the industry thrives on: (1) good infrastructure, particularly telecommunications and power; (2) a skilled labour pool; and (3) access to funding. The vast majority of firms in South Africa are thus concentrated in the large metropolitan areas.

Broadly the sector comprises four types of firms (SAITIS, 2000):

1. A small number of growing large indigenous companies, some of which have achieved multinational status.
2. Several state-owned enterprises (SOEs) that are major players in the ICT market.
3. A growing base of small, micro and medium enterprises (SMMEs).
4. A number of foreign-owned multinational corporations (MNCs) that have established a presence and business relationships in South Africa.

All these firms interact to different degrees with each other within the sectoral and the national system of innovation.

Much of the sector's current strength derives from the presence of large indigenous firms and the foreign MNCs established in South Africa. These large corporations already have a substantial share of the local ICT market, and are also active globally. They include Telkom SA, Dimension Data, Oracle, Datatec, IBM South Africa, among others. The establishment of foreign firms in South Africa has been partly fostered by deliberate policy action to attract foreign direct investment (FDI). Between 1994 and 2001, the IT and telecommunications sub-sectors registered the highest share of FDI in the country.[5] Despite this high level of foreign investment, the growth of the sector in South Africa is currently driven by domestic consumption rather than by exports (Moleke, 2003; BMI-Tech, 2005).

With the increasing convergence of technologies (that is, telephony and Internet) on a global scale, new technologies have made possible new ICT services, facilitating the entry of a wider range of firms in the industry. That is also the case for South Africa where telephony firms (Telkom and Vodacom) and state-owned enterprises, for example Eskom, Transcom and SABC, have transformed themselves into broad ICT firms encompassing telecommunications infrastructure and services, applications and content, recognizing, in particular, the opportunities brought about by the Internet (SAITIS, 2000). These firms have adapted to the evolving domestic and global market opportunities.

However, the sector is increasingly populated by small and medium-sized enterprises (SMEs), and the need to promote the competitiveness of these firms has become a central concern for policy. SMEs are a recognized source of employment and innovation for new products, services and applications. This is more so due to the strong demand by small and medium-sized enterprises for IT products and services which is currently driving the growth of the industry in South Africa (BMI-Tech, 2005). This includes all segments: hardware, software and IT services.

The Hardware Sector

There has been no concerted effort by the government to develop a computer manufacturing industry in South Africa. Despite the lack of encouragement from government, the PC assembly industry took off in South Africa in the mid-1990s.

State policy has been one of non-intervention as the computer hardware industry has enjoyed some of the lowest tariff levels in South Africa.[6] The beginnings of trade liberalization under the General Agreement on Tariffs and Trade (GATT) have seen tariffs on computer equipment come down in the early 1990s to a flat rate of 6 per cent for both hardware and imported components (Hodge and Miller 1997).[7]

Several major brands stimulated local personal computer (PC) assembly because of the flexibility that it provides for servicing the local PC market. The South African Foresight Report (1999) stated that hardware manufacturing and assembly capabilities within South Africa opened the opportunity to export, particularly into Africa. However this market is still small and according to recent figures from the Department of Trade and Industry (DTI) export values are declining. Although exports of technology-intensive products grew 36 per cent between 2001 and 2005, imports of technology intensive products also did, at 50 per cent. For the particular case of computing machines, the trade imbalance is even higher, showing an increase in imports of 73 per cent opposed to a decrease in exports of 17 per cent within the same period.

These figures show that while there is some PC assembly in South Africa, almost all hardware is imported from Europe, North America and the Far East, and marketed and distributed in South Africa. Hodge and Miller (1997) estimated that in 1997 over 95 per cent of hardware revenue by local firms came from imported products and components. Given that most of the local hardware production in South Africa is still focused on assembling foreign components, this percentage is estimated to remain at similar levels in 2007.

Major Players

According to the BMI-Tech report (2005), the South African PC market boomed in 2004. The PC market value increased 42.2 per cent annually to US$1448.88 million. However, the benefits of this 'expansion' are not equally distributed across the industry. In that year, the top ten vendors together accounted for 74.5 per cent share of the total PC sales in South Africa. In revenue terms the top ten vendors held a 79.8 per cent share of the market, higher than the 76.7 per cent and 70.7 per cent reported in 2002 and 2001 respectively (BMI-Tech, 2005).

Hewlett-Packard is the leading PC brand in terms of shipments and also in value (accounting for 23 per cent of the total value of shipments in US dollars). Meccer, a local brand produced by Mustek Co., is placed second in the market with a 16 per cent share of unit shipments. Dell, Acer and IBM also have a significant and growing presence. However other locally assembled PCs such as Proline and Sahara are also establishing themselves among these top ten vendors.

It is often difficult to define what constitutes a local or a foreign PC, since some of the foreign firms import components and assemble locally, and also local firms source foreign generic components and sell them assembled as foreign-branded PCs. Taking this into account, international brands in this case include IBM, Acer, Dell, Siemens and Hewlett-Packard among others. Major local brands include Meccer, Proline and Sahara. The other players in the local assembly market are Rectron and African Gateway.

Given the differences in locally assembled PCs and international brands (the latter are significantly more expensive), local assemblers focus on lower income groups – they sell PCs to local retail stores, where customers can purchase a PC on payment terms (BMI-T, 2005). In relation to the composition of the industry, the PC market is largely dominated by desktop sales, accounting for 77 per cent of the shipments, followed by notebooks with 20 per cent.

Demand

The number of installed personal computers in South Africa rose significantly from 1992 (541 582) to 1999 (3 091 949) at a rate of nearly 30 per cent per year. This growth has been persistent since 2000 and according to a new study by technology research firm World Wide Worx, the number of personal computers in use in South Africa passed the 5 million mark for the first time in 2006.[8]

The main consumers of hardware computers in 2000 were the finance, insurance and real estate; manufacturing; retail; transportation, communications and electricity; public administration; and consumer sectors, in that order. A more recent study by BMI-Tech (2004) confirms the concentration of PC demand around the services sector.

In terms of number of shipments to end-users in the period 2001–04, the segment that absorbed the higher number of PC units in 2004 was the small business sector (with 279 555 units), taking the first position from the very large business segment in 2001. However, the most dynamic demand of PCs is in the education sector, which has experienced a 51 per cent annual growth since 2001, followed by government with 39 per cent annual growth.

The creation of the State Information Technology Agency (SITA)[9] by the end of 2001 had the objective to consolidate the government's IT infrastructure. Since then, government expenditure in South Africa on IT has experienced a consistent increase, reaching R5 billion in 2003 and expected to grow at a rate of 9.1 per cent to reach approximately R8 billion by 2008 (BMI-Tech, 2005).

However, government purchases tend to favour internationally branded computers, a result of the existent industrial policy which does not give preferential treatment for one single vendor. SITA recently announced the list of preferred suppliers including local and international brands such as HP, Mustek, IBM, AST, Pinnacle, Sahara Computers, Dell, Siemens and Rentworks. Since the government is a major consumer of IT products, most IT vendors are adapting their market strategies to acquire more public sector customers. In 2002 and 2003 around 65 per cent of government IT hardware expenditure was spent on locally assembled PCs. However there was a shift in 2004 and only 41 per cent of the government IT hardware spend was locally produced.

Locally assembled computers are still preferred by the educational sector and SMEs, although they are losing share. Nevertheless, the increasing number of SMEs in South Africa indicates that this segment represents a great potential for the industry.

7.5   POLICY AND SUPPORT STRUCTURES

South Africa has over time effected a major process of transformation and reformulation of its innovation and technology policy. The end of Apartheid in the mid-1990s and the new economic and social imperatives refocused attention on the innovation system. This resulted in the emergence of numerous policies and institutions designed to accelerate domestic technology development and improve the absorption of imported technologies.

Following the 1994 elections the Reconstruction and Development Programme (RDP) gave a high priority to ICT-related issues. Two important events followed in 1996. The White Paper on Science and Technology emphasized the role of ICT in the context of the Growth and Development Strategy (GDS), particularly its value to the development of science and technology (S&T).

The South Africa Information Technology Industry Strategy (SAITIS) project was conceived in this context. An important goal of the project was to bridge the global development gap between the international ICT community and the South African ICT sector.

An important institutional strategy included the Telecommunications Act which established a three-tier separation of roles: (1) the Ministry and Department will formulate policy and manage shareholding in Telkom; (2) the South African Telecommunications Regulatory Authority (SATRA); and (3) the Universal Service Agency (USA) will ensure implementation of the Act, including the awarding of licences.

National Institutions and Policies

The first national attempt to develop a sector-specific initiative was the launching of the South African Information Technology Industry Strategy (SAITIS) in 1995. This resulted in the formation of a group of 37 stakeholders as an Advisory Group to the SAITIS Project representing key organizations and agencies.[10]

Subsequently there was the release of the South African ICT Sector Development Framework in November 2000, with the following objectives:

- Accelerate growth of SMEs and support their continued growth.
- Develop the nascent IT clusters, particularly in Gauteng and the Western Cape (mainly Cape Town).
- Leverage South Africa's local market for IT and foster its presence in the South African regional and global markets, particularly the expanding developing country markets.

Special emphasis is placed on creating and supporting new entrants in the IT Sector, particularly SMEs. In particular the need is observed to foster incubator and entrepreneur centres in research facilities and on university and technikon campuses across South Africa to provide a full range of scientific, technological and management services to small ICT start-up firms, to foster early-stage entry and growth.

Following the release of the ICT Sector Development Framework, the ICT Development Council was established in 2000 by the Department of

Trade and Industry. The council represents all sectors of the industry and includes multinational corporations as well as large, small and medium-sized local firms.

Strategic Industrial Projects (SIPs) started being implemented in 2001 and are managed by the DTI. The incentives derived from these projects provide between 50 and 100 per cent tax allowance to encourage investments into South African operations from local and foreign investors. The programme aims to promote computer and computer-related activities such as hardware consultancy, software consultancy and supply, data processing and database activities.

Import duties on IT hardware and software were abolished in 2003. Firms importing into South Africa only pay a value-added tax (VAT) to the South African Customs. This scheme had practical benefits for software firms as most firms import hardware from abroad. Release from import duties highly benefits South African small firms, which rely largely on imported technology.

Provincial Initiatives

The 'Smart Province' of Gauteng
As mentioned earlier, the Gauteng province is the leading economic region of South Africa. Covering only 1.4 per cent of the country's land area, it generates 10 per cent of the African GDP and 33 per cent of South Africa's GDP. The city of Johannesburg itself generates 40 per cent of Gauteng's and 16 per cent of South Africa's GDP.

The province has its economic and historic roots in the gold industry that was sparked off by the discovery of gold in Johannesburg in 1886. Based on this background, Gauteng grew as the business and financial centre of South Africa, concentrating the bulk of production in South Africa. However in 1997, the Gauteng Department of Finance and Economic Affairs' Trade and Industrial Strategy (TIS) diagnosed the inability of the provincial economy to sustain a long-term job-creating growth on the sole reliance on its historically favoured primary production industries (mostly gold, iron and steel) and its low value-added and internationally uncompetitive manufacturing sector. The strategy therefore identified three ways to grow GDP and employment in the province: develop 'smart industries', move toward high value-added manufacturing and enhance the service sector (from financial and business services to tourism). This realignment of priorities from the provincial economy derived in the launch of the Blue IQ programme in 2002.[11] The first phase of the Blue IQ involved the delivery of 11 strategic projects; the second phase of commercialization is expected to be dependent on private sector participation. One of these projects was the creation of the

Innovation Hub, an ICT incubator and Science Park. The Innovation Hub and other similar ICT-incubating activities are at the centre of the technology support services strategy directed at small entrepreneurs in Gauteng.

The Innovation Hub (IH)[12] is thus part of the Gauteng Development Strategy. Born from an investment of over R300 million by Blue IQ, the IH was established to 'act as a catalyst for the next wave of knowledge-intensive industry growth in the country, and is set to become the preferred address for high-tech start-up companies, as well as leading local and international players seeking to access a prime source of South African skills', according to Gauteng MEC, Mr Jabu Moleketi.[13]

The hub is the first internationally accredited science and technology park in sub-Saharan Africa.[14] Its aim is to function as a catalyst for improving South African technology and productivity, and to promote black economic empowerment by acting as an incubator for innovative black start-up companies. It houses a variety of technology-related businesses including electronics, ICT and bio-science. Despite its short period of operations, by March 2006 the IH hosted nearly 50 tenants.

Softstart-BTI (SBTI)[15] is an incubator that also provides technology support to ICT SMEs. SBTI was formed as a recent merger[16] between two existing incubators (Softstart and Bodibeng Technology Incubator), part of the former GODISA programme (now SEDA Technology Initiative). The services offered by SBTI include mentoring and coaching, new product assessment, business plans, office space and infrastructure, and access to finance and legal services, among others. The merger of these two incubators has resulted in the largest IT incubator in South Africa. SBTI has recently acquired new buildings and hosts around 150 ICT firms in Midrand, one of the largest industrial belts of South Africa and home to a number of major global ICT companies.

These programmes are in line with Gauteng's concentration of ICT activity. In 2004, Gauteng hosted 66 per cent of the industry (with 85 per cent of the telecommunications industry sub-sector and 65 per cent of the IT industry sub-sector). Gauteng accomodated 3541 ICT firms in 2003 of which 1681 belonged to the software development sub-sector, 1020 to the computer industry, 400 to the telecommunications segment, 360 to the media industry and 80 to electronics. The knowledge-intensive sectors represent about 15 per cent of the Gauteng economy, employing 70 per cent of South Africa's hi-tech workforce (Pejout, 2004). The sector in Gauteng contributes 6.4 per cent of the provincial gross domestic product.

The Western Cape: the growing ICT hub
The Western Cape Province has recently started challenging the dominant position of Gauteng in its 'knowledge-intensive' profile. The Western Cape

provincial government, along with the municipality of Cape Town, are devoting efforts to promote the Western Cape into a growing hub for ICT activities, and various policies are directly focused on the strengthening of the sector.

The Cape Information Technology Initiative (CITI)[17] was launched in June 1998. Registered as a non-governmental organization (NGO), it is an independent development agency supporting the growth of the ICT cluster of businesses in the Western Cape. CITI is a non-profit organization funded by the Western Cape province and city of Cape Town governments, as well as more than 40 corporate members including UUNET, Microsoft, Telkom, and other national, regional and local businesses. CITI is grounded in the concept of cluster development[18] with the idea of attracting high-tech investment to the province. CITI provides business incubation, venture capital, IT education, industry research and marketing, and networking of individuals and organizations. It works in collaboration with local universities and performs regular sector scans through surveying.

One of its major 'subsidiaries' is the Bandwidth Barn (BWB). The BWB houses around 70 small businesses in one building, and facilitates networking and outsourcing, minimizing basic operation costs such as office space, reception, telephone lines and Internet connectivity. CITI is now partnering with other small business clusters, such as the Innovation Hub in the Gauteng Province, and other incubators in Ireland and the United Kingdom.

The Western Cape hosted about 1200 ICT companies in 2004, among which three-quarters are located in the city of Cape Town. The two main activities of Western Cape-based firms are ICT services (consulting, HR recruitment, education and training, maintenance and repair) and software activities, with respectively 28 per cent and 25 per cent of firms involved in these sub-sectors.

The research from which this chapter draws covered the activities of these organizations as well as a sample of firms in each of these incubator supports.

7.6   SURVEY RESULTS

Basic Characteristics of Firms

The general characteristics of the surveyed firms in terms of size and age show that most of them are typical SMEs, although there is some representation of larger firms: 35 per cent have less than ten employees, 51 per cent have between 11 and 100 employees and 13 per cent have more than 101 employees (only 2 per cent have more than 500 employees). The average number of employees was 26 for software-related firms and 202 for hardware-related firms, while the average size of the firm for the total sample was 67. Hardware firms tend to be larger than software companies; however, for this sample this might be partly due to the inclusion of major national hardware assemblers in the sample such as Mustek and Rectron.

In terms of revenues, most surveyed firms (55 per cent) reported turnover of less than R10 million in 2004, and only 12 per cent of them reported sales of more than R100 million. However there are significant differences between hardware and software firms in terms of sizes and turnover. While software firms tend to be smaller (62 per cent reported less than R10 million turnover) hardware companies are mostly large and 53 per cent of the surveyed firms reported more than R100 million turnover.

Given the recent development of the IT industry in South Africa, it is not surprising to find that firms are rarely older than 20 years and most existing firms were established between five and ten years ago. In our sample, 48 per cent of the firms are older than six years old (established before the year 2000) and 52 per cent were established within the six years since 2001.

Interviews were conducted in the largest two IT hubs, the Western Cape (Cape Town) and the Gauteng province (Johannesburg and Pretoria). We found a representative number of firms in each geographical area, 46 per cent in the Western Cape and 54 per cent in Gauteng. Regional representation has also been pursued in terms of the number of firms that obtain direct support from provincial initiatives, where 40 per cent of the firms are part of the support programmes and 60 per cent of the companies are 'independent'.

The majority of the firms in the sample were local companies and only 12 per cent of them had some share of foreign ownership while only 6 per cent were listed on the stock market.

Software development, IT consultancy, hardware reselling and Internet services are the leading activities. Although packaged software reselling represents a small proportion of the responses of the total survey sample, it is generally embedded in the 'solution' offered by those firms involved in IT consultancy. In other words, firms tend to offer a complete IT solution that involves the acquisition of packaged software which they customize to the particular needs of the client, which includes IT training, implementation and technical support.

Knowledge Base of the Sectoral System

Technology is not always easy to define in the IT sector, particularly for those activities where software, hardware and skills become one product and production processes do not necessarily follow the traditional model of clearly defined inputs, technologies for production and outputs. Products and services are difficult to differentiate. The 'products' that firms elaborate are sometimes only used to enhance the services they provide to their clients, and at the same time these 'products' are indicative of the technological base of the firm. For instance, the provision of final 'solutions' is very much linked to the firm's human resources and skills to write new software, for example. From this point of view, firms generally understand that human capabilities are their main input for production as well as their main source of technology.

Technical skills

The ability to learn and upgrade in a firm largely depends on the base and nature of the skills within the organization. The sector, much like the Nigerian computer component sector, has a significant number of educated owners. The majority (76 per cent) of the owners of the firms have a university degree or a technical diploma.[19] The interviews showed that the type of qualification and previous skills of the owners are not necessarily related to IT, and in many cases they have backgrounds in the markets towards which their products and services are oriented (that is, medical, law, public sector, and so on). In this sense, the know-how and previous experience of the owner becomes a key aspect for business competitiveness.

However, that is not the case for the employed staff, where a very high density of university degrees and technical diplomas can be found. The average percentage of university degrees and diplomas in relation to the total amount of employees in the firm is high. For the total sample, the average percentage of highly skilled staff (university degree or technical diploma) in the surveyed firms is 72 per cent; these averages are higher in the case of the software sector, where 79 per cent of owners have a university degree (Table 7.2).

Table 7.2   Educational level of the staff (%) in 2006

	All firms	Software	Hardware
University degree	36	79	63
Technical	36	17	5
High school	26	8	32
Elementary	2	2	0
No education	0	0	0

Source: Authors' survey.

Both software and hardware sectors are thus large absorbers of skilled IT personnel. The rest of the 'unskilled' staff (high school or elementary level) are generally employees in administrative or sales positions. In the latter case, they also receive technical information and training on the products, which is normally provided by the suppliers.

Production and technology inputs

As mentioned above, production inputs for the IT industry are not easy to define. Most activities are very intense in knowledge, which is embodied in people. The interviews show that the firm directors considered human resources as their main input for production, composed in the main of domestic labour (only 20 per cent of the firms surveyed employ one or more foreign employees, which are in all cases technical staff). Most interviewees mentioned that the shortage of the necessary skills for the firm to grow and the willingness to introduce new foreign technologies prompted them into employing foreign specialized staff. However, the process has been hindered by the strict immigration laws in South Africa.

We also examined the sources of inputs (shown in Table 7.3) which refer to 'material' inputs for production, excluding human resources. In the case of the software industry the inputs mostly involve software licenses and packaged software as well as some hardware. For hardware firms they mostly involve hardware equipment and/or hardware components as well as a small amount of software. Most firms employ a combination of foreign and local inputs. Only 5 per cent of the firms reported the utilization of local inputs exclusively, and 12 per cent reported exclusive use of foreign inputs.

The results show that the industry in South Africa still relies largely on foreign inputs, particularly the hardware industry (86 per cent of the hardware firms reported the use of foreign inputs compared to 49 per cent for software). Open source is gradually being introduced in production, especially for software-related activities. SMEs especially make greater use of open source inputs for some of their clients to save on development costs.

Table 7.3   Source of inputs (%) in 2006

	All firms	Software	Hardware
Local inputs	33	39	13
Foreign inputs	58	49	86
Open source	9	12	1

Source: Authors' survey.

Table 7.4   Key constraints in importing inputs in 2006

	All firms	Software	Hardware
High tariffs	1.3	1.1	1.9
Customs formalities	2.0	1.5	3.5
Finance	1.6	1.4	2.5
Information on source	1.2	1.1	1.7
Import duties	1.3	1.2	1.7
Multiplicity of taxes	1.1	1.0	1.3
High rates of rent	1.1	1.1	1.0
Transportation (Internal)	1.5	1.2	2.6
Security of goods	1.9	1.4	3.5

Source: Authors' survey.

A large percentage of the inputs come from the USA and European suppliers, although increasingly more firms have turned to the Far East, particularly China, Taiwan, Hong Kong and Korea. However, it must be noted that most respondents found it difficult to identify the actual origin of the inputs because of the global nature of the supply chain (for example Dell is a largely supplied from Ireland but it is a US brand). According to the responses, 83 per cent of the software firms import from the US, which confirms that not much has changed since 1995 in this regard, since a study conducted in 1995 by Hodge and Miller (1997) found similar results. Hardware assemblers and resellers are increasingly turning to China due to the low price of Chinese hardware products and components (see Chapter 2 of this book).

The facilitation of imports brought by low tariffs in South Africa for hardware and software products and components is reflected in the low tariff rates given to the main constraints in importing inputs by the respondents.[20] Software firms generally acquire their software on a licensing basis and the small amount of hardware is obtained from local distributors; therefore they are not affected by these restrictions, apart from access to finance. However, hardware firms seem to be significantly affected by customs formalities, the security of goods and local transportation of the products. Goods are sometimes lost during customs formalities (Table 7.4).

When firms were asked about their source of technology, including inputs and processes, the majority of companies (70 per cent) described it as a combination of local and foreign expertise. However, there are significant differences between hardware and software companies. None of the hardware firms operates only with local sources of technology, while nearly

Table 7.5   Level of innovation (%) in 2006

	All	Software	Hardware	Small	Large	Sup	Nsup
New products	66	75	37	70	36	76	58
New services	76	78	68	76	73	88	67

Notes: Sup = supported by government; Nsup = not supported by government.

Source: Authors' survey.

20 per cent of software firms do. Hardware firms rely on foreign inputs to the tune of 47 per cent, compared with 6 per cent for software.

A very large percentage of the firms are 'innovators', as 66 per cent of them have been involved in a new product development within the last five years of operations, and 76 per cent have developed a new service. Table 7.5 shows that software-related firms are more innovative than hardware firms (75 per cent versus 37 per cent), small than larger corporations (70 per cent versus 36 per cent) and those receiving support against those than do not (76 per cent versus 58 per cent). Also hardware activities seem to be more focused on service innovation rather than product innovation. This is because hardware activities are based on assembling and distribution of foreign hardware. Some firms reported that given the high competition with other local distributors and foreign suppliers, the key to success is the development of innovative services to maintain the old and to keep new customers.

Most of these new products and services were obtained through own development, particularly in the case of software companies. The results show that hardware firms rely more often on licensing and foreign technical support (Table 7.6).

About one-third of the firms consider themselves 'global' innovators. This percentage is even higher for the software industry. This result at first contrasts with the lower exporting rate observed for the software industry; however most respondents mentioned that their innovations were based on their deep knowledge of local needs and their ability to respond creatively to those needs and the constraints in the South African and African environments. When innovations are based in strong 'localization', the incidence of low exports is not so surprising.

Quality control and reverse engineering are the major upgrading paths for the firms surveyed (Table 7.7). Significantly, 38 per cent of the firms are mostly concerned with quality control systems, although in the majority of the cases it is an internal quality control system, based on internal quality

Table 7.6   Origin of innovation (%) in 2006

	All	Software	Hardware	Small	Larger	Sup	Nsup
Licensing	22	24	16	23	18	21	21
Own development	88	95	63	92	64	91	85
Foreign technical support	17	17	16	17	18	18	15
Others	6	3	16	6	9	9	4

Notes: Sup = supported by government; Nsup = not supported by government.

Source: Authors' survey.

Table 7.7   Nature of upgrading (%) in 2006

	All	Software	Hardware	Smaller	Larger	Sup	Nsup
Quality control	38	40	32	39	27	33	40
Reverse engineering	38	44	16	41	18	45	33
Original design	32	38	11	37	0	45	23
Original brand	6	3	16	4	18	3	8
Adaptive engineering	1	2	0	1	0	0	2
Others	68	65	79	68	73	67	71

Notes: Sup = supported by government; Nsup = not supported by government.

Source: Authors' survey.

check of products before they go into the market. In very few cases (less than 25 per cent) is there an external system of quality control, and even in those cases it is limited to firms with a parent company or a single customer. The 'other' upgrading factors involve different dimensions such as growing interaction with their customers' needs and learning by doing.

Support for Innovation

Despite the above-mentioned efforts from national and provincial governments to support small entrepreneurs and the IT sector, only 13 per cent of the firms have received a grant or funds from government sources. According to the results across sub-samples, government assistance does not seem to be directly related to sector, size or participation in an incubation programme.

Interviews revealed that there is a general discontent with government support for the firms surveyed. The issues arousing dissatisfaction include weak support for innovation and other crucial aspects of business, such as finance, taxation and provision of infrastructure services. Much of government supports were rated as 'weak' or 'not sufficient'. State policy instruments of support that were ranked 'average' include science parks and clusters especially by firms that receive government support, and intellectual property protection in the sub-sample of large corporations (Table 7.8).

Most firms rely on private sources in their search for technical services, which consist largely of information provision, technical training, quality control, and research and development services. Only about one-quarter of the firms receive technical support from government in the form of information and only 13 per cent had received some kind of training support since 2002. Significantly, even those involved in a support programme or incubator do not report the existence of concrete technical support. The support they receive is mostly directed towards training and general business operations, rather than technical functions. A number of interviewees remarked that in terms of technical support they were 'on their own'.

The provision of technical support from government sources is in the main rated as 'weak'. IT firms seem to have responded to this lack of technical support by turning to private sources, which they rate as 'very good' on average. Perhaps as a result of this, the majority of firms do not find technical competence a major constraint for competitiveness or innovative performance. For hardware activities, the role of suppliers is crucial, as most training and technical assistance is provided by them.

Finance

Firms' access to finance is a crucial element in the innovation process, particularly for SMEs, especially in translating the results of R&D into commercial outcomes.

The interviews showed that very few firms rely on external sources of finance, and only 30 per cent of the respondents have acquired a loan either for capital or operations. The financial support, mostly required to start up the business and for new product development, has been generally obtained from personal sources. For example 49 per cent of financing is used for start-up, 52 per cent for new product development and 12 per cent for export and finance. Financial support is a clear constraint for

Table 7.8   Assessment of government support in 2006

	All	S	H	S	L	Sup	Nsup
Government incentives for innovation	1.4	1.4	1.3	1.4	1.5	1.4	1.4
Available scientific/ skilled manpower	1.3	1.3	1.2	1.2	1.5	1.2	1.4
Local universities support for technical and R&D collaboration	1.3	1.3	1.4	1.3	1.4	1.3	1.4
R&D institutions support for technical solutions	1.1	1.1	1.2	1.1	1.4	1.1	1.1
Intellectual property protection	1.4	1.4	1.6	1.3	2.1	1.5	1.4
Quality of IT support services	1.3	1.3	1.2	1.2	1.5	1.3	1.3
Availability of venture capital	1.3	1.3	1.4	1.3	1.6	1.3	1.4
Bank loans	1.2	1.1	1.4	1.1	1.8	1.0	1.3
Subsidy for innovation	1.5	1.5	1.5	1.5	1.5	1.6	1.4
Taxation policy	1.1	1.1	1.2	1.1	1.4	1.2	1.1
Science park/cluster advantage	2.1	2.2	1.7	2.2	1.5	3.2	1.4
Government procurement policy	1.4	1.3	1.6	1.3	2.0	1.1	1.6
Special support for SMMEs	1.6	1.6	1.6	1.6	1.5	1.9	1.4

Notes: Rating: 1 = weak, 5 = very strong; Sup = supported by government, Nsup = not supported by government.

Source: Authors' survey.

business competitiveness and innovation processes, which was rated as 'quite severe' by most firms, particularly small businesses.

Government and private banks were generally rated low, and firms tend to rely on their private sources for engaging in new investments. Infrastructure such as roads and water are regarded favourably but the high cost of telecommunications remains one of the major barriers to competitiveness. According to national statistics, fixed-line call charges have escalated at a rate of more than 21 per cent since 1997, lowering growth in vital new sectors such as IT. The high tariff of telecommunications services was

Table 7.9   How firms would rate lack of technical support as a constraint in 2006 (%)

Firms	Technical	Financial	Infrastructure
All	2.1	3.5	3.7
Software	2.3	3.6	3.8
Hardware	1.8	1.8	3.6
Small	2.3	3.7	3.8
Large	1.2	2.1	3.6
Supported	2.4	3.8	3.6
Non-supported	2.0	3.4	3.9

Note: Rating: 1 = weak, 5 = very strong.

Source: Authors' survey.

repeatedly mentioned by the firms interviewed as one of the major factors pushing down the industry's competitiveness and their ability to export.

Delays in the licensing of competitors such as the Second Network Operator (SNO) and the ban over the use of Voice over Internet Protocol (IP) and least-cost routing services until February 2005 allowed Telkom to enjoy a de facto monopoly while the businesses suffered high costs. Very recent interventions have sought to drive affordable access to communication services and encourage smaller entrants, and after this survey was conducted, in November 2006, a second network operator entered the market.

According to the results, Internet is the lowest-rated service, followed by transport services, electricity and telephony. Although provision is rated as 'average', the cost is what firms mostly complain about.

The negative effect of infrastructure on business performance is rated as significantly high. However, software firms seem to have a worse experience than hardware companies, as do small rather than larger corporations, and those unsupported more than the ones receiving support.

Market access and export
The desire to be globally competitive features noticeably in the market strategy of firms. More than half of the firms surveyed (56 per cent) oriented part of their main products and services towards international markets. This strategy is increasingly important in both hardware and software sectors (with an increase from 48 per cent of exporting companies in 2004 to 54 per cent in 2005 in the software sector, and from 47 to 58 per cent in the hardware sector). Southern Africa (South African Development Community – SADC countries) and the EU are the target markets for all firms surveyed. However,

this is more evident for the case of hardware exporters where 100 per cent of the exporters address part of their foreign sales to Southern African countries, contrasting with only 47 per cent of the software exporters. This shows the growing opportunities and potential of the African market for South African IT products, particularly in the hardware sector. In the case of software, exporting activities seem to be limited in many cases by the need for proximity to the client for the provision of after-sales and technical services.

However exporting is not a major concern for many of the firms surveyed, as market orientation partly depends on the nature of their customer base. For those providing highly advanced products for the public and government sector, the export strategy is demand-driven. However, firms with a majority of SMEs as their customer base tend to adopt a clearer export orientation. When asked why exporting was important for them, 37 per cent of those exporting to developed countries such as European and US markets mentioned the advantages of the exchange rate. For instance 30 per cent export due to specific demand, while 50 per cent do so to diversify risk, expand their market or attenuate poor domestic demand.

Again government support tends to be limited as 90 per cent of the firms receive some type of marketing support, albeit mostly through private sources. Firms that belong to one of the incubation programme sub-samples received the most significant marketing support from non-private sources. Marketing 'abroad' was mentioned by several interviewees as 'a risk they cannot afford'.

7.7 INNOVATION AND PERFORMANCE OF FIRMS

This section analyses the determinants of innovation and firm performance in the South African computer sector, which consists of specialized software and hardware firms. We use t- and z-tests to stress the differences between the software and hardware sectors. A probit model of innovation is estimated by maximum likelihood, and a linear and a censored regression model carried out for firm-level performance. The linear regression model is estimated using ordinary least squares, instrumental variables, limited information maximum likelihood and generalized method of moments, and the censored regression is estimated using maximum likelihood. The next section presents innovation and performance analysis. More specifically, we describe the data and estimate the model of innovation and of performance. Table 7.10 presents the definition of the dependent and independent variables used in the innovation and performance analysis, and reports descriptive statistics for the whole sample contrasted with those of the hardware computer firms.

Dependent Variables

We examined four dependent variables namely: product innovation, productivity in 2005, export intensity and increased net profit. Table 7.10 suggests that 66 per cent of all firms are involved in new product development while only 37 per cent carry out product innovation among the hardware firms. Hence, the percentage of firms that are involved in new product development in the software sector is much higher than in the hardware sector. Productivity, that is, sales per employee (in millions of dollars), is higher in the computer hardware sector than in the computer software sector. In other words, sales per employee are on average about $1 million dollars in the whole computer sector and twice as much in the computer hardware sector. The figures for export intensity, that is, the share of export sales in total sales and increased net profit, are on average similar for the computer hardware and software sectors. More specifically, export intensity is (on average) about 17 per cent in the whole sector and 13 per cent in the hardware sector, and net profit has increased for 88 per cent of all firms and for 84 per cent of the computer hardware firms.

Independent Variables

Table 7.10 also shows that 23 per cent of the firms are computer hardware firms which consist of a lower percentage of staff with university or technical degrees (human capital) than in the software sector. Indeed about 73 per cent of workers in the whole sector have a university or technical degree while the percentage is only 55 per cent in the hardware sector. The figures for size, upgrade activities, technology source, government support, customer demand, technical capability and training in the whole sector are contrasted with those of the same variables in the hardware sector as follows.

Size
The three variables that reflect size, that is, the number of employees, total sales (in millions of dollars) and the percentage of large firms (with more than 100 employees), show that on average firms are much larger in the hardware sector than in the software sector. More specifically, firms in the hardware sector are on average three times as large in terms of employees, and four times as large in terms of sales as firms in the software sector.

Upgrade activities
The percentage of firms that upgrade with reverse engineering and original design is on average larger in the software sector than in the hardware sector; that of firms upgrading with original brand is larger in the latter

Table 7.10   *Descriptive statistics of the dependent and independent*
              variables

Variable	All firms				Hardware computer firms			
	Mean	(Std. Dev.)	Min.	Max.	Mean	(Std. Dev.)	Min.	Max.
Product innovator[†]	0.659	(0.477)	0	1	0.368	(0.496)	0	1
Productivity in 2005[*] $	0.995	(1.715)	0.019	13.462	2.026	(2.931)	0.167	13.462
Export intensity	0.171	(0.292)	0	1	0.133	(0.271)	0	0.98
Increased net profit	0.878	(0.329)	0	1	0.842	(0.375)	0	1
Size[*]	66.866	(159.639)	2	1162	198.316	(290.389)	2	1162
Large firms[*]	0.134	(0.343)	0	1	0.421	(0.507)	0	1
Turnover in 2005[*]	148.992	(533.796)	0.075	3500	576.121	(1013.127)	1.200	3500
Hardware firms	0.232	(0.425)	0	1	–	–	–	–
Human capital[†]	0.725	(0.257)	0.138	1	0.550	(0.281)	0.138	1
Asian competition	0.183	(0.389)	0	1	0.158	(0.375)	0	1
Quality control	0.378	(0.488)	0	1	0.316	(0.478)	0	1
Upgrade, reverse engineering[†]	0.378	(0.488)	0	1	0.158	(0.375)	0	1
Original design[†]	0.317	(0.468)	0	1	0.105	(0.315)	0	1
Original brand[*]	0.061	(0.241)	0	1	0.158	(0.375)	0	1
Local expertise[†]	0.146	(0.356)	0	1	0.000	(0.000)	0	0
Foreign expertise[*]	0.159	(0.367)	0	1	0.474	(0.513)	0	1
Combination[†]	0.695	(0.463)	0	1	0.526	(0.513)	0	1
Licensing from clients[†]	0.744	(0.439)	0	1	0.474	(0.513)	0	1
Buyers[†]	0.183	(0.389)	0	1	0.053	(0.229)	0	1
Joint venture partner	0.622	(0.488)	0	1	0.474	(0.513)	0	1
Component suppliers[*]	0.280	(0.452)	0	1	0.579	(0.507)	0	1
Transfer from parent firm	0.146	(0.356)	0	1	0.158	(0.375)	0	1

Table 7.10 (continued)

Variable	All firms				Hardware computer firms			
	Mean	(Std. Dev.)	Min.	Max.	Mean	(Std. Dev.)	Min.	Max.
Managers/ skilled employees[†]	0.866	(0.343)	0	1	0.737	(0.452)	0	1
Suppliers of equipment	0.951	(0.217)	0	1	0.947	(0.229)	0	1
Univ. and public inst.[†]	0.195	(0.399)	0	1	0.053	(0.229)	0	1
Tech. source, reverse engineering[†]	0.512	(0.503)	0	1	0.211	(0.419)	0	1
Gvt. Assistance	0.134	(0.343)	0	1	0.158	(0.375)	0	1
Gvt. supp., innov. incentives[†]	0.280	(0.452)	0	1	0.158	(0.375)	0	1
Gvt. supp., avail. skilled manpower	0.171	(0.379)	0	1	0.158	(0.375)	0	1
Gvt. supp., local univ. for R&D col.	0.220	(0.416)	0	1	0.263	(0.452)	0	1
Gvt. supp., R&D inst. for tech. sol.[*]	0.073	(0.262)	0	1	0.158	(0.375)	0	1
Gvt. supp., IPP	0.305	(0.463)	0	1	0.263	(0.452)	0	1
Gvt. supp., quality of IT sup. serv.	0.183	(0.389)	0	1	0.158	(0.375)	0	1
Gvt. supp., avail. venture capital	0.232	(0.425)	0	1	0.263	(0.452)	0	1
Gvt. supp., bank loans[*]	0.110	(0.315)	0	1	0.211	(0.419)	0	1
Gvt. supp., innov. subsidy	0.329	(0.473)	0	1	0.263	(0.452)	0	1
Gvt. supp., taxation policy	0.085	(0.281)	0	1	0.105	(0.315)	0	1

Table 7.10   (continued)

Variable	All firms				Hardware computer firms			
	Mean	(Std. Dev.)	Min.	Max.	Mean	(Std. Dev.)	Min.	Max.
Gvt. supp., science clust. advant.[†]	0.537	(0.502)	0	1	0.316	(0.478)	0	1
Gvt. supp., procurement policy	0.232	(0.425)	0	1	0.263	(0.452)	0	1
Gvt. supp., spec. supp. for SMEs[†]	0.451	(0.501)	0	1	0.316	(0.478)	0	1
Gvt. dem., faster deliv. time	0.561	(0.499)	0	1	0.526	(0.513)	0	1
Gvt. dem., packaging quality[†]	0.305	(0.463)	0	1	0.158	(0.375)	0	1
Gvt. dem., conf. to standards	0.549	(0.501)	0	1	0.474	(0.513)	0	1
Gvt. dem., price	0.634	(0.485)	0	1	0.737	(0.452)	0	1
Gvt. dem., product quality	0.768	(0.425)	0	1	0.684	(0.478)	0	1
Capability, more manag. training	0.512	(0.503)	0	1	0.474	(0.513)	0	1
Capability, more techn. training	0.756	(0.432)	0	1	0.842	(0.375)	0	1
Capability, improve quality	0.683	(0.468)	0	1	0.579	(0.507)	0	1
Capability, product innovation[†]	0.598	(0.493)	0	1	0.368	(0.496)	0	1
Training, in-house technical	0.927	(0.262)	0	1	0.947	(0.229)	0	1
Training, in-house management	0.671	(0.473)	0	1	0.684	(0.478)	0	1

Table 7.10   (continued)

Variable	All firms				Hardware computer firms			
	Mean	(Std. Dev.)	Min.	Max.	Mean	(Std. Dev.)	Min.	Max.
Training, overseas technical*	0.354	(0.481)	0	1	0.579	(0.507)	0	1
Training, overseas management*	0.073	(0.262)	0	1	0.158	(0.375)	0	1
Training, local training*	0.659	(0.477)	0	1	0.789	(0.419)	0	1
Number of firms		82				19		

Note: [†]These figures are larger on average in the software sector.
*These figures are larger on average in the hardware sector.

Source: Authors' calculations.

sector than in the former; and that of firms upgrading with quality control is on average similar across the two sectors.[21]

Source of technology
When comparing the figures for technology source in the whole sector with those of the hardware sector, we find that the software sector obtains knowledge mainly through local expertise (or a combination of local and foreign expertise), licensing from clients, buyers, hiring mangers and skilled employees, universities and public institutes, and reverse engineering, while technology source in the hardware sector mainly comes from foreign expertise and component suppliers. The two sectors equally rely on technology from joint venture partners, transfer from parent firms and suppliers of equipment.

7.8   GOVERNMENT SUPPORT

In general, government support is directed equally towards software and hardware firms as indicated by the figures in Table 7.10. These include government support regarding innovation incentives and science parks and clusters, and special support for small and medium-sized enterprises (SMEs) that are mainly directed towards the software sector,[22] while

Uneven paths of development

government support regarding R&D institutions for technical solutions and bank loans is mainly directed towards the hardware sector.

7.9   EMPIRICAL RESULTS OF INNOVATION ANALYSIS

Table 7.11 reports maximum likelihood (ML) estimation results of the probit model that studies the likelihood of being involved in new product development.[23] The estimated coefficients as well as their standard errors are reported in the first pair of columns, while the slope parameters (marginal effects) and their standard errors are reported in the second pair of columns.

The first pair of columns suggest that, other things being equal, the use of original design, upgrade activity, government assistance, overseas technical training, and the threat of severe and very severe challenge from Asian competition have a strong and significant effect on the likelihood of being involved in new product development. Pressure from more demanding customers with regards to conformity to standards has a positive effect, although not strongly significant. Finally, improved capability through more managerial training and belonging to the hardware sector decreases the likelihood of being involved in new product development. The latter

Table 7.11   Probit estimation results and marginal effects: new product development

Variable	Coefficient	(Std err.)	Slope	(Std err.)
Original design	2.125**	(0.732)	0.385**	(0.083)
Gvt assistance	2.255*	(0.900)	0.259**	(0.083)
Capability, more manag. training	−1.611**	(0.494)	0.399**	(0.115)
Training, overseas technical	1.166*	(0.542)	0.252*	(0.104)
Cust. dem., conf. to standards	0.816†	(0.428)	0.215†	(0.113)
Asian competition	1.454*	(0.648)	0.233**	(0.081)
Hardware firms	−1.756**	(0.609)	0.566**	(0.190)
Intercept	0.070	(0.368)	–	–
Number of firms			82	
Log-likelihood			−27.758	

Note: Significance levels: †: 10 per cent *: 5 per cent **: 1 per cent.

Source: Authors' calculations.

does not surprise as most firms are involved largely in computer hardware assembly and sales, whereas software firms engage in continual changes to suit customers.

The second pair of columns shows the magnitude of the effects of the explanatory variables on the likelihood of being involved in new product development.[24] *Ceteris paribus*, involvement in upgrade activity with regard to original design, receiving government assistance, investment in overseas technical training, facing more demanding customer demand with regard to conformity to standards, and facing severe and very severe challenge from Asian competition significantly increase the probability of being involved in new product development by respectively 0.385, 0.259, 0.252, 0.215 and 0.233.

7.10   FIRM-LEVEL PERFORMANCE

The two measures of economic performance that are considered in this chapter are productivity, as proxied by sales per employee, and export intensity as measured by the share in total sales of export sales.[25]

Productivity

We consider a linear regression model where firm's i productivity, denoted by y_i, is explained by explanatory variables described in Table 7.12 and included into the vector x_i. Formally, the model is written as:

$$y_i = \beta' x_i + \varepsilon_i, i = 1, \ldots N, \tag{7.1}$$

where ε_i consists of unobserved factors that affect productivity. The model as defined in equation (7.1) is estimated using ordinary least squares (OLS), instrumental-variable/two-stage least squares (IV/2SLS), limited information maximum likelihood (LIML), and generalized method of moment (GMM) depending on the assumptions on the regressors and the error term of the model.

OLS

In order to estimate equation (7.1) by OLS, the assumptions of the classical linear regression model must be satisfied. One of the assumptions is that the explanatory variables included in x_i are exogenous, that is, $E[\varepsilon_i | x_i] = 0$ The resulting OLS estimator is given in Greene (2003).

IV/2SLS

If the exogeneity assumption is rejected, that is, $E[\varepsilon_i | x_i] \neq 0$ the OLS estimator is inconsistent and the parameter vector must be estimated by IV-type techniques. For instance, in our application, we explain productivity by among others being involved in new product development and export sales which are assumed to be endogenous. These two variables need to be instrumented.

LIML

If furthermore the error terms are assumed normal, the LIML estimator can be used. The derivation of the log-likelihood function is explained in detail in Theil (1971), and Davidson and MacKinnon (1993).

GMM

To gain efficiency with respect to the IV/2SLS or LIML estimator, GMM techniques can be used.

Empirical Results of Productivity Analysis

Table 7.12 presents the estimation results of the linear regression model of productivity. The OLS estimates are reported in the first pair of columns in which case all the explanatory variables are assumed to be exogenous. In the remaining pairs of columns of the table, the regressors that capture firms' involvement in new product development and export sales are assumed to be endogenous. The endogeneity of these regressors are tested using a Durbin–Wu–Hausman (DWH) test which states that the OLS estimates are consistent and no IV-type estimation technique is required.[26] As a result, we shall comment on the OLS estimated. For instance, *ceteris paribus*, being involved in new product development decreases sales per employee, and a 1 per cent increase in the number of employees (size) increases productivity by approximately 0.4 per cent. The other coefficients are interpreted similarly, for instance rising exports and pressure from customers also contributes to sales per employee by 0.233 per cent when increased by 10 per cent and 0.65 per cent when raised by 1 per cent respectively.

   In what follows we explain the second measure of performance considered in this report, namely export intensity.

Table 7.12   Estimation results of the linear regression model of productivity

Variable	Coeffi-cient	(Std err.)	Coeffi-cient	(Std err.)	Coeffi-cient	(Std err.)	Coeffi-cient	(Std err.)
Product innovator	−0.685**	(0.224)	−0.898*	(0.432)	−0.933*	(0.456)	−0.859*	(0.406)
Export sales (in log)	0.023*	(0.010)	0.038*	(0.015)	0.040*	(0.016)	0.038**	(0.014)
Size (in log)	0.395**	(0.071)	0.388**	(0.071)	0.386**	(0.072)	0.377**	(0.065)
Quality control	0.791**	(0.192)	0.805**	(0.193)	0.809**	(0.195)	0.806**	(0.187)
Upgrade with reverse engineering	−0.596**	(0.208)	−0.586**	(0.222)	−0.581*	(0.226)	−0.590**	(0.212)
Capability, more manag. training	−0.415*	(0.205)	−0.515*	(0.228)	−0.529*	(0.233)	−0.461*	(0.204)
Licensing from clients	−0.393†	(0.217)	−0.314	(0.223)	−0.303	(0.226)	−0.278	(0.214)
Suppliers of equipment	0.790†	(0.440)	0.891*	(0.438)	0.905*	(0.443)	0.615	(0.576)
Cust. dem., faster deliv. time	0.605**	(0.205)	0.590**	(0.197)	0.589**	(0.198)	0.606**	(0.178)
Cust. dem., price	−0.453*	(0.199)	−0.506**	(0.194)	−0.512**	(0.196)	−0.490**	(0.167)
Intercept	11.888**	(0.504)	11.912**	(0.499)	11.919**	(0.505)	12.103**	(0.585)
Number of firms				82				

Note: Significance levels: †: 10 per cent *: 5 per cent **: 1 per cent.

Source: Authors' calculation.

Export Intensity

Unlike productivity which has a rather symmetrical distribution, 52 per cent of the firms have no export sales, hence resulting in a zero value of export intensity. The linear regression model is no longer appropriate, hence the use of a censored regression model also known as a Tobit model to analyse export intensity.

Export Intensity Results

Table 7.12 reports ML estimation results of the tobit model that studies the determinants of export intensity. We report the estimated coefficients and their standard errors in the first pair of columns, and the slope parameters and their standard errors in the second pair of columns.

The results suggest that, for instance, sourcing technology source from a joint venture partner has a positive effect on export intensity while technology source through licensing from clients has a negative effect.

More specifically, the share of export sales in total sales is, *ceteris paribus*, 75 per cent more for firms with technology sourced from joint ventures and 60 per cent less for firms with technology sourced from licensing from clients. Furthermore, export intensity of firms with Internet protocol provider (IPP) government support increases by more than 100 per cent and that of firms with local training decreases by approximately 100 per cent.

Significantly, the two sub-sectors differ in terms of product innovation, productivity, size, human capital, upgrade activities, technological source and training. The two sub-sectors have similar characteristics regarding export intensity, increased net profit, government support, customer demand and capability. Again several factors encourage new product development which tends to occur more often in the software sector. While product innovators (surprisingly) have smaller sales per employee than firms that are not involved in new product development, and larger firms have larger sales per employee than smaller counterparts, there is no difference between these types of firms in terms of export intensity. In other words while these two sub-sectors tend to share rather similar generic technological platforms, there are considerable differences that point to the need for differentiated policies.

7.11 SUMMING UP

The IT sector evolved from the late 1990s from a relatively immature market to a significant growth sector in South Africa. Both hardware and software activities have developed largely in the absence of national coordinated strategies specifically to promote these sub-sectors.

IT activities in South Africa are very heterogeneous and unevenly distributed across regions. The firms are concentrated in the large metropolitan areas where hardware reselling and assembling represent the largest sub-sector, comprising over 40 per cent of the total IT revenues.

Although much of the sector's revenues are distributed among a few large indigenous firms and foreign MNCs – in hardware and software activities – the sector is increasingly populated by SMEs. The competitiveness and survival of SMEs have become a focus for policy, particularly considering their potential contribution to employment creation, innovation and skills development in the country. To a large extent, the future of South Africa's IT industry depends in part on the growing dynamics of these small, micro and medium-sized entrepreneurs.

A number of initiatives affecting the IT sector have been developed at national and provincial levels. However, results from this study show that government support is generally considered weak by the firms surveyed. Similarly, only a small percentage of firms seem to benefit from government assistance for innovation and new product development, mostly funded with private resources.

Surveys also show that both hardware and software firms are increasingly expanding their market abroad, particularly in Southern Africa (mainly SADC countries) and the EU. South Africa's relative advantage in terms of skills and experience in technology-intensive activities opens opportunities to expand the sector. However, the lack of a specific and defined strategy in relation to specialization and niche markets puts South Africa in a weaker position compared to other developing countries discussed in this book that have already developed very concrete and dynamic strategies.

Again, the results of this study show that the South African IT sector is highly innovative. Despite the larger share of hardware activities in overall revenues, results from our sample show that innovation is most significant for small software firms versus large hardware firms. The dynamism and potential of these small software entrants should be considered as a central point for future sectoral policy.

There is considerable dynamism in the sector. Most firms are expanding their networks and growing linkages with domestic and international actors, both within the same sector and with other sectors of the economy. Existing policies seem to benefit cluster-based firms and facilitating networking and formation of linkages to some extent. In a similar way, policy clearly facilitates imports of IT components, favouring the 'consuming' habits of the South African IT industry of foreign IT products and components. Nevertheless, access to finance and high prices of telecommunications were repeatedly mentioned as major constraints to the industry's competitiveness and ability to penetrate export markets.

Policy needs to reflect and address the potential as well as the constraints that the majority of domestic IT firms are currently facing in their competitiveness and innovation dynamics. Understanding this, and developing concrete sectoral strategies for the hardware and software sub-sectors, constitute the first step to a sustainable and competitive IT industry in South Africa.

NOTES

1. SAITIS (2000). This study was developed under separate contract by the Canadian International Development Agency (CIDA) to the International Development Research Centre (IDRC) office in South Africa.

2. DACST was divided into two departments in 2002: the Department of Arts and Culture and the Department of Science and Technology.
3. Hodge and Miller (1997); Day (1998).
4. Firms receiving support from the above-mentioned initiatives were contacted with the assistance of the supporting institutions (Innovation Hub and SBTI in Gauteng and CITI in the Western Cape).
5. R16 billion (Moleke, 2003).
6. During the 1980s tariffs on computers were 15 per cent compared to an average level of 35 per cent, while in the 1990s tariffs were reduced to 6 per cent compared to a country average of 25 per cent.
7. Although South Africa is a member of the World Trade Organization (WTO), it has not signed the Information Technology Agreement (ITA), consisting of the total elimination of tariffs and other duties on most IT goods.
8. See http://www.theworx.biz/.
9. See http://www.sita.co.za/.
10. The outcome was a Project Design Document (PDD) to guide the direction of the project and the establishment of a Project Steering Committee (PSC).
11. Through Blue IQ, the Gauteng local government is investing R3.7 billion in 11 projects for 'strategic' industries and value-added manufacturing to restructure the composition of the provincial economy.
12. See www.theinnovationhub.com.
13. Perunal communication.
14. Full member of the International Association of Science Parks (IASP).
15. See http://www.bti.co.za/.
16. Under the guidance of their respective boards and a merger steering committee, Softstart and BTI merged on 1 April 2006 to form SoftstartBTI.
17. See http://www.citi.org.za/.
18. CITI was the result of informal discussions among members of the private sector, academia and provincial government during 1997.
19. Note that the percentages do not add up to 100 per cent, given that some companies have more than one owner with different qualifications.
20. Companies were requested to rate from 1 (not a problem) to 5 (very severe).
21. See Table 7.2 for more details on the percentages.
22. The fact that special support for SMEs is mainly directed towards the software sector makes sense as firms in that sector are on average smaller than those in the hardware sector.
23. We always report estimation results that include only the jointly significant explanatory variables.
24. Since all the explanatory variables reported in Table 7.11 are binary, their marginal effects are calculated as discrete changes of those variables from 0 to 1.
25. In the regressions, natural logarithm transformation of productivity and export intensity have been considered.
26. The result of the test is somewhat surprising as we would expect the two regressors to be endogenous. Indeed, we explained the likelihood of engaging in new product development and firms' export intensity. However, the sample is not sufficiently informative to support the endogeneneity assumption of the two regressors.

8. Taiwan's move from follower to leader[1]

8.1 INTRODUCTION

The successful insertion of Taiwanese firms to the global information hardware (IH) value chain was greatly supported by the systemic and institutional environment developed through smooth coordination between government, institutions and firms. Government policy was particularly important in stimulating technological upgrading and research and development (R&D) activities. The Taiwanese government adopted policies that were complementary to its vertically decentralized structure and encouraged the development of technological capabilities. The flexibility enjoyed by small size and strong bonds of trust helped Taiwanese firms to harness the advantages of scope offered by global production chains. From original equipment manufacturing (OEM), strong coordination from markets and trust, and government participation in the stimulation of R&D activities helped transform Taiwanese computer and component firms to enter original design manufacturing (ODM) and own brand manufacturing (OBM).

Although foreign direct investment has remained small, significant diffusion of foreign technology to local computer and component firms took place in Taiwan. Lin's (1986) study of cathode ray tubes (CRT) found that the manufacturing capability of personal computers and peripherals, such as monitors and computer terminals, originated from the manufacture of colour television (CTV) sets in the 1970s. The assembly of radios and black and white television sets in the 1960s, particularly by Japanese manufacturers, laid the foundation for technological capability building in the industry. Modern manufacturing technology was developed only since 1969 when foreign joint ventures started producing CTV sets in Taiwan. CTV used transistors and thus used printed circuit boards and components that go into computers and peripherals.

While foreign technology through the operations of consumer electronics firms laid the initial foundation, firms' participation in R&D activities in the computer and component industry depended extensively on the development of the high-tech infrastructure by the government. The role of the Industrial Technical Institute (ITRI) was transformed following the launching of the science and technology projects (STP) in 1979 but especially from 1983 when the emphasis on public–private coordination helped resolve market and government failures. The sectoral focus of the Taiwanese government on computer and component products in the ITRI is handled by the Electronics Research and Service Organization (ERSO). Effective coordination between the high-tech infrastructure and firms helped drive Taiwan into becoming a major producer and exporter of computer and related components by the 1980s.

Using the framework advanced in the introductory chapter, this chapter attempts to examine the four pillars of the systemic quad that helped make Taiwan a major success in the computer and components industry. The rest of the chapter is organized as follows. Section 8.2 presents the methodology and data used in the chapter. Section 8.3 evaluates the state of the four systemic pillars from the lenses of firms. Section 8.4 examines the knowledge depth and technological intensity of the firms using taxonomic and trajectory categories, and section 8.5 presents the conclusions.

8.2   METHODOLOGY AND DATA

As advanced in the introduction chapter, the strength of development of the four pillars advanced in the systemic quad – basic infrastructure (BI), high-tech (HT) infrastructure, nature of global integration (GI) in value chains and markets, and network cohesion (NC) – will have a strong impact on firm-level technological intensities and complexities (see also Rasiah, 2006). Hence, the methodology used in this chapter first examines firms' assessment of the four pillars defining the embedding environment in Taiwan, before the evaluation of technological intensities and complexities is carried out.

Following the illuminating work of Amsden (1985), Fransman (1985), Wade (1990), Amsden and Chu (2003), Mathews (1997, 2005, 2006) and Mathews and Cho (2000), the state of the four pillars of the systemic quad in Taiwan can be expected to be strong. While the pivotal role of government in facilitating firms' participation in learning and innovation as well as global integration has been discussed extensively by these works, in computer and components manufacturing Mathews (2006) pointed out the strategic role and timing of government intervention to support Taiwanese firms' entry during times of crisis. Rasiah and Lin (2005) advanced the simultaneous and integrated coordination role of markets, government and trust in resolving information and collective-

Table 8.1   *Technological intensities, computer and components, Taiwan sample, 2001*

Variable	Proxies	Specification
HR	Training expenditure in payroll, cutting-edge HR practices, scale of HR operation (training centre (4), department (3), staff with training responsibility (2) and training undertaken externally (1)	Normalized using formula: $(x_i - x_{min})/(x_{max} - x_{min})$
Process technology	Age of machinery and equipment, cutting-edge process (inventory and quality) technology (TPM, TQM, JIT, MRPI, MRPII), expenditure on physical reorganization of the firm as a share in sales	Normalized using formula: $(x_i - x_{min})/(x_{max} - x_{min})$
Process R&D	Process R&D expenditure	Actual percentage in sales
Product R&D	Product R&D expenditure	Actual percentage in sales

Notes: TPM – total preventive maintenance; TQM – total quality management; JIT – just in time; MRPI – materials resource planning; MRPII – integrated materials resource planning.

Source: Rasiah (2008).

action problems in driving learning and innovation in computer and component firms.

The chapter uses two-tailed t-tests to compare statistical differences of firms' assessment of institutional and systemic instruments facing them, as well as technological intensities of foreign and local firms in Taiwan. Likert scale scores ranging from 1 to 5 were used to score firms' rating of use and quality, and connections and coordination of the critical institutions. A score of zero was given when firms reported non-existence of connections (either directly or indirectly) with any particular institution. The estimation of the technological variables is shown in Table 8.1. Trajectories and taxonomies were used to differentiate technology, and technological intensities were captured by normalizing related proxies (see Table 8.2). A sixth category was included in the knowledge depth typology to include especially firms' funding either in their own R&D labs or through contract R&D scientists working on new processes and products.

The chapter draws from a two-industry survey conducted in 2002 on the electronics and auto-parts industry in Taiwan. Information on the

Table 8.2   Technological complexity, computer and components, Taiwan sample, 2001

Knowledge depth	HR	Process	Product
(1) Simple activities	On the job and in-house training	Dated machinery with simple inventory control techniques	Assembly or processing of low value-added components
(2) Minor improvements	In-house training and performance rewards	Advanced machinery and problem-solving	Precision engineering and CKD assembly
(3) Major improvements	Extensive focus on training and retraining	Cutting-edge inventory control techniques, SPC, TQM, TPM	Cutting-edge quality control systems (QCC and TQC)
(4) Engineering	Hiring engineers	Process adaptation: layouts, equipment and techniques	Product adaptation
(5) Development-related R&D	Hiring R&D personnel and devising new modes of HR development	Process R&D: layouts, machinery and equipment and processes	Product development (e.g. ODM and OBM)
Frontier product development			New patent-seeking R&D scientists

Notes: QCC – quality control circles; TQC – total quality control; SPC – statistical process control; CKD – completely knocked down.

Source: Developed from Rasiah (1992).

computer and related components firms was extracted from this survey. The national consultants engaged in the survey used a sampling frame supplied by the national statistics department to select for study.[2] Of the 150 firms that were selected 69 responded (see Table 8.3). In addition to the Asian Development Bank (ADB) survey conducted in 2002, also accessed are interviews carried out with general managers, engineers and chief executive officers on the participation of the firms in global value chains (see Rasiah and Lin, 2005). Unless otherwise stated all information presented is for the year 2001.

Table 8.3   Breakdown of sampled data, computer and related component firms, Johor and Penang, 2004

	Ownership		Size	
	Foreign	Local	Large	SM
Selected sample	21	129	50	100
Mailed	21	129	50	100
Full response	7	62	30	39
Interviewed	3	7	4	6

Note: Firms were classified as foreign once foreign ownership reached 50 per cent of overall equity; Firms were classified as large when employment size exceeded 500 and the remaining firms were classified as small and medium-sized (SM).

Source: ADB Survey, 2002.

8.3   SYSTEMIC DEVELOPMENT

The four pillars of the systemic quad are used to examine the state of Taiwan's embedding environment from the lenses of computer and component firms.

Basic Infrastructure

Taiwan's basic infrastructure (BI) institutions evolved smoothly not only to raise literacy rates and provide healthcare, transport, utilities (water and power) and housing to ensure that labour force participation was high, but it also provided an excellent telecommunications infrastructure to ensure smooth logistics coordination.

Using Likert scale scores (1–5 with rising strength) firms were asked to rate the quality of each of the institution stated in the questionnaire. The mean scores were evaluated using two-tailed tests by ownership and size. An initial pilot interview with three foreign and seven local, four large and six small and medium-sized firms showed that there were no industry-specific basic infrastructure services sought by computer and component firms. Telecommunication services enjoyed a high mean score irrespective of ownership and size (see Table 8.4).

The mean scores recorded on all the BI institutions have been high irrespective of ownership and size (see Table 8.4). Local firms enjoyed a statistically significant lead over foreign firms only in the communication skills of employees. Since the questionnaires were replied to by professional

Table 8.4   Basic infrastructure, Taiwan sample, 2001

	Ownership			Size		
	Foreign	Local	t	Large	SM	t
Secondary school graduates	3.201	3.973	−1.012	3.873	3.911	−0.010
Communication skills of workforce	3.231	4.641	−2.633*	4.612	4.413	0.684
Healthcare	3.331	3.452	−0.971	3.481	3.410	0.091
Roads	3.834	3.831	0.069	3.993	3.712	1.017
Air and sea transport	3.567	3.972	−0.634	3.997	3.888	0.035
Telecommunications	4.222	4.375	−0.101	4.441	4.301	0.057

Note: * 1 per cent level of statistical significance.

Source: Compiled by ADB survey (2002).

personnel it is very likely that the problem of communication arose between foreign managers and local employees rather than between local managers and local employees. Interviews suggest that Mandarin is the main language of communication but English is used in some form, owing to the technical drawings, and references dealing with designs, orders and specifications.

Size produced no obvious statistically significant difference with respect to basic infrastructure institutions (see Table 8.4). Unlike the biases typically enjoyed by larger firms in most developing economies, the results suggest that basic infrastructure institutions have connected with firms irrespective of their scale of operations. Basic infrastructure institutions in Taiwan obviously enjoy high standards and they are accessible to firms irrespective of size.

High-Tech Infrastructure

Taiwan's computer and components industry has been supported by high-tech infrastructure institutions, especially since the 1980s. The initiation into high-tech operations began in 1979 following the introduction of R&D grants under the STP, but significant intermediation between the R&D labs of ITRI, universities and private firms only took place after 1983 when the government introduced a matching system to the grants offered, which helped connect the R&D labs to firms' needs and remove free-rider problems. ERSO, the division within ITRI that focuses on electronics research and services, has kept its relentless emphasis on R&D operations with new high-tech firms continuously spun out from its incubators. Taiwan Semiconductor Manufacturing Company (TSMC) – which in the first half of 2006 generated the fourth-highest revenue among IC manufacturers behind Intel, Samsung and Texas Instruments – is one of several high-tech companies that have benefited from the high-tech infrastructure developed in Taiwan (see Box 8.1).

BOX 8.1   TAIWAN SEMICONDUCTOR MANUFACTURING COMPANY (TSMC)

Taiwan Semiconductor Manufacturing Company (TSMC) was launched from Taiwan's Industrial Technical Research Institute (ITRI) with its headquarters in Hsinchu Science Park. Attempts to move on to higher value-added chips led to the establishment of a joint venture with Philips in 1987 with 49 per cent equity by the former and 51 per cent equity by the latter. Philips's efforts to move out of semiconductors have seen its share falling to 12.8 per cent in March 2007. The company has since been listed on the Taiwan Stock Exchange and on the New York Stock Exchange.

In 2006 TSMC engaged in cutting-edge fabrication of 4-, 8- and 12-inch silicon wafers (including nanotechnology) with plants in Hsinchu, Tainan. In 2005 the company carried out fabrication processes, including CMOS logic, mixed-mode/RF, volatile and non-volatile memory, BiCMOS, High Voltage and CMOS Image Sensor. In 2002 TSMC ranked among the top ten IC companies based on worldwide sales. The company enjoyed sales of US$8.2 billion to rank eighth among IC producers in 2005. With sales reaching US$4.9 billion TSMC managed to rise to fourth place among IC producers in the first half of 2006.

TSMC epitomizes the successful high-tech companies in Taiwan that benefited from strong government support. The government negotiated the relocation of Chairman Morris Chang (who enjoyed enormous amount of experiential and tacit knowledge of the industry when he was hired), establishment of the joint venture with Philips and provided grants and other support for the growth of TSMC. Located in the Hsinchu Science Park and enjoying the R&D synergies from the Electronics Research and Service Organization (ERSO), TSMC has enjoyed frontier innovation support throughout its existence.

Source: Compiled by Rajah Rasiah and Yeo Lin.

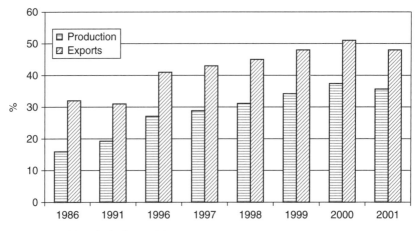

Source: Rasiah and Lin (2005: 406).

Figure 8.1   *Share of electronics production and exports in manufacturing,*
Taiwan, 1986–2001

The 1980s were also characterized by significant firm-level learning in the industry. Video gaming equipment assemblers shifted to Apple II clones in 1982 when public pressure on gambling pushed demand down. The assembly of Apple clones through reverse engineering also closed down quickly following legal action from the Apple Computer firm. The learning experience from these activities snowballed into a pool of entrepreneurs equipped with the technical know-how to manufacture computer components and completely knocked down (CKD) parts. Computer assembly know-how grew further after local assemblers such as Teco Corporation obtained orders to assemble mainframe computer monitors in 1983 (see Rasiah and Lin, 2005).

The phasing out of the labour-intensive stages to China since 1991 coincided with further upgrading in the industry. The absorption of public–private coordination from long-developed traditional networks in the country helped avert market and government failure (see Rasiah and Lin, 2005). The computer and components industry grew rapidly as a consequence to become the leading generator of production and exports in Taiwanese manufacturing in the period 1981–2001 (see Figure 8.1). Taiwan's share in global markets reached almost 50 per cent in notebooks, over 50 per cent in monitors and modems and exceeded 90 per cent in scanners in 1999 (see Figure 8.2).

As explained in the previous section, Likert scale scores (1–5 with rising strength) were used by firms to rate the importance (frequency of

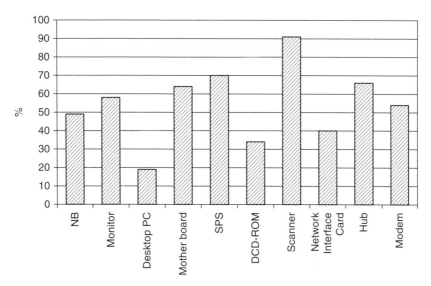

Source: Rasiah and Lin (2005: 416).

Figure 8.2 Taiwanese share in global market, 1999

use and quality of service offered) of each of the institutions stated in the questionnaire. The mean scores were tested using two-tailed t-tests by ownership and size. An initial pilot interview with three foreign and seven local, four large and six small and medium-sized firms showed that there were industry-specific high infrastructure services sought by computer and components. Although generic and broad-based technical and engineering skills were considered important (especially in process technology), these ten firms also reported that technical and engineering skills specific to information hardware were critical in the development of product technology in computer and component manufacturing.

Local firms enjoyed a positive and statistically significant advantage over foreign firms in the use of the high-tech institutions of universities on R&D collaboration, coordination of curriculum of courses carried out and R&D labs (see Table 8.5). Given that the HT index is a measure of frequency of use and the quality of the service rendered, local firms seem to depend on these high-tech institutions much more than foreign firms. The pilot interviews with the ten firms suggested differences in the duration and nature of internships and sabaticals carried out, by ownership. Local large firms appear more inclined to take on academic staff on sabbaticals and students on internships than foreign firms. It would be interesting to explore this in greater detail in a future study. In addition,

Table 8.5   High-tech infrastructure, Taiwan sample, 2001

	Foreign	Local	t	Large	SM	t
University R&D collaboration	2.776	3.587	−5.564*	3.637	3.411	−0.203
University courses	2.998	3.345	−2.877*	3.512	3.157	2.856*
Government R&D labs	2.555	3.889	−3.375*	3.495	3.957	−1.057
Training institutions	3.667	3.746	0.108	3.575	3.851	−0.335
Quality of human capital	4.122	4.001	0.05	4.021	4.013	0.503

Note: * 1 per cent level of statistical significance.

Source: Compiled by ADB survey (2002).

the asset-specific advantage of foreign firms with access to their own plants at parent sites may explain the lower intensity of use of the high-tech institutions.

There were no obvious differences in the frequency of use and quality rating of the training institutions and the human capital hired in the firms (see Table 8.5). Indeed, the mean score on human capital was both high and fairly even.

The assessment by size produced a statistically significant difference only on university courses (see Table 8.5). Large firms seem to enjoy a stronger link and provide a higher rating of university courses. Greater interaction between students (internships) and academic staff (sabbaticals) of larger firms and these institutions may explain these differences. Also, smaller firms may be too lean to take on academic staff and students in their firms. Nevertheless, small and medium-sized firms provide similar assessments of their R&D links with universities and government R&D labs to those of the large firms. The capacity of high-tech institutions to reach out to computer and component firms of all sizes equally may explain the widespread participation in R&D activities in Taiwan.

The absence of a statistically significant difference in training institutions and human capital available by size raises another interesting dimension of learning and innovation in Taiwan. Typically small new firms invest little on sending employees out for training owing to their lean flexible operations. Taiwan may have produced an institutional environment where workers of small firms manage to access training like the large firms despite their smaller employee numbers.

Global Integration

The invention of the personal computer (PC) provided small local firms with a huge technological boost in the mid-1980s as the global decentralization of production offered strong potential for the proliferation of contract manufacturing in Taiwan. Its open architecture and modular design broke the vertically integrated production structure of mainframe computers and made outsourcing of components economic. Two major developments strengthened this trend further. First, Intel's development of the powerful 32-byte 386 microprocessor in the mid-1980s expanded the computing power of PCs exponentially. Second, Microsoft's introduction of the Windows operating system in the mid-1980s enhanced the operative capability of computers. Computer and components production in Taiwan grew by almost 60 per cent per annum in 1986–88 (Lin, 2003: Appendix Table 8.16).

The global orientation of Taiwanese firms and the introduction of cheap PCs forced some changes in Taiwan's computer and components industry. Changes in the global strategy of flagship firms such as Dell, HP and Cisco almost halted the development of Taiwan's own PC brands as the whole industry focused more on OEM operations after 1993. Falling profit margins and the problems of selling new Taiwanese brands forced several firms into OEM operations. All firms in the sample were export-oriented – irrespective of ownership and size. Acer was the only Taiwanese computer brand name that still existed in the global market in 2003.

The large number of OEM orders from computer and peripheral manufacturers across the globe helped Taiwan's vertically disintegrated industrial structure to drive differentiation and division of labour in the industry. The industry gave birth to several product species: for example PCs, casings, mice, motherboards, power switches, monitors, scanners and keyboards. The expansion of the motherboard industry was by far the most representative. Taiwan's vertically dispersed industrial structure enabled OEM firms to specialize and develop the motherboard industry independently as separate firms in the value chain.

Interviews show that the government's strategy of targeting the world for the appropriation of tacit knowledge – conceptual, production and marketing knowledge from experience gained in world-class R&D institutions, universities and firms – helped attract quality Taiwanese human capital to run R&D labs and high-tech firms from the 1980s.[2] Acer was founded in 1984, and Quantum and ASUS were founded by engineering professionals in 1989 who had returned from abroad under the 'brain gain' programme. Rising demand for contract manufacturing helped boost new firm entries in the computer OEM market. Integration in global human capital supply markets – particularly human capital from flagship firms – helped raise participation in OEM and R&D activities (Chao, 1999). Acer developed an Intel-based 80386 (32-byte) microcomputer. ASUS developed an Intel 486 microprocessor-compatible motherboard, and Quantum added innovation in notebooks. Acer is among the largest computer systems manufacturers. ASUS is the leading motherboard manufacturer. Quantum is one of the leaders in notebook PC production.

The strong integration of firms in global value chains and the intensification of differentiation in the industry obviously acted as a springboard in the mushrooming of computer component firms in Taiwan. OEM firms in the computer and component industry hence grew from 1709 in 1985 to 4400 firms in 1988 – an expansion of 160 per cent in just three years (Lin, 2003: Table 2). Kawakami (1996) found that monitor producers increased tenfold: from 20 in 1984 to 201 in 1990.[3] Taiwan's CC production reached US$1 billion for the first time in 1985 and by 1987 it had become the largest monitor producer in the world, accounting for more than 40 per cent of the global market share (Lee and Pecht, 1997: 33).

Network Cohesion

Strong basic and high-tech institutions and global integration are not the only necessary conditions for the smooth operation and development of high-tech firms. In addition, the conduct and performance of firms are also affected by the connections and coordination between these institutions and firms. A combination of markets, government and trust (loyalty) helped strengthen the connections and coordination of links between these institutions and firms in Taiwan (see Rasiah and Lin, 2005).

Two-tailed t-tests of firms' responses on network cohesion by ownership and size produced statistically significant differences on ownership only involving the frequency of use of universities and chambers of commerce (see Table 8.6). Otherwise connections and coordination between the economic agents in the computer and component industry appear strong irrespective of ownership and size. Quite clearly these results show that computer and component firms in Taiwan are highly integrated with the embedding environment.

Interviews from the pilot study of four foreign and seven local firms (four large and six small) suggest that foreign firms tend to enjoy less network cohesion because of the less-developed sabbatical and internship programmes between them and universities, and their lower participation

Table 8.6   Network cohesion, Taiwan sample, 2001

	Foreign	Local	t	Large	SM	t
Universities	2.815	3.771	−2.412*	3.887	3.517	1.116
Buyer and ancillary firms	3.336	3.753	−1.511	3.769	3.669	0.127
Chambers of commerce	3.367	3.811	−2.013*	3.626	3.856	−0.307
R&D labs	3.671	3.789	−0.001	3.763	3.795	−0.001
Logistics companies	4.012	4.125	−0.069	4.029	4.181	−0.051
Training institutions	3.988	4.057	−0.113	3.957	4.122	−0.217
Local government	3.779	3.855	−0.307	3.935	3.779	−0.101

Note: * 5 per cent level of statistical significance.

Source: Computed from ADB (2002) survey.

in the activities of the chambers of commerce. Nevertheless these differences have not affected connections between foreign firms, buyers and suppliers, R&D labs, logistics companies, training institutions and local government, which could be because these institutions and the networks have already achieved developed status.

8.4   TECHNOLOGICAL INTENSITY AND COMPLEXITY

The strong embedding environment unravelled in the previous section is expected to be reflected in the human resources, process technology and R&D intensities of computer and component firms in the sample. As in the previous section the empirical evidence is examined here by ownership and size.

Technological Intensities

The statistical means of local firms in all the technological categories – HR, PT and RD – were higher than those of foreign firms but were only statistically significant in product R&D (see Table 8.7). Local firms tend to show significantly higher utilization of product technology which is likely to be

Table 8.7   Technological intensities, Taiwan sample, 2001

	Foreign	Local	t	Large	SM	t
HR	0.518	0.528	−1.106	0.650	0.424	4.896*
PT	0.496	0.556	−1.148	0.623	0.484	3.967*
Process R&D	0.333	0.486	−1.656	0.516	0.432	1.449
Product R&D	0.266	0.369	−3.054	0.304	0.399	1.080

Note: * Refers to 1 per cent level of statistical significance.

Source: Computed from ADB (2002) survey.

a consequence of the access foreign firms have to their parent firms. Local firms are obviously engaged in strong host-site development of product technology since they are currently reaching the frontier end of the 'S' curve of learning.[4] Nevertheless foreign firms also showed fairly strong participation in R&D activities which was reflected in no obvious statistical difference in process R&D activities. Firms – irrespective of ownership – reported strong participation in improvements to quality and inventory control systems. The statistical means of process technology were almost even, demonstrating the use of similar process technologies in computer and component firms competing in a similar environment.

Significant statistical differences on the basis of size only emerged in HR and PT intensities (see Table 8.7). Large firms generally had either a training department or a training centre, compared to most small and medium-sized firms which were equipped with the most training departments. Medium-sized firms fared equally well as the large firms on HR practices and PT intensity. These results suggest that small firms tend to access training institutions much more than large firms because the latter enjoy the resources to internalize their activities much more than the former. Taiwanese training institutions appear to offer state-of-the-art training, so that small firms have the option of externalizing their training requirements.

There were no obvious size-based differences on R&D intensities. Although large firms showed higher means they were not statistically significant (see Table 8.7). It appears that the institutional and systemic framework in Taiwan has produced no R&D biases with respect to size. Small and medium-sized firms seem to enjoy similar access to the embedding institutions to undertake R&D, both process and product. Although interviews show that a few large firms have managed to become high-volume global contract and OBM manufacturers with internalized R&D activities (see also Rasiah and Lin, 2005) Taiwan's strong high-tech infrastructure – including smooth access to government R&D labs and those in universities – has stimulated small and medium-sized firms to participate equally with large firms on R&D activities.

Technological Complexities

The strong development of the systemic quad discussed in section 8.3 is reflected in an impressive depth of participation in complex knowledge activities in Taiwan. All firms, irrespective of size and ownership, reported participation in at least level 4 activities where engineers are important to their activities, and frequent layout and other process changes, and product adaptation are carried out (see Table 8.8).

Differences by ownership and size only appear on the levels of 5 and 6 (see Table 8.8). Five of the seven foreign firms in the sample reported participation in development-based R&D activities – in the three taxonomic categories of HR, process technology and R&D – supporting Ernst's (2006) arguments on R&D offshoring. Seven firms also reported participation in the uncertain level 6 knowledge depth activities with a successful record of being granted patents by the United States patent office. Level 6 activities were dominated by local firms. Two of the six local firms reported specialization in research-oriented operations within their ownership. The rest of the firms with level 6 operations reported undertaking these activities through contract research. Unlike level 5 operations, level 6 operations seem to require the requisite human capital in-house as the incidence of firms' participation is the same in HR, process technology and product R&D.

All large firms and 31 of the small firms reported participation in the level 5 category of HR and process technology. Also, interestingly, all large

Table 8.8   Technological complexity, Taiwan sample, 2001

	HR				Process technology				Product technology			
	Foreign	Local	Large	SM	Foreign	Local	Large	SM	Foreign	Local	Large	SM
1	7	62	30	39	7	62	30	39	7	62	30	39
2	7	62	30	39	7	62	30	39	7	62	30	39
3	7	62	30	39	7	62	30	39	7	62	30	39
4	7	62	30	39	7	62	30	39	7	62	30	39
5	5	57	30	31	5	57	30	31	5	52	30	27
6	1	6	5	2	1	6	5	2	1	6	5	2

Source: Computed from ADB (2002) survey.

firms and 27 of the 39 small and medium-sized firms reported participation in the level 5 category (see Table 8.8) of the product technology category. The high incidence of participation in developmental R&D activities may be one of the main reasons why Taiwan has moved swiftly up the technology ladder in computer and component manufacturing.

However, the participation of computer and component firms in level 6 activities have been largely confined to large firms: five (16.7 per cent of sample) large and two (5.1 per cent of sample) small and medium-sized firms. The two small and medium-sized firms engaged in research activities and patent take-up in the United States exceeded 400 employees, suggesting that scale was important for firms to take part in risky research activities.

Overall it can be seen that a strong systemic and institutional environment has stimulated component and components firms – irrespective of ownership and size – to participate strongly in high-tech operations. The exceptions were in product R&D operations where local firms enjoyed a significant advantage over foreign firms, and in HR and PT where large firms enjoyed a significant advantage over small and medium-sized firms. Local large firms also dominated participation in research-oriented R&D activities with successful take-up of patents granted by the United States patent office. Local firms' lead in product technology over foreign firms could be explained by the access enjoyed by the latter in their plants abroad. Nevertheless, Taiwan's advanced high-tech infrastructure has also stimulated strong participation of foreign firms in developmental R&D activities.

8.5   SUMMING UP

This chapter has attempted to examine the state of the four pillars of the systemic quad that helped drive learning and innovation in the computer and components industry in Taiwan. All the four pillars – basic infrastructure, high-tech infrastructure, global integration and network cohesion – have been so developed that they not only enjoyed high Likert scale scores but also produced few differences by ownership and size. The effective coordination of government, markets and trust helped drive the development of the four systemic pillars effectively so that small and medium-sized firms were able to avoid the typical barriers they face in other developing economies to compete successfully with large firms. Institutionally it is only in collaboration with R&D and the course curriculums of universities that local large firms enjoy statistically significant stronger links than foreign and small and medium-sized firms.

The strong development of the systemic quad explains the high technological intensities – HR, process technology and R&D – in firms irrespective of ownership and size. However, asset-specific advantages enjoyed by foreign firms (from R&D subsidiaries abroad) and the higher reliance of local firms on the host-site's embedding environment, have produced differences in R&D intensities. Hence, local firms show higher and statistically significant R&D intensities than foreign firms. Although foreign firms showed a high incidence of participation in developmental R&D in Taiwan, local firms dominated when it came to research-based R&D accompanied by take-up of patents in the United States.

This chapter has considerable implications for technology policy. Government intervention in evolving economies should connect simultaneously with the four systemic pillars so that the simultaneous promotion of basic and high-tech infrastructure institutions, integration in global value chains and markets, and network cohesion helps drive learning, innovation and competitiveness. The experience of ERSO under ITRI and the specificity of high-tech operations have also been critical in promoting upgrading in electronics firms. Computers and components are a sub-component of the electronics industry.

NOTES

1. Chu W.W., Lin Yeo and Rajah Rasiah carried out the fieldwork in Taiwan.
2. See Rasiah and Lin (2005).
3. Kawakami (1996) argued that this figure is likely to be larger owing to the presence of unaccounted small-scale subcontractors.
4. The 'S' curve of learning posits that newcomers will find it difficult to learn in the initial phase but will learn much more quickly after a critical mass of knowledge is absorbed, until they reach the frontier when learning becomes difficult again as this phase involves knowledge creation.

9. Conclusions and policy implications

9.1 INTRODUCTION

We start this concluding chapter by recalling our central proposition that the diverse set of polities that define learning and innovation in particular industries in individual countries follow imperfect and uneven paths of industrial and technological evolution. Variations in initial conditions and policy support have largely differentiated these countries. The systemic quad with its four pillars was used as a heuristic model to locate the drivers of learning, innovation and competitiveness. The model emphasized the need for the simultaneous evolution of the four pillars. The chapters assessed the information technology industry to capture the evolutionary elements of learning and innovation.

The presence of these learning factors is indicative of the base conditions in building a dynamic system of innovation. However, in order to understand how the different countries' experiences help explain the importance of institutions and institutional change we reiterate once more the critical drivers that are important in driving learning, innovation and competitiveness.

9.2 EXPLAINING UNEVEN OUTCOMES

While the systemic quad offered a simple and concise way to approach development policy, we emphasize the fact that the policy instruments that are necessary to drive the four pillars are rooted in different institutional regimes. In order to understand the process of uneven development shaping the sectoral innovation system within a given historical context but using the capability framework, we suggest a typology of sectoral systems that emerged out of the different country case studies. While initial conditions and the accumulation of sectoral knowledge bases are important, governance should emphasize four pillars of the systemic quad: basic infrastructure, high-tech infrastructure, network cohesion and global integration. A multitude of institutions constitute the four pillars. The selection of an industry and the participation of all critical economic agents in the development of these elements should be coordinated by a stakeholder coordination council.

The path-dependent nature of a Sectoral Innovation System (SIS) and the ways in which it evolves in uneven fashions in the different countries is evident from the empirical chapters. Initial conditions are important because historical precedent was clearly evident in all the countries; we have proceeded on the a priori assumption that like all industrialization processes the evolution of the information hardware (IH) industry is also an evolutionary process. Institutions and systems are therefore closely connected because they co-evolve. As David (1994: 215) observed: 'Institutions typically evolve new functions and because these are added sequentially they are shaped by internal precedents.'

Evolving sectoral systems are conceptualized in dynamic terms and are therefore placed within a component band or spectrum. A sectoral system has a number of components which we set out earlier. For instance, while the Taiwanese IH industry is a more advanced SIS, it is placed in the same band as the Chinese SIS. The first SIS is a dynamic and rapidly learning system, termed the Dynamic System of Learning Innovation (SLI1), while the second is a non-dynamic system that is slow to learn, termed the Non-Dynamic System of Learning Innovation (SLI2). What distinguishes the two systems are:

- The depth of computer hardware activities (assembling, manufacture, design, systems integration); see Chapters 3, 4 and 8 for quantitative analysis.
- The sophistication of physical and high-tech infrastructure; Chapters 3, 4, 6, 7 and 8.
- Quality of human capital required for computer hardware (CH) manufacturing, design and new products.
- Global integration into the CH value chain; see Chapters 2, 4 and 8.

The sectoral policy focus on IH and related industries directly and indirectly starts from phase 2 in Table 9.1 and increases in intensity as regions evolve to the frontier phase. The evidence from the country chapters in the book shows that only Taiwan has reached phase 4 with semiconductor firms participating in frontier research activities in DRAM microchips. Computer and components firms are also engaged in frontier activities in Taiwan. All four systemic pillars are rated highly by both foreign and local firms in Taiwan, though; local firms utilize the research and development (R&D) institutions much more than foreign firms. Indeed, the extensive accumulation of knowledge synergies in the IH industry has been driven systematically through a sectoral policy focus by the Electronic Research and Services Organization (ERSO).

China is very much in the catch-up phase with no firms engaged yet in

Table 9.1   Policy focus on driving systemic pillars

	Basic infrastructure	High-tech institutions	Network cohesion	Integration in global markets
Initial conditions (1)	Political stability and efficient basic infrastructure.	Critical mass of economic agents.	Social bonds driven by the spirit to compete and achieve.	Integrated in global economy.
Learning phase (2)	Strengthening of basic infrastructure with better customs and bureaucratic coordination.	Import, learning by doing and duplicative imitation. Human capital development.	Expansion of tacitly occurring social institutions to formal intermediary organizations to stimulate connections and coordination between economic agents.	Access to foreign knowledge through machinery and equipment import and FDI. Integration in global value chains.
Catch-up phase (3)	Smooth integration with all institutions in 4 pillars.	Import, creative duplication and innovation. Developmental research. Creative destruction is a major source of technological catch-up (Schumpeterian Mark I).	Participation of intermediary and government organizations in coordinating technology inflows, initiation of commercially viable R&D.	Access to foreign knowledge through licensing, acquisition of foreign companies and imitation. Access to imports and exports. Upgrading in global value chains.
Frontier phase (3)	Novel basic infrastructure support instruments to support short lead times.	Basic research (Schumpeterian Mark II system).	Participation of intermediary organizations in two-way flow of knowledge between producers and users.	Access to R&D human capital and collaboration with R&D institutions, high-tech resources and markets abroad.

frontier research activities (Schumpeterian Mark II). Although the largest IH firms are only engaged in assembly and test activities, the institutional support in China has evolved to support strong operations in wafer fabrication and developmental research activities, including IC design. Although design and R&D activities are dominated by local firms, flagship foreign multinationals such as Intel have also started R&D and wafer fabrication activities in China.

Malaysia is very much still in the learning phase in the computer and components industry. A handful of the computer firms (for example Dell) and component firms (for example Intel and AMD) in Penang reported participation in developmental R&D but none in Johor. Firms in Penang enjoyed stronger network cohesion and global integration than firms in Johor. Basic infrastructure in the two states was similar. However, institutional efforts to support the catch-up process has so far been stalled by poor coordination between the institutions in the high-tech pillar and firms (see also Best and Rasiah, 2001). Several organizations were created to encourage upgrading but they have failed owing to discontinuities in coordination between them and the firms. While critical organizations – for example the Malaysian Institute of Microelectronics Systems (MIMOS), the Human Resource Development Council (HRDC), the Multimedia Development Corporation (MDC), the Multimedia Super Corridor (MSC), the Malaysian Technology Development Corporation (MTDC), the Small and Medium Industries Development Corporation (SMIDEC) and the Malaysian Industry, Government High Technology (MIGHT) – were created in the period 1985–97, the human capital selected to lead them were neither picked on their qualifications and experience nor required to meet specific milestones of performance. In addition, these organizations enjoyed little interface with IH firms. Hence, these organizations more often than not turned out to be white elephants (see also Rasiah, 1999).

Without a sectoral emphasis on driving catch-up the IH industry is still limited to assembly and test activities in Indonesia, Mauritius, Nigeria and South Africa. Local firms are engaged in the assembly of computers and components for the domestic markets. The emphasis in Indonesia, South Africa, Nigeria and Mauritius has largely been on how best to use rather than produce information and communication technology (ICT). Liberal government policies in these countries have not given a fillip to the drive for upgrading in the IH industry (also software in South Africa). Hence, lacking in institutional support, IH manufacturing in these countries has largely been limited to small-batch localized assembly of final IH goods such as computers. Hence IH firms are hovering between phases 1 and 2 in these countries.

The results point us to issues that help to explain uneven development of the IH industry. Some of these features are captured in Table 9.2.

Table 9.2 Comparative sectoral systems of IT

Country	Actors	Prime operation in value chain	Policies	Institutions	Organizations and network forms
China	MNCs and local firms	Integrated operations with R&D, and labour intensities assembly operations	JVs between local and MNCs; central and provincial government demand to stimulate local production; etc. Strategic Interventionist	Rules change to integrate research and industry; to convert military to civilian research centres, unique laws to form quasi public-private business partnerships	Economic zones that form high-tech clusters; state-like enterprises that operate with measures of business autonomy
Taiwan	World class local firms	High value-added R&D driven operations	Strategic interventions to drive upgrading	ERSO, Hsinchu Science Park play important role in driving learning and innovation	Highly developed and integrated IH Cluster Frontier knowledge linkages
Malaysia	Dominated by MNCs	Labour-intensive assembly and test	Incentive driven	MIMOS is a failure in driving learning and innovation. MITI's success in coordinating investment continues to sustain MNC-driven assembly	A promising knowledge link between MNCs and local firms in Penang has started to fade from the late 1990s owing to weak institutions Truncated operations in Johor

Indonesia	Dual structure: MNC assemblers of components; Local computer assemblers	Labour-intensive assembly	Liberal with no emphasis on IH manufacturing. Promotion of ICT use	No specific instrument to promote IH manufacturing	Truncated operations and designated zones
South Africa	MNCs Local assembling	Labour-intensive assembly	Liberal with no emphasis on IH manufacturing Promotion of ICT use	No specific instrument to promote IH manufacturing	Designated zones or regions
Nigeria	Local assemblers	Labour-intensive assembly	State procurement but weak policy	Weak knowledge base and poor institutions of finance	Spontaneous cluster
Mauritius	Local service producers	Labour-intensive assembly of computers	Policy towards services	No specific instrument to promote IH manufacturing	Designated but underdeveloped IH incubators

Five key dimensions emerge from the evidence from the seven countries. Variations in IH industry development in these countries can be captured under: (1) composition in production mix; (2) demand structures; (3) firm-level technological capabilities; (4) network cohesion; and (5) institutional differences.

9.3   COMPOSITIONAL DIFFERENCES

The composition of the IH industry varies in all the countries examined. Taiwan enjoys leadership in almost all the IH products manufactured by firms in these countries. Manufacturing in Mauritius and Nigeria is confined strictly to labour-intensive assembly of a limited range of IH goods such as computers for the domestic market.

Following successful upgrading and rising production costs Taiwanese firms relocated the labour-intensive segments of assembly and test operations of IH components, completely knocked down (CKD) and completely built up (CBU) to Southeast Asia initially from the mid-1980s, but especially China from the 1990s. Hence, Taiwan managed to support upgrading with human capital deepening in the IH industry.

Taiwan's information hardware is dominated by a large number of small and medium-sized enterprises (SMEs) and a few powerful sets of large firms that drive the sector through R&D, design and manufacturing. Taiwan was one of the world's leading producers of laptop computers, monitors, desktop PCs, scanners and motherboards in 2000 (see Rasiah and Lin, 2005).

With a huge domestic market and the world's largest labour force, China has attracted major multinational corporations and spawned domestic firms into a range of IH activities in the country. China's sheer size has attracted component, high-end and integrated operations. Almost all the leading IH multinationals have both low-end and high-end operations in China, and in addition local firms have acquired IBM and entered into integrated circuit (IC) design, fabrication and assembly of a number of IH CKDs and CBUs. Indeed China has low-assembly operations in locations such as Pearl River Valley and high-end operations in places like Shenzen and GanSu.

In Malaysia, multinational-driven component manufacturing in low value-added assembly and testing still dominates IH operations. Multinationals assemble a range of microchips, ink cartridges and printers, capacitors and resistors, monitors and motherboards. Only a handful of multinational firms assemble computers, motherboards, scanners and monitors (Dell, Acer and Agilent) and one has been engaged in wafer fabrication in 2006 (Infineon).

However, unlike Taiwan and China, IH firms in Malaysia, including the multinationals that attempted unsuccessfully to upgrade in the early 1990s, still specialize only in labour-intensive assembly and test operations. Yet Intel, AMD and Hitachi in components, Dell in computers and Motorola in hand phones did start, and some have still retained, a large engineering presence to carry out designing activities in 2006, but without much catch-up movement. While exports dominate, production-orientation firms such as Dell have since the late 1990s started manufacturing within Malaysia.

None of the foreign IH hardware firms in Indonesia, Mauritius, Nigeria and South Africa are engaged in microchips and designing activities. The focus is still very much on low value-added activities. Some firms have entered computer assembly and hand phone assembly in all four countries. However, only local brands are produced and sold in the domestic markets.

Export-oriented IH firms – both foreign and local – in Indonesia specialize in low printed circuit board assembly, though one firm reported specializing in surface mount technology to carry out high-end printed and flexible board assembly. These firms enjoy no links with the locally owned computer assembler serving the domestic market.

Both the CKD and CBU computer assemblers in Mauritius and Nigeria largely sold their brands in the local market, with some exports going to other African countries. Semiconductor firms are still absent in these countries. Imports still dominate domestic demand in IH products in these countries.

Despite enjoying superior infrastructure and human capital compared to Indonesia, Mauritius and Nigeria, the lack of industrial policy support in IH development has reduced South Africa to being largely an importer of IH products. Although the level of capability achieved falls below that of firms in Taiwan and China, South Africa's IH firms are significantly different from the Chinese and Taiwanese firms. South Africa's sector comprises four types of firms: (1) a small number of large, growing indigenous firms, some of which have achieved multinational status; (2) several state-owned enterprises (SOEs) that are major players in the ICT market; (3) a growing base of ICT SMEs; and (4) a number of foreign-owned multinationals that have established a presence and business relationships in South Africa. However, apart from software these firms specialize more in services rather than manufacturing.

In South Africa, telephony firms (Telkom and Vodacom) and state-owned enterprises, (for example Eskom, Transcom, and SABC) have transformed themselves into broad ICT firms encompassing telecommunications infrastructure and services, applications and content, recognizing, in particular, the opportunities brought about by the Internet (SAITIS, 2000). These firms have changed to adapt to the evolving domestic and global market opportunities.

9.4   DEMAND CONDITIONS

Demand coordination has been a critical driver in the growth of sectoral production systems. The prime demand drivers in the growth of IH firms in the Asian and African countries examined vary considerably.

China enjoys by far the largest domestic market and labour force, and hence has attracted the largest production base. Multinationals engaged in the assembly and testing of IH products supply the domestic as well as export markets. Local firms engaged in wafer fabrication and designing activities largely sell in the domestic market. However, China's production and export structure is diversified extensively and hence no one product has more than 15% of the share of total export (see WTO, 2006).

China's large domestic market (income per capita is a rough guide to the size of market and this differs significantly in the two sectoral systems) has provided a strong stimulus for innovation (Kline and Rosenberg, 1986). Amsden (1977, 1985) has presented insightful accounts of the machine tools sector in Taiwan which points to the ubiquitous ways in which the size and type of markets shape the rate of knowledge creation as well as the division of labour. The 'extent of market' or 'size of market' refers to the purchasing power, rather than to a geographic area or large population and 'the capacity to absorb a large annual output of goods'.[1] Amsden makes a distinction between the notion of 'size' and 'type' of market. Two markets of equal purchasing power may be qualitatively different in their capacities to consume large amounts of goods.[1] Markets in the three African countries are relatively small in size (and thrive on personal exchanges of kinship relations, personal loyalty and social connections) and in very many respects fit markets characterized by low profitability, limited economies of scale and low-intensity learning that slow long-run technological capability building.

Due in large part to active state interventions, industrialization in Taiwan has been driven by export demand. The IH industry itself grew with strong integration in export markets. Contract manufacturing for exports dominated the evolution of Taiwanese firms from original equipment manufacturer, own-design manufacturer and own-brand manufacturer (OEM to ODM and OBM) activities. The export-intensity shares of IH firms in Taiwan have been high. As production costs increased, the labour-intensive segments of IH manufacturing were relocated to other Southeast Asian countries starting from the mid-1980s, and China from the 1990s.

The foreign firms that dominated the IH industry in Malaysia are also integrated strongly in export markets. IH products constituted over 50 per cent of Malaysia's exports in 2005 (see WTO, 2006). Links with giant multinationals helped connect Malaysian exports to global buyers. Although the domestic market has increased its absorption of intermediate demand (for example components and CKDs) and final demand (for example Dell computers), export markets have remained the prime propellant of IH growth in Malaysia.

Indonesia has a dual structure, with multinationals relying on export markets and domestic computer firms focused on supplying the domestic market. Foreign firms dominate low-end assembly operations for regional buyers in Singapore and Johor. Apart from one local firm that uses surface mount technology to assemble printed and flexible circuit boards, the remaining local firms either assemble low-end CKDs for foreign firms or computers for the local market.

Mauritius is characterized by the smallest domestic market. The Nigerian market is larger and hence supports more domestic assembly of IH CBU products such as computers. Although some local brands are exported to the African continent, production of IH CKDs and CBUs is largely geared to the domestic market in both countries.

The preponderance of foreign firms in South Africa has been partly fostered by deliberate policy action to attract foreign direct investment (FDI). Between 1994 and 2001, the IT and telecommunications sub-sectors registered the highest share of FDI in the country. However, despite the high level of foreign investment, the growth of the sector in South Africa is currently driven by domestic consumption rather than by exports (Moleke, 2003; BMI-T, 2005).

Overall the IH manufacturing industries of Taiwan, Malaysia and China are integrated strongly in export markets and hence the technological effects of creative destruction (Schumpeter's Mark I system) is seen most in these economies. Despite the large domestic market, exports markets are still critical for China. South Africa is also fairly strongly integrated but the focus is primarily in software, including programming and support. Hence, South Africa remains highly import-dependent on IH products. Mauritius and Nigeria's IH industry is the least integrated despite the former being strongly connected to export markets in other sectors such as garment and clothing.

9.5   UNEVEN TECHNOLOGICAL CAPABILITIES

Firms in the IH industry in the seven countries examined show different levels of technological capabilities. The knowledge and technological capabilities demanded by these operations are very uneven. Only Taiwan has reached the frontier with the R&D capability to design and engineer frontier semiconductor chips. For example, the microchips engineered and fabricated by TSMC are among the key drivers of IH CKDs and CBUs. Taiwanese firms also have the capacity to produce OEM, ODM and OBM versions of IH products. Chinese firms are headed in that direction with involvement in such operations but currently still largely utilize microchips to assemble Chinese OEM, ODM and OBM IH products. Firms in Malaysia are largely confined to assembly and test operations of components and IH CKDs. A handful of firms assemble IH CBUs such as computers and fabricate low-end wafers. IH firms in Nigeria, Mauritius and South Africa are limited to assembly of IH products for the domestic market. Apart from software firms in South Africa, IH firms are not engaged in high-end operations in the three African countries studied.

The key human capital capabilities required to stimulate innovation at the frontier in IH firms are technicians, engineers and scientists. The segments in IH value chains comprise: (1) product design; (2) component manufacturing; (3) assembly; (4) software development; (5) marketing; and (6) distribution. Each of these sub-stages requires a combination of different kinds of knowledge and skills of actors from various disciplines; some as diverse as physics, informatics and computer science are required to facilitate innovation. The demand for engineers and scientists is highest in the stages of product design and software development.

Taiwan has developed the highest level of technological capabilities with the requisite development of human capital. The key actors in Taiwan's CH sector fall into three categories, namely own-brand manufacturer (OBM), original equipment manufacturer (OEM), and a mix of OBM and own-design manufacturer (ODM).[2] In 2000, Taiwan's[3] hardware information technology industry (domestic and overseas combined) had a total production value of US$47 billion, up 17.9 per cent from the previous year's US$39.9 billion, making it the most important foreign exchange earner of the country.

The particular combination of capabilities that contributes the most effectively to innovation and to increased competitiveness evidently varies at different levels of SIS. For instance the portfolio of capabilities needed to foster competitiveness in a context purely devoted to computer assembly typically differs from those required in computer systems integration, to take one extreme. Movement into a more complex set of activities naturally involves developing concomitant sets of capabilities. The Taiwanese and Chinese cases illustrate this most emphatically.

Across the IH sector, the set of and particular combination of knowledge resources that contribute most effectively to competitiveness change over time. For the different countries that we examined, the change runs within an innovation spectrum starting from pure imitation right up to the phase where the country has developed the capabilities to compete with global leaders at the frontier. Our set of case studies shows that countries maintain dynamic competitiveness only by continuous and explicit investment in a wide range of resources that deepen existing extant knowledge bases.

The findings demonstrate the cumulative and path-dependent nature of knowledge growth (Schumpeter, 1942; Nelson and Winter, 1982; Malerba, 1992, 2006). The changing bases of the sectoral system are triggered by a host of factors, not least of which is export into sophisticated markets. Capabilities are built to take advantage of emerging opportunities, and where this opportunity is missed systemic evolution is slowed or in some cases halted. As the SIS evolves from simple assembly to complex design and manufacturing, the key elements of the knowledge bases change over time as firms build up capabilities to manufacture complex products for foreign markets or claim new domestic market niches.

For instance, Taiwanese and Chinese firms adapted imported technologies, acquired foreign companies and built new microchips and computer models in order to integrate Mandarin characters, and through this process created an entirely new domestic market. One of the keys to their success is mastering the core components of IH, which include integrated circuits, chip design and software mould. Also, the international semiconductor and computer markets played a very important demonstrative role at the initial as well as latter stages of development. Initially, Taiwanese and Chinese firms learnt by responding to international consumers' needs and making changes to old computer models through supply service and sales of imported computer. While Taiwanese firms are at the frontier of shaping new technologies, by 2006 Chinese firms were comfortably transiting the catch-up phase.

IH firms in Malaysia still specialize in assembly and test activities. A tight labour market and changing technological conditions favouring regional specialization in design had raised demand for upgrading in foreign multinationals in the 1990s (see Rasiah, 1996). However, the lack of effective institutional responses stalled upgrading so that only a handful of firms undertake re-engineering activities in Malaysia.

The production experience gained from the early 1970s and integration in global markets helped subsidiaries in Malaysia to carry out efficient ramping-up operations in Southeast Asia. Foreign multinational and local supplier firms located in Penang also show higher technological capabilities than IH firms located in Johor. Although the basic infrastructures in the two locations are similar, better network cohesion, stronger integration in global markets and larger numbers of flagship firms such as Intel,

AMD, HP and Dell helped Penang drive stronger process technology and engineering activities than in IH firms in Johor. The lack of institutional support for high-tech operations stalled further upgrading in the whole country.

In both China and Taiwan the sectors progressively moved from producing for low-income and within low-labour cost regimes to higher-income and innovation-based competition. This situation contrasts with Malaysia which has made considerable progress but has not built as deep a knowledge base as Taiwan and China, but remains a much bigger base for IH manufacturing compared to Indonesia and the African countries examined.

Although some CBU assemblers in the IH industry in Mauritius and Nigeria undertake designing activities, the technological capabilities of these firms is built largely around labour-intensive and imitational capabilities. Lacking in scale and lock-ins with lead firms as well as effective institutional support, local firms in these countries are constrained simply to absorb and internalize prevailing technology to assemble computers and mobile phones for the domestic and African continental market. These products lack the quality and price to compete in major export markets.

IH firms in South Africa excel especially in software technology. However, these firms do not have strong linkages with local IH manufacturing operations. Instead software firms largely support the service sector, providing software solutions in South Africa and the regional market.

Overall, IH firms in Taiwan and China are clearly either already at the technology frontier or show clear movement towards it. IH firms in Malaysia have been stagnant since 1997 as institutional weaknesses have impeded movement to the catch-up phase. The lack of effective industrial policy has been a major reason why IH firms in Indonesia, Mauritius, Nigeria and South Africa have been unable to make the leap in the IH manufacturing trajectory, though the last has both human capital and market networks to make the transition.

9.6   UNEVEN NETWORKING

The nature of connections and coordination between economic agents – firms and institutions – influences production and innovation synergies. Geographic space represents knowledge bases but these have manifested themselves differentially in the different systems (Saxenian, 1994; Rasiah, 1994, 2002). An industrial cluster is a dense sectoral and geographical concentration of enterprises comprising a multiplicity of actors such as producers, suppliers, users and traders. When an agglomeration of enterprises exhibits strong attributes of an innovative cluster it becomes more than a geographic space where firms co-locate. In such a cluster, we have strong inter-firm interaction and specialization (Best, 2001; Oyelaran-Oyeyinka and McCormick, 2007).

Strong clustering is associated with high rates of learning and knowledge accumulation that continually alter the knowledge base of the cluster. There is demonstrable evidence of a dense network of formal and informal institutions in Taiwan (see Rasiah and Lin, 2005). Clustering in Taiwan, China and Penang in Malaysia all shows evidence of high connectivity and coordination and, hence, high economic performance. In Johor in Malaysia, Indonesia, Mauritius, Nigeria and South Africa, which exhibit weaker degrees of inter-firm collaboration, these also have a lower intensity of learning and poorly developed institutions.

Clusters in Taiwan, China and Penang in Malaysia are strongly integrated in global factor and final product markets. Among the seven countries examined only Taiwan exhibits integrated networks throughout the country. Even then there are wide regional differences in the character of these clusters in China and Malaysia, dictated in the main by their differential knowledge characteristics. For example, Penang in Malaysia is better networked than Johor. Although the manufacturing bases are concentrated in the Guangdong, Jiangsu and Fujian provinces and the Shanghai and Beijing main cities, in these regions production is localized in three locations including the Yangzi River Delta, Pearl River Delta and Loop Bo Sea Region, which have transformed into the computer manufacturing industrial clusters in those regions. However, the three areas are defined by different knowledge features: for instance, the Pearl River Delta has very strong coastal manufacturing based on import processing; the Loop Bo Sea Region is the most highly knowledge-intensive region with a large number of low-cost science and technology personnel; while the Yangzi River Delta combines the above two factors, although it does not have such a concentrated knowledge base as the Loop Bo Sea Region.

The nature and intensity of cluster cohesion achieved in these economies also differ. For instance, active involvement of the state government and its successful attempt to bring together the critical economic agents to coordinate security, production, buyer–supplier, training and distribution needs helped spawn the birth of new firms and technology flow to other firms in Penang, Malaysia. However, the hands-off approach to industrial coordination by state development corporations outside Penang limited their capacity to promote inter-firm relationships. The uneven roles – the more interventionist role of the Penang Development Corporation in Penang and the hands-off role of other state development corporations after firms obtained their operating licenses – resulted in uneven outcomes (see Rasiah, 2002). Consequently, the strength of the systems in regional clusters differs significantly, even within a single country. The Penang cluster has enjoyed far stronger network cohesion than have other regions in Malaysia. The strong relationships between the Penang Development Corporation (and the state government) and firms (multinational corporations, MNCs, as well as local firms) helped forge strong systemic coordination in the Penang cluster. Outside Penang, by contrast, there are few links beyond the allocation of land and the coordination of trade. The Klang Valley, where key ministries and the Malaysian Industrial Development Authority (MIDA) are located, has weak network connections, while the state economic development corporations of Selangor, Negri Sembilan, Melaka, Johor, Kedah, Perak and Sarawak have limited their support activities to the provision of land.

The IH locations are poorly linked with institutions and among themselves in Indonesia. Indeed, printed circuit board (PCB) assemblers in Indonesia reported very weak links with firms higher in the value chains.

In Mauritius and Nigeria organizations to *inter alia* promote interactions have emerged largely through the chambers of commerce, although effective coordination is still underdeveloped. There are also weaknesses in connections between IH firms and basic institutions such as banking and the capital market.

South Africa provides a different experience. Lacking in industrial policy support to stimulate IH manufacturing, the South African government especially at the regional level has encouraged strong networking to encourage IT use across the country. Notably, software firms have multiplied through such networks to support IT services in South Africa.

Overall, Taiwan has developed the strongest networking – formally and informally – among the concentrations of IH firms in the seven countries. China and to a less extent Penang in Malaysia have also enjoyed fairly strong connections and coordination among the critical agents. The extent of network cohesion among IH firms in Johor in Malaysia, Indonesia, Mauritius, Nigeria and South Africa have been less well developed, but regional locations have supported strong integration in software segments in South Africa.

9.7 UNEVEN INSTITUTIONAL SUPPORT POLICIES

The policy frameworks supporting IH industries in the seven countries can be examined through two sets of institutional categories, namely, basic infrastructure and high-tech infrastructure. Given the differential drivers and their consequences it is appropriate to examine them separately.

Basic Infrastructure Institutions

Taiwan (from the 1960s), Malaysia (from the early 1970s), China (from the 1980s) and Indonesia (from the 1990s) introduced FDI policies by providing basic infrastructure at export-processing zones. The provision of security, smooth customs, beaureacratic and investment coordination, repatriation guarantees of profits, liberal ownership conditions and coordination of utility suppliers, and the access to low-wage but literate and trainable labour, acted as a big incentive to attract large-scale labour-intensive operations from abroad. Tax holidays helped augment further the attractions of these sites. By and large the export processing zones in China, Malaysia and Taiwan have managed to provide excellent basic infrastructure.

Malaysia remains a good example of a country that has done well in providing good basic infrastructure to attract labour-intensive IH activities. Indonesia did the same with the leasing out of Batam's export processing zone to Singapore-owned Temasik Holdings. However, security considerations and customs problems have discouraged further expansion of IH activities in other parts of Indonesia.

The lack of financial incentives and weaknesses in infrastructure to support short lead times and knowledge-intensive operations has discouraged large-scale export-oriented assembly activities in Mauritius and Nigeria. Also, investment coordination for IH firms remains poorly developed in these economies. Not surprising, foreign ownership is rare in IH activities in these countries.

Several regions enjoy excellent basic infrastructure in South Africa. However, the lack of special financial incentives to attract FDI into IH manufacturing has discouraged the relocation of FDI-driven IH component, CKD and CBU firms in South Africa. Hence, many of the IT firms in South Africa are confined to local-owned software operations supporting the service sector.

High-Tech Institutions

There exists much higher variance in policies supporting high-tech institutions than basic institutions in these countries. Whereas strong basic insititions are critical to coordinate labour-intensive low value-added activities, upgrading to higher value-added activities require similar support from high-tech institutions.

Taiwan has provided support to IH firms' participation in strong creative accumulation activities. Starting from low value-added activities, government policy was transformed in the 1970s to support upgrading through investment in high-tech institutions. The initial targeting from government came from the creation of the Industrial Technical Research Institute (ITRI) in 1973, which led to its electronics wing, ERSO, driving catch-up in electronics technology. The acquisition of RCA in the late 1970s and subsequently the joint venture with Philips in 1986 helped Taiwanese firms incubated in ERSO to make the catch-up in DRAM and ASIC technology. Other IH firms also made significant strides in technological catch-up in components, CKD CBU products through support from ERSO, the facilities offered at Hsinchu Science Park and the science and technology policy grants (see also Mathews and Cho, 2000; Rasiah and Lin, 2005). Smooth coordination and the participation of firms in the development of human capital in technical institutes and universities, and R&D coordination with university and other labs (for example ERSO), have helped the strong movement of Taiwanese firms to the technology frontier.

In China the support for catch-up activities has been consistently strong. Although foreign multinationals have relocated wafer fabrication and R&D operations in IH activities into China, much of the design activities are carried out by local firms. Nevertheless, institutional support has successfully driven catch-up in these firms. Among the many examples is Lenova's acquisition of IBM's computer manufacturing division which has also assisted catch-up in the industry. As in Taiwan, strong coordination with the university system in designing courses and working with R&D labs has also helped firms' movement up the technology ladder.

In addition, human capital policies in Taiwan and China co-evolved strongly with upgrading: mastering modern production and manufacturing capabilities with engineers as well as skilled technicians, and mastering design and redesign of already matured products. Engineers rather than research scientists tend to dominate this set of activities. The locus of activity here is the factory and manufacturing centres.

Taiwan and China have thus been able to deepen these activities through the graduation of IH firms progressively from OEM to ODM and finally to OBM activities. Another critical step is the shift into the design and engineering of components, which involves systematic engineering and scientific specification of products, processes and systems including computer hardware and software. The importance of design was shown by the evolution of the Chinese computer hardware which literally took off on the wings of redesign rather than simply learning to produce.[4]

Significantly differential policies have led to the differences in the geography of knowledge clusters and ensured that access to local and global knowledge and information is uneven. The unusual success of Chinese computer hardware illustrates how access to both a domestic pool of scientific knowledge in government research institutes and, more significantly, to global knowledge through MNCs' investment combined well with firm-level efforts through technological upgrading required for meeting export quality. In the first instance, foreign firms dominate the computer export business, one of the most significant sources of wealth generation for China since the mid-1990s. Through foreign firms located in clusters and special economic zones – a deliberate investment coordination policy of China – the country has risen to global leadership. Unlike Malaysia which has also targeted exports, the key objective has been not just employment creation but also the accumulation of technological capability in very specific areas. What might well be considered market distortion in neoclassical economics, for instance, the deliberate use of coercive mechanisms to forge joint ventures with local firms, and protection of the domestic market for computers and related components that formed the basis for the emergence of new markets, made the decisions by foreign investors to locate in China relatively easy. China was for a long time vilified for weak intellectual property rights (IPR) enforcement but this singular action, as with the deliberate abolishment of product patents in India, gave domestic firms the platform to acquire relevant capabilities. This strong nexus of a local–global capability platform which has simultaneously spawned strong domestic CH firms in collaboration with equally strong foreign firms explains in large part the rapid rise of the IH sector.

The drive to export is another inducement mechanism to the rapid upgrading of the sector. In the same way that foreign actors have been instrumental in the deepening of the domestic manufacturing base, so foreign market dynamics is a spur for deepening the product quality of Chinese exports, as it had been for Taiwan before it. There are three reasons. First, as a new entrant, a latecomer faces stiff competition from established producers in external markets. In order to compete, it has to upgrade rapidly both manufacturing processes as well as products. In doing this local firms benefit from joint-venture arrangements with partners with superior technologies. Second, signals from buyers and intermediate suppliers in typical user–producer interactive learning fashion (Lundvall, 1988), provide valuable market information to local firms that are determined to succeed. This is the case with the Taiwanese unique OEM–ODM–OBM arrangements by which local Taiwanese firms learnt to make superior products through technical arrangements with global leaders. Third, the pathway to export success in electronics has two dimensions, namely, the modular nature of the semiconductor industry that opens the way for firms to participate at different stages of manufacturing. Again there are a multiplicity of learning sources that admit different actors within the global value chain, from simple assemblers to systems integrators. The uneven paths that admit Taiwanese (largely small and medium-sized) firms equally permitted the participation of initially state-owned Chinese companies as well as large multinationals.

The Taiwanese and Chinese governments moved from basic framework conditions to support targeted products such as integrated circuits, newly typed electronics components and three circuit (3C) products. Notably, integrated circuit (IC) and newly typed electronics components are related to the computer core software manufacturing from the 1970s and 1990s respectively, which directly influence computer product added values. One of the most visible interventions was the setting up of the IH industry bases and IH industry parks in both countries. Enterprises in the identified national electronics information industrial bases or industrial parks could apply for specific state and industry development funds to support investment in fixed assets and industrialization projects. Local governments were mandated to support the industrial bases and parks. The government in both countries adopted active global networking strategies to access critical technologies from MNCs abroad. Both governments also initiated an export strategy to stimulate learning and innovation in electronics manufacturing.

The opening of the Malaysian Institute of Microelectronics Systems (MIMOS) in 1985 and the Action Plan for Industrial Technology Development (APITD) of 1990 and subsequent institutional development offered considerable promise for catch-up to occur in the IH industry in Malaysia. However, institutional failures have limited the effectiveness of these institutions. Unlike China and Taiwan, incentives for building capabilities and for stimulating higher-level manufacturing and R&D activities have not been well developed in Malaysia. Although government incentives were generous, they were unsuitable for firms on the lower rungs of technological development and seem more appropriate for mature innovators and for MNCs seeking to offset the risks of relocating developmental R&D activities. The implementation of R&D grants also bypassed start-ups and potential individual innovators. In contrast to the other high performers, incentives and grants tended to reward innovators after the fact. The fact that tax holidays were available based on different criteria – such as level of investment and strategic classification – made the R&D incentives redundant for many firms. In other words, the uneven paths to policy choices contributed to the uneven outcomes in building domestic capabilities.

Also, the uneven choices of policy instruments in different countries equally led to differentiated outcomes. For instance in Malaysia the mechanisms for identifying potential entrepreneurs and innovators, for drawing them into the policy process, and establishing a legal framework to connect venture capitalists with innovators, have been poorly developed. The outcome is that few firms have been born. Therefore in contrast to China and Taiwan, where local firms quickly moved into high-end products as original equipment, own-design and own-brand manufacturers, Malaysia's IH firms are largely multinationals and foreign affiliates that rely on the technological capability of parent firms. In addition to foreign multinationals having dominated IH manufacturing, the lack of interface between MIMOS and university human capital programmes and R&D labs undermined a major channel for catch-up for firms in Malaysia. Also, while the country has successfully attracted considerable FDI, created jobs, engendered diversification and promoted exports, manufacturing has been limited to low value-added activities drawing on a relatively shallow knowledge base.

Whereas there has been strong growth in the supply of human capital – including those attracted back under their talent attraction programmes that has brought back tacit knowledge – in Taiwan and China, the lack of human capital has discouraged upgrading in Malaysia. Learning and catch-up in Malaysia effectively stalled from the 1990s so that most IH firms are engaged in labour-intensive activities.

In addition, while Malaysia's export-oriented policies have been successful in attracting large-scale assembly operations from foreign multinationals, the lack of effective export-oriented upgrading strategies meant that the few local firms that emerged in component and CKD manufacturing have remained as contract suppliers without any sign of a transition to either Schumpeterian Mark I or Mark II activities. The acquisition of VLSI Technology in the late 1990s was not backed up with a deliberate catch-up strategy and hence the potential synergies were simply dissipated.

The lack of proactive policies to support upgrading activities in IH manufacturing in Indonesia, Mauritius, Nigeria and South Africa means that these countries have remained without a significant concentration of IH firms.

From the typology, the observed differences in SIS have as much to do with policy choices and initial conditions as with institutional evolution, all of which influence economic performance (North, 1990). The comparative study carried out by Nelson (1993) on national SIS showed that countries generally develop different knowledge bases in both R&D and the capacity for innovation. For instance, he noted the differences that size makes in SIS: 'The differences in the innovation systems reflect differences in economic and political circumstances and priorities [while] size and the degree of influence matter a lot' (Nelson, 1993: 507). In other words, policy political choices in a given institutional context influence the shape and direction that the sector takes.

For instance, while dynamic and interactive policies were at the heart of successful catch-up and transition to frontier operations in China and Taiwan respectively, uncoordinated and ineffective policies limited

Malaysia's capacity to make the transition to the catch-up stage. The poorly developed high-tech institutions throughout the country, poor network cohesion and weak global integration outside Penang have stifled the progress of IH firms on the technology ladder in Malaysia.

For example, financial institutional incentives were instrumental in offsetting the risks associated with relocating to a new and potentially risky site in the early 1970s, but there has been no review of these generous tax holidays.[5]

Problems of security and customs coordination and poor infrastructure led to Indonesia, Mauritius and Nigeria creating industrial estates (and also export processing zones in Indonesia) to locate IH firms. However, the lack of policy emphasis to support learning and catch-up beyond investment and employment generation has meant limited innovation in Indonesia and Mauritius. Policy framework in Nigeria does even include IH as a major promotional industry.

In South Africa, there is evidence of rather broad framework-type government intervention at regional levels to support the diffusion of ICT activities, but the lack of specific catch-up strategies has now encouraged the utilization of its superior human capital, basic infrastructure and domestic market to support catch-up in IH manufacturing.

Innovative activities in geographic space are localized to the Gauteng area in South Africa, while in Nigeria firms have agglomerated spontaneously in the Lagos area unaided by any sort of coherent policy choices by local, state and federal governments. Clearly the role of municipal and local governments could be decisive, and the participation by local authorities in promoting industrial activities to different levels of success is evident in China, Taiwan and Malaysia.

9.8   SUMMING UP

The information hardware sector is made up of complex production sub-systems underpinned by structures of knowledge comprising closely located clusters as well as knowledge bases in far-flung locations all over the world. The path of innovation generation is uneven and is characterized by constant changes as the sector develops, including through making difficult policy choices. Low-income countries are often disadvantaged in terms of cognitive and geographic proximity to knowledge bases and markets, because the sector thrives on links with global knowledge systems in order to access technical and scientific expertise. Local firms drove catch-up in the IH industry in Taiwan. Multinationals have dominated IH manufacturing in Malaysia. Export-oriented IH manufacturing in components and CKD products in Indonesia is dominated by multinationals, but local firms dominate ownership of computer and mobile phone assembly for the domestic market. Local firms dominate manufacturing in Mauritius and Nigeria, which is largely targeted to the domestic market. Despite strong basic infrastructure and software capabilities, IH goods are largely still imported from abroad to South Africa.

In addition to links with global networks, local links with key actors have been important particularly for Taiwan and China. China has turned what could have been an institutional burden to a dynamic advantage, illustrating in very direct ways the impact of initial conditions. The role of scientific and technological manpower built up in the communist era in China and the quality of pre-existent national human and industrial capabilities meant for other purposes such as the military were successfully transformed to commercial IH production. The institutional transformation of the relationship between universities, research institutes and the IH industry that subsequently emerged illustrates the persistence of institutions and the power of path-dependent development. Institutional deepening over time in Taiwan – especially strong high-tech institutions – and cohesive integration between firms and these institutions were instrumental in firms upgrading to OEM, ODM and OBM operations.

Policies that reintroduced generous tax incentives and the maturation of Malaysia's labour force, combined with imports of cheap foreign labour from Indonesia and Bangladesh, led to the relocation of labour-intensive low value-added firms in Johor, Malaysia. The synergies created by these firms, as well as the high cost of operations in Singapore, attracted IH component and CKD assembly firms to Johor from the 1990s. Even though China and Vietnam began to offer attractive financial incentives to all firms from 1998 to attract more investment, several labour-intensive multinationals stayed in Malaysia. However, this strategy along with ineffective coordination with upgrading institutions has restricted Malaysia's capacity to follow Taiwan, and it has now been overtaken by China on the technology ladder. Quite evidently, knowledge bases, strategic policy choices, initial conditions, differentiated coordination mechanisms and institutions exert considerable impact on the evolution of sectoral systems.

9.9 POLICY IMPLICATIONS FOR LATECOMERS

From the foregoing, it becomes clear that governments have to deal with a greater variety of new and complex conditions arising from the systemic nature of innovation processes. We identify three broad features.

First, the heterogeneity of actors in a user–producer framework means that policy-making will move away from a focus on the supply side to managing interfaces between the supply and demand sides. This will involve a continuous balancing of autonomy and embeddedness as policy-makers seek to make innovation more widely integrated into the broader socio-economic process. This will involve not just the simple task of managing technology transfer processes, but will also require greater awareness creation and stimulating demand for innovation through a variety of policy instruments (Metcalfe, 2005). It will mean redressing the organizational and institutional failures related to: (1) bridging the gap between theory and practice (for example, university–industry linkages, public research organizations (PROs) and users; (2) facilitating connections between different knowledge bases within the national economy; and (3) raising the knowledge and technological capabilities of the different organizations to perform their roles better and to become more competent in collaborative activities.

Policy-making will have to address coordination and informational externalities arising from systems failure. Second, far from the traditional conception of technology as a ready-made good that is easily transferred between organizations, the process of innovation is inherently complex, unpredictable and characterized by uncertainty in its outcome. Actors do not possess perfect information and, as Metcalfe points out, the adaptive policy-maker functions under the same bounded rationality as the agents that are involved in the process. The policy-maker under the evolutionary framework is not omniscient and is subjected to the same heuristic search process of trial and error of the innovating entity. Economic systems do not give one but multiple responses to a well-known problem. In other words, problem-solving is an evolutionary process, not a search for an optimal outcome. The evolutionary policy-maker is an adaptive policy-maker (Metcalfe, 1993) rather than an optimizer. Policy has to act at several levels and be conscious of the changes inherent in different phases.

The role of policy is: (1) to build institutions to attenuate uncertainty – this can be done by providing information to help firms and organizations make short- and long-term investments; (2) to provide incentives and establish organizations or strengthen existing ones where they are performing poorly – this includes intermediary organizations that mediate transfer processes and ensures pay-off to innovation, and those that take the risk element from the process such as venture capital; and (3) to provide the tools and environment for learning.

Third, systemic failure manifests itself as missing institutions and organizations; and dysfunctional connections between organizations in national systems. The implication of this is that the state has a role in: (1) building knowledge infrastructure; (2) establishing regulations and organizations to enforce the rules; and (3) formulating policies that generate networking in systems.

Basic Infrastructure Institutions

Although investment approval and coordination, security, customs coordination and other basic infrastructure support such as water and power supply, supply of literate labour and transport are common to all industries, the specific characteristics of IH that require short lead times and knowledge-intensive workers mean that governments must also provide this infrastructure to support even labour-intensive low value-added operations in the industry.

Taiwan, China and Malaysia in the initial stages attracted foreign firms in the IH industry by providing good basic infrastructure in export processing zones. Whereas Taiwan and China have moved up the ladder to high-tech operations, the large labour force still supports labour-intensive operations in export processing zones such as the Pearl River Valley. Malaysia continues to provide good basic infrastructure and has maintained demand for labour-intensive operations despite rising wages by importing labour from Bangladesh and Indonesia. Malaysia has even maintained tax incentives to compete with newly emerging sites in Indonesia, the Philippines and Vietnam.

Foreign-owned IH assembly has evolved considerably in Batam, Indonesia. Security and customs coordination outside Batam has continued to discourage large-scale IH assembly in Indonesia. South Africa and Nigeria have failed to attract such IH assembly of components on a large scale owing to problems with incentives, while in Mauritius a critical mass of knowledge-intensive workers is also lacking. In these countries, however, locally owned IH assembly (for example in computers) exists largely to supply the domestic markets – and Mauritius, Nigeria and South Africa also export within the African continent. Apart from South Africa the others still require significant improvements in basic infrastructure to attract large-scale and diversified IH operations.

Learning and Innovation Infrastructure as the Driver of Economic Development

Countries have certain levels of STI; however, the nature of the science, technology and innovation (STI) and the innovation process vary depending on the stage of development of the economy. In the relatively low-income countries, innovation is more about the adoption of foreign technologies and incremental innovations implemented through new management techniques or the introduction of new businesses to the market. In low- to middle-high-income economies (advanced followers), innovation is more knowledge-intensive and has more to do with technology adaptation, and sometimes creation and invention. A number of countries have developed autonomous endogenous capacity for higher-level learning and relatively strong innovation capacity.

Human Capital

Taiwan and China managed to engender the human capital to drive learning and catch-up, and in the case of the former even frontier IH innovations. In addition, basic education – primary and secondary – technical training and education at the tertiary level are all important. In addition to activities associated with human capital developed domestically both countries have in place effective talent attraction policies to attract back their human capital who have gained experiential knowledge working in cutting-edge R&D institutions and flagship firms abroad. The IH industry has not progressed to the catch-up phase in Malaysia because of the failure of the requisite institutions to match human capital supply with the need for upgrading. Instead of focusing on attracting human capital from abroad its talent attraction policies have been ineffective, and large-scale unskilled labour imports from Indonesia and Bangladesh have only undermined upgrading in the country. Latecomer countries thus must be ready to create these institutions to facilitate firms' movement from the elementary learning to the advanced catch-up phase.

   IH firms in these countries used graduates initially to engage in operational, problem-solving activities and engineering activities. It is only when these firms are passing from the learning phase to the catch-up phase that R&D engineers and scientists become important. The latter become pertinent when IH firms reach the technology frontier. One of the fundamental functions promoted by institutions is R&D learning that creates the absorptive capacity of nations. The state has historically played a leading role in both the early 'industrializers' as well as in the more recent dynamic economies such as Taiwan and South Korea (Mowery, 2005). For example, the role of universities has received considerable attention as a source of trained personnel and streams of scientific and technological knowledge, and as a facilitator, for example through the mobility of scientists between university and industry, and the diffusion of new knowledge and human capital.

   Taiwan managed to achieve these developments and hence a number of IH firms in the country have reached the frontier. Chinese firms are strongly poised to reach the frontier with similar development of human capital. Malaysia's failure to implement effective human capital policies has stunted its efforts to reach the catch-up phase. Indonesia, South Africa, Mauritius and Nigeria have no purposive policy to drive firms in this direction, though South Africa is endowed with considerable human capital.

High-Tech Parks

The key to facilitating the dissemination and exploitation of specialized sectoral knowledge is a reliable infrastructure (ICT, export processing zones, software parks and links with industry) that functions in a coordinated and systemic manner, and strengthens linkages and encourages the exchange of knowledge. Taiwan, China and Malaysia created high-tech parks to drive learning and innovation. Whereas IH firms in high-tech parks have achieved considerable innovation capabilities in Taiwan and China, the lack of connections and poor coordination has severely restricted such developments in Malaysia. Whereas effectively using matching grants to support R&D has also been successful in Taiwan and China, in Malaysia financial incentives for similar operations did not bring the same results. Government was central in the creation of these high-tech parks in all three countries. No explicit high-tech parks to support IH innovation are present in Mauritius, Nigeria and South Africa, and hence this missing platform is an additional reason why these countries are unlikely to follow the path of Taiwan and China in their IH firms making the transition to high value-added activities.

R&D Labs

Government R&D labs supported by ERSO in Taiwan and similar organizations in China were instrumental in several successful incubation activities that helped the creation of high-tech IH firms. Indeed, almost all the high-tech firms that have succeeded in or passed the catch-up stage evolved from government-driven incubators in Taiwan and China.

However, the lack of connections and poor coordination have resulted in none of the Malaysian Institute of Microelectronics (MIMOS) incubators reaching the catch-up stage. Without any government policy for supporting upgrading in IH firms, none of the IH firms in Indonesia, Mauritius, Nigeria and South Africa are poised to enter the catch-up phase. It is only in software technology, where strong government support is not a necessary condition, that South Africa has successfully spawned innovative firms.

Global Integration

Integration in global markets helped Taiwan and China not only to appropriate scale and scope economies to expand IH production, but also access scarce knowledge to speed up the catch-up process. Global markets were also central to the integration of low value-added exports from Malaysia and Indonesia, but the lack of institutional dynamism restricted the capacity of the firms to move up the value chain. However, in the computer assembly industry the main actors in Indonesia are small and medium-sized assemblers with little connection to global players.

Global integration also acted as a vital channel for firms to access scarce foreign knowledge – via direct investment, licensing arrangements, and the transfer of experiential knowledge embodied in human capital from MNCs to local firms. Taiwan and China have benefited considerably from the inflow of technology through all these channels to drive upgrading. Malaysia appropriated considerable direct investment advantages but has not successfully developed the mechanisms for effective upgrading, including through licensing, to move up the value chain. An ethnic-driven development policy has also discouraged productive networking among the critical institutions of learning and innovation to drive upgrading in the nature of integration enjoyed by firms in global value chains in Malaysia. Gripped by political fragility, Indonesia has yet to even frame an effective upgrading policy for information hardware industries.

Among the sub-Saharan Africa (SSA) economies, South Africa is the best placed to enjoy export growth, but only in software activities. Much of the hardware assembled in the SSA economies is either sold in the domestic markets or in Africa. The lack of policy focus on upgrading in these countries has reduced both foreign and local firms to assembly and test operations. Much of the R&D undertaken is new only to the firms or the domestic economies. In the computer assembly industries in Nigeria and Mauritius the main actors are small and medium-sized assemblers with little connection to global players.

The lack of rapid expansion has reduced the demand for human capital and hence Malaysia's problem of a severe scarcity in human capital supply is not typical of the IH firms in the SSA economies. Indeed, South Africa and Nigeria seem to have sufficient human capital to stimulate deepening in R&D activities.

Demand Structures

One of the keys to a successful catch-up has been integration in global markets. Taiwan relied almost completely on export markets while the large domestic market only complemented the pressures and opportunities of export markets that drove catch-up in China. Malaysia has continued to retain a major position in IH manufacturing only because of integration in global markets. Indonesia has achieved some export success in low-end activities, but problems outside Batam have restricted rapid expansion in such markets. IH manufacturing in Nigeria, Mauritius and South Africa remains little integrated in export markets, though imports continue to feature strongly in the latter two economies. Hence, any latecomer seeking to introduce and upgrade in IH value chains must integrate into global markets.

Cluster Networks

Cluster cohesion or integration constituted one of the pillars driving the creation and appropriation of systemic synergies involving learning and innovation. The successful countries in the IH industry have managed to achieve stronger cluster cohesion than the less successful ones.

The experience of the successful catch-up of Taiwan and China, as well as the transition to frontier activities in the former, is also driven by the nature of networks connecting and coordinating the activities of the firms and institutions. The interactive flow of information between economic agents in an atmosphere of competition and cooperation helped reduce government and market failures and collusion in these countries.

Apart from Penang, IH operations in Malaysia have been characterized by truncated activities and hence little learning and innovation has taken place in these locations. Although IH manufacturing is smaller and shorter in experience in Indonesia, Mauritius, Nigeria and South Africa, the lack of systemic instruments to foster stronger networking to resolve collective action problems suggests that these countries resemble Johor rather than Penang in Malaysia. Ethnic policies that have created severe polarization in Malaysia – partly explaining the lack of integration in Malaysia – should be avoided in latecomer countries. In addition, at least in the formative years, institutional support through intermediary organizations such as chambers of commerce and the state development corporations should play an active role to build and strengthen productive inter-firm and firm–institution networking.

NOTES

1. R16 billion (Moleke, 2003).
2. Examples of original brand manufacturers (OBM) include Acer and BenQ. The two largest of the seven are OEM Quanta and Compal.

3. Information on Taiwan can be found at 'Questions and Answers About the Republic of China (Taiwan)', http://www.gio.gov.tw/taiwan-website/5-gp/q&a/page_07.htm.
4. For instance in this category, 13 per cent of science and engineering S&E manpower is employed in the US, while close to 20 per cent work in non-S&E fields of project management and related areas.
5. In Malaysia, the government established the Kulim and Bukit Jalil high-tech parks in the 1990s. To attract strategic high-tech firms engaged in R&D activities to the parks, it offered pioneer-status tax incentives. Electronics firms became the prime beneficiaries of this initiative, although the rate of take-up has been relatively low compared to that of the FTZs and LMWs.

References

Abramovitz, M. (1956), 'Resource and Output Trends in the United States since 1870'. *American Economic Review*, 46, pp. 5–23.

Amsden, A. (1977), 'The Division of Labour is Limited by the Type of Market: The Case of the Taiwanese Machine Tool Industry', *World Development*, 5(3), pp. 217–33.

Amsden, A.O. (1985), 'The Division of Labour is Limited by the Rate of Growth of the Market: The Taiwan Machine Tool Industry in the 1970s', *Cambridge Journal of Economics*, 9(3), pp. 271–84.

Amsden, A. (1989), *Asia's Next Giant: South Korea and Late Industrialization*, New York: Oxford University Press.

Amsden, A.O. and W.W. Chu (2003), *Beyond Late Development Taiwan's Upgrading Policies*, Cambridge, MA: MIT Press.

Amsden, A., T. Tschang and A. Goto (2001), 'Do Foreign Companies Conduct R&D in Developing Countries?', Working Paper No. 14, Tokyo: Asian Development Bank Institute.

Ariffin, N. and P.N. Figueiredo (2004), 'Internationalization of Innovative Capabilities: Counter-evidence from the electronics industry in Malaysia and Brazil', *Oxford Development Studies*, 32(4), 559–83.

Audretsch, D. (2002), 'The Dynamic Role of Small Firms: Evidence from the US', *Small Business Economics*, 18(1–3), pp. 13–40.

Barry, Frank and Chris Van Egeraat (2005), 'The Eastward Shift of Computer Hardware Production: How Ireland Adjusted', paper prepared for presentation to conference on Relocation of Production and Jobs to CEECs: Who Gains and Who Loses?, Hamburg, 16–17 September.

Bell, M. and K. Pavitt (1995), 'The Development of Technological Capabilities', in I.U. Haque (ed.), *Trade, Technology and International Competitiveness*, Washington, DC: World Bank.

Best, M. (1990), *The New Competition*, Cambridge, MA: Harvard University Press.

Best, M. (2001), *The New Competitive Advantage*, Oxford: Oxford University Press.

Blomstrom, M. and F. Sjoholm (1999), 'Technology Transfer and Spillovers: Does Local Participation with Multinationals Matter?', *European Economic Review*, 43: 915–23.

BMI-TechKnowledge (2002), *An Overview of the IT Industry in South Africa.*

BMI-TechKnowledge (2003), *An Overview of the IT Industry in South Africa.*

BMI-TechKnowledge (2004), *An Overview of the IT Industry in South Africa.*

BMI-TechKnowledge (2005), *An Overview of the IT Industry in South Africa.*

BMI-TechKnowledge (2006), *An Overview of the IT Industry in South Africa.*

Booth, A. (1998), *The Indonesian Economy in the Nineteenth and Twentieth Centuries: A History of Missed Opportunities*, Basingstoke: Macmillan.

Booth, A. (1999), 'Initial Conditions and Miraculous Growth: Why is South East Asia Different from Taiwan and South Korea?', *World Development*, 27(2), pp. 301–22.

Brusco, S. (1982), 'The Emilian Model: Productive Decentralisation and Social Integration', *Cambridge Journal of Economics*, 6(2), pp. 167–84.

Chang, H.J. (1994), *The Political Economy of Industrial Policy*, Basingstoke: Macmillan.

Chang, H.J. (2003), *Kicking Away the Ladder*, London: Anthem Press.

Chang, M.C. (2001), 'From Vertical Disintegration to View the Foundation of Taiwan's Economic Society and Policy Implication', *Industry Forum*, 1(3), pp. 245–66.

Chang, M.C. and C.C. Chen (2001), 'Competitiveness of SMEs: An Analysis of Vertical Disintegration', in J. Lee (ed.), *Taiwan's Economic Development and the Role of SMEs*, Taipei: Chung-Hua Institution of Economic Research.

Chang, P.L. and C.W. Hsu (1998), 'The Development Strategies for Taiwan's Semiconductor Industry', *IEEE Transactions on Engineering Management*, 45(4), pp. 349–56.

Chao, C.M., J.C. Wang and K.H. Tsai (2002), 'Innovation and Economic Development: The Case of Taiwan's Information Industry', working paper, Taipei: Chung-Hua Institute for Economic Research.

Chao, F.Y. (1999), *The Legend of the ASUS*, Taipei: Shon-Chao Publishing.

Chau, C.C. (2000), 'The Classification of the Industrial Structure of Taiwan's Information Electronics Industry', Masters Thesis, Taipei: National Central University.

Chu, W.W. (1997), 'Causes of Growth: A Study of Taiwan's Bicycle Industry', *Cambridge Journal of Economics*, 21, pp. 55–72.

CIA (1999), *The World Factbook 1999 – Maurtius*, Washington, DC.

Cohen Wesley. M. and Daniel A. Levinthal (1990), 'Absorptive Capacity: A New Perspective on Learning and Innovation', *Administractive Science Quarterly*, 35, pp. 128–52.

Cripps, F. and R. Tarling (1973), *Growth in Advanced Capitalist Economies, 1950–1970*, Cambridge: Cambridge University Press.

Dalhman, C. and C. Frischtak (1993), 'National Systems Supporting Technical Advance in Industry: The Brazilian Experience', in R.R. Nelson (ed.), *National Innovation Systems: A Comparative Analysis*, New York: Oxford University Press.

Darwent, D. (1969), 'Growth Poles and Growth Centers in Regional Planning: A Review', *Environment and Planning*, 1, pp. 5–32.

Day, R.S. (1998), 'The State of the Information and Communications Technologies in South Africa', www.dacst.gov.za/foresight.

Dhanani, S. (2000), *Indonesia: Strategy for Manufacturing Competitiveness, Vol. II: Main Report*, Jakarta: UNIDO/UNDP Project.

Dosi, G. (1982), 'Technological Paradigms and Technological Trajectories', *Research Policy*, 11(3), pp. 147–62.

Dunning, J. (1974), *Economic Analysis and the Multinational Enterprise*, London: Allen & Unwin.

Easterly, W. (1989), 'Policy Distortions, Size of Government, and Growth', NBER Working Paper 3214, National Bureau of Economic Research.

Edquist, C. and S. Jacobssen (1987), 'The Integrated Circuit Industries in India and South Korea in an International Techno-Economic Context', *Industry and Development*, 21, pp. 1–62.

Edquist, C. (2004), 'Systems of Innovation: Perspectives and Challenges', in J. Fagerberg, D.C. Mowery and R.R. Nelson (eds), *The Oxford Handbook of Innovation*, Oxford: Oxford University Press.

Ernst, D. (2003), 'Global Production Networks and Local Development', research proposal, mimeo.

Ernst, D. (2006), 'Innovation Offshoring: Asia's Emerging Role in Global Innovation Networks', East–West Center Special Report 10, East-West Center, Hawaii.

Ernst, D., T. Ganiatsos and L. Mytelka (eds) (1998), *Technological Capabilities and Export Success: Lessons from East Asia*, London: Routledge.

Ernst, D. and P. Guerrieri (1998), 'International Production Networks and Changing Trade Patterns in East Asia: The Case of the Electronics Industry', *Oxford Development Studies*, 26(2), pp. 191–212.

Ernst, D. and D. O'Connor (1989), *Technology and Global Competition: The Challenge for Newly Industrializing Economies*, Paris: Organisation for Economic Co-operation and Development.

Figueiredo, P.N. (2002), 'Learning Processes Features and Technological Capability Accumulation: Explaining Inter-Firm Differences', *Technovation*, 22, pp. 685–98.

Figueiredo, P.N. (2003), 'Learning, Capability Accumulation and Firms Differences: Evidence from Latecomer Steel', *Industrial and Corporate Change*, 12(3), pp. 607–43.

Foster, William, Zhang Cheng, Jason Dedrick and Kenneth L. Kraemer (2006), *Technology and Organizational Factors in the Notebook Industry Supply Chain*, CAPS: Center for Strategic Supply Research and The Personal Computing Industry Center.

Fransman, M. (1985), 'International Competitiveness, Technical Change and the State: The Machine Tool Industries in Taiwan and Japan', *World Development*, 14(12), pp. 1375–96.

Freeman, C. (1987), *Technology Policy and Economic Performance: Lessons from Japan*, London: Pinter.

Freeman, C. (1989), 'New Technology and Catching-Up', *European Journal of Development Research*, 1(1), pp. 85–99.

Friedmann, J. (1972), 'A General Theory of Polarized Development', in N.M. Hansen (ed.), *Growth Centres in Regional Economic Development*, New York: Free Press.

Garofoli, G. (ed.) (1992), *Endogenous Development and Southern Europe*, Aldershot: Avebury.

Gereffi, G. (2002), 'International Competitiveness in the Global Apparel Commodity Chain', *International Journal of Business and Society*, 3(1), pp. 27–60.

Gereffi, G., J. Humphrey and T. Sturgeon (2005), 'The Governance of Global Value Chains', *Review of International Political Economy*, 12(1), pp. 78–104.

Gerschenkron, A. (1962), *Economic Backwardness in Historical Perspective*, Cambridge: Belknap Press.

Hamilton, A. (1791), 'Report on Manufactures', 5 December, available at: http://www.oberlin.edu/~gkornbl/Hist258/ReportMfres.html, accessed on 13 December 2005.

Hill, H. (1988), *Foreign Investment and Industrialisation in Indonesia*, Singapore: Oxford University Press.

Hill, H. (1995), *The Indonesian Economy since 1966: Southeast Asia's Emerging Giant*, Cambridge: Cambridge University Press.

Hill, H. (1996), 'Indonesia's Industrial Policy and Performance: "Orthodoxy" Vindicated', *Economic Development and Cultural Change*, 45(1): 147–74.

Hirschman, A. (1958), *The Strategy of Economic Development*, New Haven, CT: Yale University Press.

Hirschman, A. (1970), *Exit, Voice and Loyalty: Responses to Decline in Firms, Organizations, and State*, Cambridge, MA: Harvard University Press.

Hobday, M. (1995), *Innovation in East Asia*, Aldershot, UK and Brookfield, US: Edward Elgar.

Hobday, Mike, Alan Cawson and S. Ran Kim (2001), 'Governance of Technology in the Electronics Industries of East and South-Asia', *Technovation*, 21, pp. 209–26.

Hodge, J. and J. Miller (1997), 'Information Technology in South Africa: The State of the Art and Implications for National IT Policy', www.uct.ac.za/depts/dpru.

Hou, C.M. and Gee San (1993), 'National Systems Supporting Technical Advance in Industry: The Case of Taiwan', in R. Nelson (ed.), *National Innovation System*, Oxford: Oxford University Press.

Hsing, Y.T. (1999), 'Trading Companies in Taiwan's Fashion Shoe Networks', *Journal of International Economics*, 48, pp. 101–20.

Hsu, C.W. and H.C. Chiang (2001), 'The Government Strategy for the Upgrading of Industrial Technology in Taiwan', *Technovation*, 21, pp. 123–32.

Huang, C.Y. (1995), *ROC: The Republic of Computer*, Taipei: Tien-Sha Publication.

Johnson, C. (1982), *MITI and the Japanese Miracle*, Stanford: Stanford University Press.

Kaldor, N. (1957), 'A Model of Economic Growth', *Economic Journal*, 67, pp. 591–624.

Katz, J. and N. Berkovich (1993), 'National Systems of Innovation Supporting Technical Advance in Industry: The Case of Argentina', in R.R. Nelson (ed.), *National Innovation Systems: A Comparative Analysis*, New York: Oxford University Press.

Kawakami, M. (1996), 'Development of the Small-And-Medium-Sized Manufacturers in Taiwan's PC Industry', Discussion paper No. 9606, Taipei: Chun-Hua Institute for Economic Research.

Kim, L. (1993), 'National System of Industrial Innovation: Dynamics of Capability Building in Korea', in R.R. Nelson (ed.), *National Innovation Systems: A Comparative Analysis*, New York: Oxford University Press.

Kim, L. (1997), *From Imitation to Innovation*, Cambridge, MA: Harvard Business School Press.

Kim, L. (2003), 'The Dynamics of Technology Development: Lessons from the Korean Experience', in S. Lall and S. Urata (eds), *Competitiveness, FDI and Technological Activity in East Asia*, Cheltenham, UK and Northampton, MA, USA: Edward Elgar.

Kim, L. and R. Nelson (eds) (2001), *Technology, Learning and Innovation: Experiences of Newly Industrializing Countries*, Cambridge: Cambridge University Press.

Kline, S.J. and N. Rosenberg (1986), 'An Overview of Innovation' in R. Landau and N. Rosenberg, *The Positive Sum Strategy*, New York: National Academy Press, pp. 275–305.

Kong, Xinxin (2006), *Studies on the Growing Dynamics of the Electronics Industry in China*, Beijing: Economy and Management Press.

Krueger, A.O. (ed.) (1981), *Trade and Employment in Developing Countries*, Chicago, IL: University of Chicago Press.

Lall, S. (1992), 'Technological Capabilities and Industrialisation', *World Development*, 20(2), pp. 165–86.

Lall, S. (1996a), *Learning from the Asian Tigers*, Basingstoke: Macmillan.

Lall, S. (1996b), 'Creation of Comparative Advantage: The Role of Industrial Policy', in I.U. Haque (ed.), *The Trade and Technology and International Competitiveness*, Washington, DC: World Bank.

Lall, S. (2001), *Competitiveness, Technology and Skills*, Cheltenham, UK and Northampton, MA, USA: Edward Elgar.

Lall, S. and P. Streeten (1977), *Foreign Investment, Transnationals and Developing Countries*, Basingstoke: Macmillan.

Lan, K.C., J.C. Wang and K.H. Tsai (1992), 'The Effectiveness of Government Incentives on R&D, Pollution Prevention and Automatic Production', Industry Development Bureau, Taipei: Chung-Hua Institute for Economic Research.

Lawrence, P. and C. Thirtle (2001), *Asia and Africa in Comparative Economic Perspective*, New York: Palgrave.

Lee, C.S. and M. Pecht (1997), *The Taiwan Electronics Industry*, New York: CRC Press.

Lewis, A. (1955), *The Theory of Economic Growth*, London: Unwin Hyman.

Lin, Yeo (1986), 'The Technological Change: A Microeconomic Study of the Consumer Electronics Industry in Taiwan', PhD dissertation, Evanston, Northwestern University.

Lin, Yeo (2003a), 'Industrial Structure, Technical Change and the Role of Government in the Development of the Electronics and Information Technology Industry in Taiwan', Working Paper, Manila: Asian Development Bank.

Lin, Y. (2003b), 'Industrial Structure and Market-Complementing Policies: Export Success of the Electronics and Information Industry in Taiwan', ADB Working paper series, Manila.

Lindauer, D. and M. Roemer (1994), *Asia and Africa: Legacies and Opportunities in Development*, San Fransisco: ICS Press.

List, F. (1885), *The National System of Political Economy*, London: Longmans, Green & Company.

Lundvall, B.A. (1988), 'Innovation as an Interactive Process: From User–Producer Interaction to the National System of Innovation', in G. Dosi, C. Freeman, G. Silverberg and L. Soete (eds), *Technical Change and Economic Geography*, London: Frances Pinter.

Lundvall, B.A. (1992), *National Systems of Innovation: Towards a Theory of Innovation and Interactive Learning*, London: Frances Pinter.

Mai, C.C., J.C. Wang and K.H. Tsai (2002), 'Innovation and Economic Development: The Case of Taiwan's Information Electronics Industry', working paper, Taipei: Chung-Hua Institute for Economic Research.

Malaysia (2001), *The Sixth Malaysia Plan 2001–2005*, Kuala Lumpur: Government Printers.

Malaysia (2007), *Eight Malaysia Plan 2001–2005*, Kuala Lumpur: Government Printers.

Malerba, F. (1992), 'Learning by Firms and Incremental Technical Change', *Economic Journal*, 102(413), pp. 845–59.

Malerba, F. (2006), 'Innovation and the Evolution of Industry', *Journal of Evolutionary Economics*, 16(1), pp. 3–23.

Malerba, F. and L. Orsenigo (1997), 'Technological Regimes and Sectoral Patterns of Innovative Activities', *Industrial and Corporate Change*, 6(1), pp. 83–117.

Malerba, F., R.R. Nelson, L. Orsenigo and S. Winter (2001), 'Competition and Industrial Policies in a "History Friendly" Model of the Evolution of the Computer Industry', *International Journal of Industrial Organization*, 19(5), pp. 635–64.

Mansfield E. (1985), 'How Fast Does New Industrial Technology Leak Out?', *Journal of Industrial Economics*, 34(2), pp. 217–24.

Marx, K. (1860), *Capital: The Process of Circulation of Capital*, Volume II, Moscow: Progress Publishers.

Mathews, J. (2002), 'Introduction: Schumpeter's "Lost" Seventh Chapter', *Industry and Innovation*, 9(1–2), pp. 1–5.

Mathews, J.A. (1995), *High-Technology Industrial Development in East Asia: The Case of the Semiconductor Industry in Taiwan and Korea*, Taipei: Chung-Hua Institute for Economic Research.

Mathews, J.A. (1996), 'High Technology Industrialisation in East Asia', *Journal of Industry Studies*, 3(2), pp. 1–77.

Mathews, J.A. (1997), 'A Silicon Valley of the East: Creating Taiwan's Semiconductor Industry', *California Management Review*, 39(4), pp. 26–54.

Mathews, J.A. (2005), 'The Intellectual Roots of Latecomer Industrial

Development', *International Journal of Technology and Globalization*, 1(3/4), pp. 433–50.

Mathews, J.A. (2006), 'Catch-up strategies and the latecomer effect in industrial development', *New Political Economy*, 11(3), pp. 312–35.

Mathews, J.A. and D.S. Cho (2000), *Tiger Technology: The Creation of a Semi-conductor Industry in East Asia*, Cambridge: Cambridge University Press.

Metcalfe, J.S. (1997), 'On diffusion and the process of technological change', in G. Antonelli and N. De Liso (eds), *Economics of Structural and Technological Change*, London: Routledge.

Metcalfe, J.S. (2005), 'Ed Mansfield and the Diffusion of Innovation: An Evolutionary Connection', *The Journey of Technology Transfer*, 30(212), pp. 171–81.

Metcalfe, S. (1993), 'The Economic Foundations of Technology Policy: Equilibrium and Evolutionary Perspectives', Mimeo, Department of Economics, University of Manchester.

Meyer-Krahmer, F. and U. Schmoch (1998), 'Science Based Technologies: University–Industry Interactions in Four Fields', *Research Policy*, 27(8), pp. 835–51.

MIC (Market Intelligence Centre) (1999), *Annual Reports on the Notebook Computer Industry*, Taipei, Taiwan.

MIC (Market Intelligence Centre) (2001), *Annual Reports on the Notebook Computer Industry*, Taipei, Taiwan.

MIC (Market Intelligence Centre) (2005), *Annual Reports on the Notebook Computer Industry*, Taipei, Taiwan.

Mill, J.S. (1844), *Principles of Political Economy, with Some of Their Applications to Social Policy*, London: John W. Parker & West Strand.

Moleke, P. (2003), 'Employment Experience of Graduates', Human Sciences Research Council Paper 3085.

MOSTI (Ministry of Science, Technology and Innovation) (2004), 'Science and Technology Data', unpublished, Kuala Lumpur: Ministry of Science, Technology and Environment.

Mowery, D. (2005), 'The Role of Knowledge-Based "Public Goods"', Industrial Development Report 2005. Background Paper Series, UNIDO.

Myrdal, G. (1957), *Economic Theory and Under-Developed Regions*, New York: Methuen.

Mytelka, L.K. (ed.) (1999), *Competition, Innovation and Competitiveness in Developing Countries*, Paris: OECD.

Nelson, R. (ed.) (1993), *National Innovation Systems*, New York: Oxford University Press.

Nelson, R.R. and S.G. Winter (1982), *An Evolutionary Theory of Economic Change*, Cambridge, MA: Harvard University Press.

North, Douglass C. (1990), *Institutions, Institutional Change, and Economic Performance*, New York: Cambridge University Press.

NSF (National Science Foundation) (2003), *Science and Engineering Indicators*.

OECD (2002), 'Measuring the Information Economy', Paris: OECD.

Okamoto, Y. and F. Sjoholm (2003), 'Technology Development in Indonesia', in S. Lall and S. Urata (eds), *Technology Development in East Asia*, Cheltenham, UK and Northampton, MA, USA: Edward Elgar.

Oyelaran-Oyeyinka, B. (2006), *Learning to Compete in African Industry: Institutions and Technology for Development*, Aldershot, UK: Ashgate Publishing.

Oyelaran-Oyeyinka, B. and K. Lal (2006), *SMEs and New Technologies: Learning, E-Business and Development*, Basingstoke, UK: Palgrave Macmillan.

Oyelaran-Oyeyinka, B. and D. McCormick (2007), *Industrial Clusters and Innovation Systems in Africa*, Tokyo: UNU Press.

Oyeyinka, B.O. (2003), 'Human Capital and Systems of Innovation in Africa', in M. Muchie, B.A. Lundvall and P. Gammeltoft (eds), *Putting the Last First: Building Systems of Innovation in Africa*, Aalborg: Aalborg University Press.

Pangestu, M. (1993), 'Indonesia: From Dutch Disease to Manufactured Exports', mimeo.

Panglaykim, J. (1983), *Japanese Direct Investment in ASEAN: The Indonesian Experience*, Singapore: Maruzen.

Pavitt, K. (1984), 'Sectoral Patterns of Technical Change: Towards a Taxonomy and a Theory', *Research Policy*, 13(6), pp. 343–73.

Perez, C. (1983), 'Structural Change and the Assimilation of New Technologies in the Economic and Social Systems', *Futures*, 15(5), pp. 357–75.

Perroux, F. (1950), 'Economic Space: Theory and Applications', *Quarterly Journal of Economics*, 64, pp. 89–104

Perroux, F. (1970), 'Note on the concept of "Growth Poles"', D. McKee, R. Dean and W. Leahy (eds), *Regional Economics: Theory and practice*, New York: Free Press.

Piore, M. and C. Sabel (1984), *The Second Industrial Divide: Possibilities for Prosperity*, New York: Basic Books.

Prasada, R. (2000), *Globalisation of Corporate R&D: Implications for Innovations Systems for Host Countries*, London: Routledge.

Pratten, C. (1971), *Economies of Scale in Manufacturing Industry*, Cambridge: Cambridge University Press.

Prawiro, R. (1998), *Indonesia's Struggle for Economic Development: Pragmatism in Action*, Kuala Lumpur: Oxford University Press.

Rasiah, R. (1987), *The International Division of Labour: The Semiconductor Industry in Penang*, MSocSc thesis approved at University Science Malaysia, in Malay; published (1993), Kuala Lumpur: Malaysian Social Science Association.

Rasiah, R. (1988), 'The Semiconductor Industry in Penang: Implications for the New International Division of Labour Theories', *Journal of Contemporary Asia*, 18(1), pp. 44–67.

Rasiah, R. (1992), 'Foreign Capital and Industrialization in Malaysia', doctoral thesis approved by Cambridge University, Cambridge (published by Macmillan, 1995).

Rasiah, R. (1994), 'Flexible Production Systems and Local Machine Tool Subcontracting: Electronics Transnationals in Malaysia', *Cambridge Journal of Economics*, 18(3), pp. 279–98.

Rasiah, R. (1995), *Foreign Capital and Industrialization in Malaysia*, Basingstoke: Macmillan.

Rasiah, R. (1996), 'Institutions and Innovations: Moving Towards the Technology Frontier in the Electronics Industry in Malaysia', *Industry and Innovation*, 3(2), pp. 433–54.

Rasiah, R. (1999), 'Malaysia's National Innovation System', in K.S. Jomo and G. Felker (eds), *Technology, Competitiveness, and the State: Malaysia's Industrial Technology Policies*, London: Routledge.

Rasiah, R. (2000), 'Globalization and International Private Capital Movements', *Third World Quarterly*, 21(6), pp. 917–29.

Rasiah, R. (2002), 'Systemic Coordination and the Knowledge Economy: Human Capital Development in MNC-driven Electronics Clusters in Malaysia', *Transnational Corporations*, 11(3), pp. 89–130.

Rasiah, R. (2003a), 'Foreign Ownership, Technology and Electronics Exports from Malaysia and Thailand', *Journal of Asian Economics*, 14(5), pp. 785–811.

Rasiah, R. (2003b), 'Manufacturing Export Experience of Indonesia, Malaysia and Thailand', K.S. Jomo (ed.), *Southeast Asia's Paper Tigers*, London: Routledge.

Rasiah, R. (2003c), 'Foreign Ownership, Exports and Technological Capabilities in the Electronics Firms in Malaysia and Thailand', *Journal of Asian Economics*, 14(5): 786–811.

Rasiah, R. (2004), 'Technological Capabilities in East and Southeast Asian Electronics Firms: Does Network Strength Matter?' *Oxford Development Studies*, 32(3), pp. 433–54.

Rasiah, R. (2005), 'Foreign Ownership, Technological Intensity and Export Incidence: a Study of Auto Parts, Electronics and Garment Firms in Indonesia', *International Journal of High Technology and Globalization*, 1(3/4), pp. 361–80.

Rasiah, R. (2007), 'Ownership, Institutions and Technological Intensities: Automotive and Electronics Component Firms in East Asia', in J. Eatwell and P. Arestis (eds), *Evidence-Based Economics: Essays in Honour of Ajit Singh*, Basingstoke, UK: Palgrave Macmillan.

Rasiah, R. (2008), 'The Systemic Quad: Technological Capabilities and Economic Performance of Computer and Component Firms in Penang and Johor, Malaysia', *International Journal of Technological Learning, Innovation and Development*, 1(2), pp. 179–203.

Rasiah, R. (2009), 'Can Garment Exports from Cambodia, Laos and Myanmar be Sustained?', *Journal of Contemporary Asia*, forthcoming.

Rasiah, R. and Y. Lin (2005), 'Learning and Innovation: The Role of Market, Government and Trust in the Information Hardware Industry in Taiwan', *International Journal of Technology and Globalization*, 1(3/4), pp. 400–432.

Reinert, E.S. (1994), 'Catching-up from Way Behind: A Third World Perspective on First World History', in J. Fagerberg, B. Verspagen and N.V. Tunzelmann (eds), *The Dynamics of Technology, Trade and Growth*, Aldershot: Hassocks.

Reinert, E. (2007), *How the Rich Countries Got Rich . . . and Why the Poor Countries Stay Poor*, London: Constable & Robinson.

Robison, R. (1986) *Indonesia: The Rise of Capital*, London: Allen & Unwin.

Rosenberg, N. (1976), *Perspectives on Technology*, Cambridge: Cambridge University Press.

Rosenberg, N. (1982), *Inside the Black Box*, Cambridge: Cambridge University Press.

SAITIS (2000), 'South African IT Industry Strategy Baseline Studies: A Survey of the IT Industry and Related Jobs and Skills in South Africa', SAITIS, www.saitis.co.za/docs/publications.

San, Gee (2001), 'The Impacts of Overseas Recruits on the High-Tech Industry Development: The Case of Hsin-Chu Science-Based Industrial Park', *Taiwan's Science and Technology Industry*, Taipei: National Central University.

Saxenian, A.L. (1994), *Regional Advantage: Culture and Competition in Silicon Valley and Route 128*, Cambridge, MA: Harvard University Press.

Scherer, F.M. (1980), *Industrial Market Structure and Economic Performance*, Chicago, IL: Rand McNally.

Scherer, F. (1992), *International High Technology Competition*, Cambridge, MA: Harvard University Press.

Schumpeter, J. (1934), *The Theory of Economic Development*, Cambridge, MA: Harvard University Press.

Schumpeter, J. (1942), *Capitalism, Socialism and Democracy*, New York: Harper and Row.

Scott, A.J. (1988), *New Industrial Spaces: Flexible Production Organization and Regional Development in North America and Western Europe*, London: Pion.

Shieh, K.S. (1991), 'Network Type Production Structure: the Subcontracting Activities in the Taiwan's Export Industry', *Ethnology Research*, Taipei: Academia Cinaca.

Sjoholm, F. (1999), 'Productivity Growth in Indonesia: The Role of Regional Characteristics and Direct Foreign Investment', *Economic Development and Cultural Change*, 47(3), pp. 559–84.

Sjoholm, F. (2002), 'The Challenge of Combining FDI and Regional Development in Indonesia', *Journal of Contemporary Asia*, 32(3), pp. 381–93.

Smith, A. (1904), *An Inquiry into the Nature and Causes of the Wealth of Nations*, London: Dent & Sons.

Stein, H. (1995), *Asian Industrialization and Africa*, London: Macmillan.

Storper, M. (1995), 'The Resurgence of Regional Economies, Ten Years Later: The Region as a Nexus of Untraded Interdependencies', *European Urban and Regional Studies*, 2(3), pp. 191–221.

Sun, K.N. (1995), 'The Evolution and Efficiency of the Tax Incentives in Taiwan', in Y.H. Yang (ed.), *Industrial Development and Policies in Taiwan*, Taiwan: Chung-Hua Institute for Economic Research.

Taiwan (2001a), *Information Electronics Industry*, Annual Report, Taipei: Government Printers.

Taiwan (2001b), 'Unpublished data', Industry Development Bureau, Taipei: Ministry of Economic Affairs.

Taiwan (2001c), *Indicators of Science and Technology*, Taipei: National Science Council.

Taiwan (2001d), *Taiwan Statistical Data Book*, Taipei: Council for Economic Planning and Development.

Thee, K.W. (2000), 'The Impact of the Economic Crisis on Indonesia's Manufacturing Sector', *Developing Economies*, 38(4), pp. 420–53.

Thee, K.W. and M. Pangestu (1998), 'Technological Capabilities and Indonesia's Manufactured Exports', in D. Ernst, T. Ganiatsos and L. Mytelka (eds), *Technological Capabilities and Export Success in East Asia*, London: Routledge.

UNCTAD (2003), *FDI Policies for Development: National and International Perspectives*, World Investment Report, Geneva: United Nations Conference for Trade and Development.

UNCTAD (2005), *World Investment Report*, Geneva: United Nations Conference for Trade and Development.

UNU-INTECH, World Bank and DFID (2004), 'Survey Data on Malaysian Industrial Firms', compiled by the Institute for New Technologies (INTECH), DCT and Pemm Consultants.

Veblen, T.B. (1919), *The Place of Science in Modern Civilisation and Other Essays*, New York: Huebsch.

Vedi, H. (1997), *Workers and the State in the New Order Indonesia*, London: Routledge.

Vernon, R. (1971) *Sovereignty at Bay: The Multinational Spread of US Enterprises*, New York: Basic Books.

Wade, R. (1990), *Governing the Market: Economic Theory and the Role of Government in East Asia's Industrialization*, Princeton, NJ: Princeton University Press.

Wang, J.C. (1995), 'A Discussion of the Efficiency of Taiwan's Industrial and Science and Technology Policy', in Y.H. Yang (ed.), *Industrial Development and Policies in Taiwan*, Taipei: Chung-Hua Institute for Economic Research.

Wang, J.C. (1999), 'The Development of SMEs in Taiwan and the Efficiency of Related Policies: The Case of the Information Electronics Industry', in T.S. Yu and C. Lee (eds), *Economic Policy and Economic Development*, Taipei: Chung-Hua Institute of Economic Research.

Wang, Yuan, Yonghong Mei and Heping Xu (eds) (2002), *China's Strategic Technologies and Industrial Development*, Beijing: Economy and Management Press.

Westphal, L.E., K. Kritayakirana, K. Petchsuwan, H. Sutabutr and Y. Yuthavong, (1990), 'The Development of Technological Capability in Manufacturing: A Macroscopic Approach to Policy Research', in R.E. Evenson and G. Ranis (eds), *Science and Technology: Lessons for Development Policy*, London: Intermediate Technology Publications.

Wignaraja, G. (2002), 'Firm size, Technological Capabilities and Market-Oriented Policies in Mauritius', *Oxford Development Studies*, 30(1), pp. 87–104.

Wong, P.K. (1999), 'University–Industry Technological Collaboration in Singapore: Emerging Patterns and Industry Concerns', *International Journal of Technology Management*, 17(3–4), pp. 270–84.

World Bank (1989), *World Development Report*.

WTO (2006), *International Trade Statistics*, Geneva: World Trade Organization.

Young, A. (1928), 'Increasing Returns and Economic Progress', *Economic Journal*, 38(152), pp. 527–42.

Index